Hitler's British Slaves

THE AUTHOR Sean Longden studied East European history at the School of Slavonic and East European Studies, University of London. After graduation he worked in photographic archives and press agencies. His first book, *To the Victor the Spoils*, was published in 2004. He is married with two children and lives in Surrey.

Hitler's British Slaves

Sean Longden

ARRIS BOOKS
An imprint of Arris Publishing Ltd
Gloucestershire

First published in Great Britain in 2005
by Arris Books

An imprint of Arris Publishing Ltd
12 Main St, Adlestrop, Moreton in Marsh
Gloucestershire GL56 0YN
www.arrisbooks.com

Text copyright © Sean Longden 2005
Map by John Taylor

ISBN 1-84437-060-7

Typeset by Windrush Publishing Services
Printed and bound in Great Britain by William Clowes Ltd, Beccles, Suffolk

Telephone: 01608 659328
Visit our website at www.arrisbooks.com
or email us at info@arrisbooks.com

Contents

Acknowledgements

There are many people without whom this book would not have been possible. My thanks must go firstly to 'Bill' Sykes, the D-Day veteran and ex-POW whose thoughtful communications from his home in California contributed much to this book. Thanks must also be given to Les Allan, the founder of the National Ex-POW Association. Les has campaigned long and hard for the sufferings of European prisoners of war to be fully recognised by the British government. I only hope this book can help contribute to a wider understanding of the subject and possibly play some small part in their sufferings being acknowledged.

Gordon Barber and Ken Wilats both provided vital details about life on farms in East Prussia. Even now, sixty years later, they remain close friends and helped colour this book with so many vivid tales. Bryan Willoughby kindly shared his tales of the battles in Arnhem and his subsequent experiences as a prisoner. Thanks must also go to Sandi Toksvig for inviting me onto her radio show to discuss my previous book, *To the Victor the Spoils*. This resulted in Alec Reynolds contacting me to tell his tales of working in the copper mines of the Third Reich. Thanks must also go to the wives of the men I interviewed, all of whom showed such great hospitality.

My thanks go to Maurice Newey, Kenneth Clarke, James Witte and Eric Laker, all of whom gave me permission to quote from their memoirs held in the Imperial War Museum. Thanks are also due to Mrs R. Eltringham, A.J. Richardson and Anne Turner who gave me permission to quote from the memoirs of their fathers, also now held in the Imperial War Museum.

Thanks must also be given to the board and trustees of the Imperial War Museum, and to the staff in both the Department of Documents and in the photographic archive whose assistance was priceless. I must also extend my gratitude to Helen Pugh and Ipsita Mandal at the Red Cross who helped me access the albums of photographs taken by the Red Cross at the work camps and Stalags across occupied Europe. Many of these are included within this book. Bryan Willoughby, Gordon Barber and Bill Sykes also kindly allowed me to use their treasured photographs within the book. As ever the staff of the National Archives in Kew provided a highly efficient service in finding all the necessary documents. Thanks must also be given to the individual at the Ministry of Defence who decided that the POW debriefing questionnaires should finally be made available to the public. The release date was just in time for me to be able to include these documents in my research.

I must also offer my gratitude to Geoff, Victoria, Bethan and Beth. Last, but not least, I must thank my wife Claire who has been so understanding when I spent so many hours sat in front of the computer.

Preface

Hitler's British Slaves? That is the correct title, it's a true description. A slave is someone who is made to work under threat to his life. If a slave tries to run away he is killed. He isn't paid. He is at the will of his masters. It was the same for us. We were given a bowl of soup and some bread made from sawdust. If you didn't do as you were told you were shot. Therefore it was slavery. *Leslie Allan, founder of the National Ex-Prisoner of War Association.*

There is an impression of World War Two prisoner of war camps that is forever engraved in the imagination of the public. In this mythologised version of events the camps are perceived as institutions whose atmosphere and conditions were like a mixture of a severe boarding school and a strict holiday camp. This was an image created by the books and films that emerged in the aftermath of war with their stereotypes later reinforced by television series and comedy shows. From Eric Williams's classic tale *The Wooden Horse*, first published in 1949, through to the 2005 television drama *Colditz,* the public have been fed a stream of misleading information. These were tales of heroism, evasion and escape – of tunnels, expert lockpickers, forgers and masters of disguise. The image was fostered of resolutely middle class officers staging escapes with 'devil may care' bravery, anxious to get home ready for another 'crack at the Hun'.

In this myth incarceration was an unwanted interruption to wartime service and escaping a matter of honour to be approached with the levity of boarding school boys sneaking out of the dorm to indulge in a forbidden cigarette. Their clothes were clean, their hair groomed and their chins shaved. These were men who read books, produced plays, listened to camp orchestras, made themselves cricket nets from the string from Red Cross parcels and studied for professional exams.

This life did exist, it is part of the story but not the whole story. Missing from this story are the experiences of the vast mass of prisoners. In short, the mythical POW camp ignores all ranks except officers. Although the POW camp of fiction could be recognised by many former officer prisoners as a sanitised version of their experiences, for those other ranks unlucky enough to experience the Stalags and work camps little comparison could be made. Left out of this rosy picture of POW life are the men who toiled in the farms, factories and mines of the Reich – the men who swept the streets of German cities and cleared its bombsites. These were the men who marched hundreds of miles into captivity, who survived on starvation rations and faced casual violence from their guards. These forgotten men were forced to manufacture munitions for the enemy and were used as slave labour to build the factories of Auschwitz. Twelve-hour shifts, often seven days a week, were the norm. Watery soups and hard, dry bread was their diet. Often clad in rags and shod in clogs, the prisoners of war were the forced miners, builders, farm labourers and quarrymen of the Third Reich, slaves to Hitler's dream of European domination.

These were the real experiences of the men who faced up to life behind the wire between 1940 and 1945. Men whose characters were built by imprisonment and whose behaviour was shaped by all they had experienced at the hands of their captors between the fall of France and the collapse of the Nazi regime. As one man later wrote of his feelings towards most of the POW books he read in the post-war years: 'I, an ex-prisoner, am increasingly left with a feeling of having heard only half a tale.'[1] Here, for him and the rest of his fellow prisoners, is the rest of that tale – the story of 'Hitler's British Slaves'.

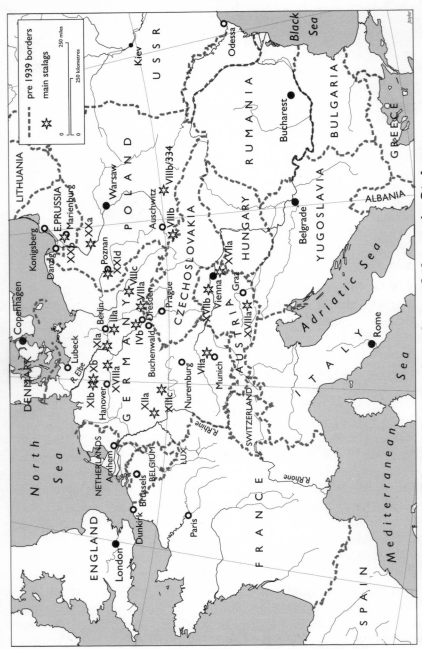

Wartime Europe 1939–45, showing locations of the main Stalags

ONE

Into the Bag

'One of the first rules of war is personal survival.' *Eric 'Bill' Sykes, 7th Parachute Battalion, captured in Normandy.*

'Treatment bad – stragglers being shot at… I saw a German officer shoot three wounded prisoners.'[1]

For a soldier there can be few more bewildering experiences than the moment of his capture. This is not what they have been prepared for – they are trained to fight and defeat the enemy, not for capitulation. Between 1940 and 1945 almost 200,000 British and Commonwealth servicemen fell into the hands of the enemy. In the early war years, with defeats in Norway, France, Greece, Crete and North Africa, streams of once proud soldiers made their way into captivity. Even once the Allies were advancing through Sicily, Italy and north-west Europe there would be a steady stream of new prisoners taking their places in the cold, damp huts of the Stalags and their work camps. Usually exhausted, dishevelled, hungry and thirsty, they had reached the end of their physical and mental endurance. Whether through the fields of France, across the sands of the desert, the parched hillsides of Crete or the shattered villas of Arnhem, they raised their hands and shuffled off to an uncertain future.

The first major influx of prisoners came with the shock defeat of the British Expeditionary Force (BEF) in France in May and June 1940. The men who had promised to 'Hang Out the Washing on the Siegfried Line' were marched off into captivity that, for most, was to last almost five years. As the Blitzkrieg smashed through the British, French and Belgian lines the Allied armies were left in disarray. Whilst some British units made organised withdrawals others were left behind, lost and alone, surrounded by the enemy. They were beaten by both tactics and technology as British tanks failed to make an impression, their guns all but useless against the enemy panzers. The mobility of the Germans shocked the British troops, many of whom were recent recruits, conscripts, or poorly trained pre-war territorials whose training was limited to the occasional exercise or evening lecture.

Unlike the Germans, who, in many cases, had years of modern military training, the British were unprepared for contemporary warfare. The British prisoners looked around at the Germans with their new vehicles and realised why they had been defeated. Much of their own transport had been civilian vehicles – butcher's lorries, delivery vans, coal trucks – which had been requisitioned and repainted in khaki. In the chaos that followed the German offensive many units found their training and supplies woefully inadequate. Medics found themselves without supplies and were forced to bandage wounded men with strips torn from blankets. Some of the more recent recruits were even without uniforms, including one man who was captured at Calais still in civilian clothing having only joined the army 24 hours previously and been shipped immediately to France to join his regiment. It was clear to such men that Britain had clearly been unprepared for war. Among them was Private Ken Wilats, captured in France in early May 1940:

> I didn't volunteer, I wasn't the military type. Like thousands of others I went because I was told to go. I was conscripted into the Queens Royal Regiment on 21 January 1940. I was in France by the end of April, I'd had about eight weeks training. You could say my military career wasn't very intensive, nor was it very successful. We were scattered through the area around Abbeville. We were subject to Stuka dive bombing. We were in a farmhouse, looking for the enemy. Out of the back of the house we could see about thirty or forty German tanks. They were the advance guard of a crack German Panzer division. The situation was ludicrous because we just had rifles and clips of five bullets each. We blazed away at these things, but I don't think we ever hit anybody. Unbelievably when we'd used our five bullets we'd report to Sgt Major Davey and say 'Excuse me Sgt Major, but I've used my five bullets can I have five more.' Then you'd put the clip in and fire until you needed another one. The tanks replied by firing tracer at us. Then we saw a small detachment of German soldiers in the farmyard. There was no struggle or fight, we were overpowered. We just put our hands up, there was nothing else we could do. It was a bit of an unequal struggle.[2]

Whilst the likes of Wilats were going 'into the bag' much of the rest of the BEF was making its way back to Dunkirk. Yet in the aftermath of the largely successful evacuation many thousands of their comrades were left behind, many of those who fought as the rearguard to protect the retreat, suffered greatly in the days between the German breakthrough and their eventual capture. Stretcher-bearer Les Allan found himself confused since his unit had managed to stop the enemy only to be told to retreat from their positions. Only later would he realise this was because flanking units had not been so successful. They kept fighting and falling back until eventually they were overcome. Allan spent his days looking after the wounded only to see most of them killed when the Germans destroyed their hospital. By the time of his capture he was already starving. He had not eaten for days, nor washed, shaved or slept. It was a grim precursor to the months, then years, of degradation that would soon follow.

Also included in the round up of the remnants of the BEF were a majority of the 51st Highland Division, surrounded at St Valery. Gunner Gordon 'Nobby' Barber was among them. He explained the chaos experienced by the defeated army:

> None of us knew where we were. All we could see were broken guns, dumped at the side of the road. They wanted volunteers to go into St Valery to find small arms, to fight our way to the beaches. We found a box of hand grenades. The sergeant said 'It would've been a good idea if you'd brought the detonators'. So that was another balls up. The outskirts of the town was a mess. We found French officers dead in their cars, like they were asleep. I went in a smashed up shop and found a big box of nylon stockings. I thought I'd be all right if I got home. Our officer, Captain Wright, he said 'Barber, you were a signaller. See if you can get a frequency on that set.' I still remember it. 'This is the BBC' – You know, the old toffee-nosed way of talking – 'The BEF have been successfully evacuated from Dunkirk.' I thought what a load of bollocks that was. There was the whole 51st Division stuck in St Valery. It was more propaganda we didn't believe. So the captain said 'I can't give you any info. Now we are going to be taken as prisoners of war.' So my mate Paddy said, 'Let's take my bike'. We put a can of petrol on the back and off we went. It was all pie in the sky. We didn't have a clue where we were or what we were doing. We were all just kids. It was a cock up from start to finish.[3]

After 20 or so miles the would-be evader 'Nobby' Barber and his mate pulled their Royal Enfield motorcycle into a farmyard only to find it full of Germans. There was no choice but to surrender. They were soon returned to St Valery and packed into a field outside the town. Initially for many among the prisoners there was little time for emotion, as Ken Wilats explained: 'The enemy, apart from the Germans, was the lack of sleep. When we were captured we hadn't slept for about 60 hours. I was extremely tired. The Germans put us in this sort of barbed wire corral and one of the first things I did was to go to sleep. Fatigue does funny things to you.'[4] This lack of emotional response was a common feature among captured soldiers, all that mattered was to have survived the battle. Seldom was it a time for tears, instead for most their emotions were submerged beneath instinct as 'Nobby' Barber recalled: 'To be honest I can't remember how I felt. We looked round and saw trucks with machine guns on them. We thought they were going to shoot us. When you're young you don't have time to cry. We didn't realise what was going to happen. From that day on it was survival of the fittest.'[5]

Both Barber and Wilats were experiencing almost identical feelings. Though both very different men – one a quiet former chef and an admittedly reluctant soldier, the other a tough and streetwise young pre-war regular – what they learned in these early days of captivity was to sustain them through the long years of imprisonment that followed. As Ken Wilats explained: 'Survival is a very emotive feeling. The progression of need in extreme circumstances is water, food, cigarettes, ladies – in that order. Without being offensive to the ladies, they come a lot further down the list than water.'[6] Little did they realise it, but their paths would later cross and they would share in a desperate battle for life.

Defeated and dejected, the remnants of the BEF were marched eastwards towards Germany. However not all began the journey immediately, some were taken to Calais where they began the task of clearing the rubble-strewn streets of the town. Another group of 700 prisoners were crammed into a single hall. For a period of three weeks they were kept inside with no exercise, no washing facilities and precious little food. Others found themselves detailed to help the victorious Germans begin to strip France of her wealth. POWs were sent to sugar refineries where they were made to load the produce into sacks to be taken back to Germany. Though they could find little pleasure in helping the enemy plunder a defeated nation, they did at least gain solace in the knowledge that the handful of sugar they ate as they worked would help keep them strong.

Those prisoners going into captivity in the summer of 1940 could hardly have known that almost five years 'behind the wire' awaited them. If they expected fair treatment from the enemy the experiences of those first few days soon changed their minds. They were marched in vast columns from France, into Belgium then on to Germany. Day after day they trudged onward, their feet blistered from their miles of marching, their crotches rubbed raw by their thick woollen trousers. The heat of summer beat down upon them, leaving their skin red and dry and their mouths parched. They spent days and weeks on the road, usually sleeping in the open, sometimes in flooded fields. There was little food – British army biscuits and soup made from boiled bones provided much of their sustenance, unless they were lucky enough to scrounge or steal food from civilians. As they marched, men broke off from the columns and took whatever they could find, running back to find their mates and hand over their haul. Without stopping, they punctured eggs and sucked out the yolk. Others dived into roadside clamps of manglewurzels and stuffed their faces with the raw vegetables that were grown as cattle feed. Despite the foul taste the men chewed them as they marched, desperate to quell the pangs of hunger. One group of men were forced to queue for three hours at an abandoned French barracks just to receive a small ration of bread. When some men were detailed to wash up after their guards had eaten their meals the prisoners received no more than bread crusts as thanks.

This treatment was sudden proof that the Germans viewed them with disfavour. The guards seemed either brutal or uninterested in the fate of the defeated men of the BEF. The only sign of any humour was when one column of prisoners was marched into a cemetery for the night. They had no choice but to laugh to themselves at what seemed to be a sick joke. Amid the beatings and the starvation there was little sign of the fabled gentlemanly respect between combatants. Instead the Germans subjected their prisoners to treatment that forced them to re-evaluate their moral code. Many among the prisoners were quick to learn tricks that would help preserve their lives. Though confused by their situation, wracked by exhaustion and with senses dulled by hunger and thirst, the survival instinct rose to the fore. The more canny prisoners realised it was always best to be at the front of the marching columns since they would be the first to rest whenever the column was called to a halt. If they were marched into a field for a break then the men at the back of the column might still not have arrived by the time the break was over. In such trying times even short breaks of 10 or 15 minutes could give precious respite from the rigours of marching.

Even brief rests could mean the difference between life and death. As the prisoners grew weaker those who fell out from the columns were punched, kicked, beaten with whips or shot. Those at the rear of the columns regularly faced more severe treatment than those at the front. To compound their humiliation they were taken on circular routes through towns to show them off to the subdued populace. Then to ensure the message of their defeat of the British army was spread far and wide, the Germans filmed the pitiful prisoners to highlight how complete had been their humiliation. In some locations they were made to run 'at the double' at bayonet point to stop them from talking to civilians. For mile upon mile they trudged: 'On that march you looked in front of you. The roads were wide, long and straight. You could see for miles. It was bloody hot and I can remember how thirsty we used to get. I've seen blokes go to a water butt and skim a dead pigeon off the top then drink the water.'[7]

In those first unnerving days of captivity the prisoners soon learned a German word they would hear almost every day for the next five years – 'Raus!'. Meaning 'out' the Germans used it whenever it was time for them to move. That summer it was their signal to rise each morning from their sleep in the fields of France, it would also soon be their cue to exit the stinking cattle wagons transporting them eastwards, and would eventually be the call they heard each morning as their guards woke them ready for a long, hard day's work in the fields or factories.

In the early days of the march there was little food apart from that thrown to them by French and Belgium civilians. One man later wrote home of his experiences: 'We got nothing for the first 12 days and had to do forced marching right through France and Belgium…. At the first peep of dawn we were herded together and made to walk until ten past 11 that night, where we lay in a lane. Then the same the next day for 12 days, living on the charities of the villages we passed.'[8] Yet for all the efforts of the civilians, it was the guards who had control over what the prisoners were allowed. When water buckets were left at the roadside by civilians for the prisoners to drink from, the guards simply kicked them over, leaving the prisoners ever more thirsty.

In their desperation the British prisoners fought for food with their allies and with each other. Fights even broke out between members of rival regiments, each accusing the other of having let them down in battle. It was little wonder that morale dropped as their humiliation on the battlefield was reinforced by the degradation endured on the marches. Ken Wilats, marching from Abbeville towards Trier in the Rhineland,

remembered the situation: 'My feelings were dulled by the extreme physical conditions. To be honest with you, the morale was defeatist. There
wasn't too much anger against the Germans – only when they kicked
the buckets of water over. I think we all thought we'd been unlucky. Let's
face it, we weren't trained soldiers, we were just there because we had to
be. So we just thought it was hard luck.'[9]

As the columns continued their journeys prisoners swarmed like lo-
custs through the local kitchens and gardens stealing all the food they
could find to fuel them on the march. For Gordon Barber it was a time
to learn to survive: 'They had guards but there were so many of us they
couldn't keep an eye on us all. So the good thing was you could nip off
now and again. Not far, but if you saw a farmhouse you could go to get
food. I remember we were going through a village and I saw a butchers
shop. I had a few francs so I went in this little shop and saw this piece
of meat hanging on a hook. I said "How much?" He said "No, no, no".
So I slapped the coin on the counter, ripped the meat off the hook, right
handed him – smacked him out of the way a bit sharpish – but he didn't
go down. And I ran back into the crowd.'[10]

It was not only the civilians who came into conflict with the marching prisoners. There was precious little camaraderie amongst the defeated Allies. British prisoners watched in amazement at the behaviour
of the Dutch soldiers among them. They had fought hard alongside
their allies but once they discovered their country had capitulated, they
cheered, mounted their bikes and rode off home. As one of the onlook-
ers recalled: 'We thought that was a little odd. They weren't exactly in a
"Churchillian" frame of mind.'[11] The ragged British prisoners were also
irritated by the sight of French soldiers who marched into captivity with
their kit intact, or the Belgians whose sudden capitulation had left the
British flank exposed. The Germans exploited these divisions, humiliating the British in front of the French where circumstances permitted.
One small group of British territorials found themselves in a hospital
with large numbers of French prisoners; whilst the Frenchmen looked
on the British were forced to clear up piles of human excrement, picking it up with their bare hands and throwing it from the windows. Later
on, during the journey into Germany, some angry British POWs threw
their French counterparts from the moving trains in order to clear space
for themselves. Gordon Barber was among those who came into contact
with his erstwhile allies: 'I saw the French getting issued dripping from
these big vats. I had a French overcoat I'd pinched, so I could go and
get my share. As I came away with mine the French spotted my British

jacket and I had to run for it. This Froggie went to grab it, he kicked my arm, so I nutted him hard. So I ran like bleedin' anything and got back to my mates. But personally I think if it hadn't have been for the French civilians we would have starved.'[12]

By night the columns stopped by the roadside. They slept in the open air or occasionally in barns, fighting each other for the best place to sleep. Whilst one column of prisoners was resting for the night in flooded fields the strong men fought for places on the dry ground whilst the weaker men had to spend the night standing in inches of water. Many of those left standing in the water found themselves plagued by months of rheumatic pain courtesy of their overnight soakings. It was little wonder they fought to stand in the dry areas, as one of the 'stronger men' later wrote: 'The evolutionary clock had been put back to the era of the survival of the fittest. Man's primitive instincts had taken over. How thin is the veneer of civilization!'[13]

Fortunately for the soldiers most were young and healthy. They were strong enough to keep going despite the shortages of food, their aching feet and their skin rubbed red raw by the heavy wool of their battledress, as one explained: 'You'd be surprised how resilient you are at that age. When you know that if you don't keep going you're going to die – they're going to fucking shoot you.'[14] One of those shot and killed during the march was a Sapper Singleton who met his end after striking a guard who had been hitting him with a rifle butt for not marching quick enough. Those lucky enough not to face such extreme violence still suffered much. One prisoner later wrote home about how the march affected his health. When he finally sat down on a hard seat he had realised he had used up all his reserves of fat and his buttocks had disappeared: 'So I'm now just gristle and bone, but as hard as iron and in good health, except for diarrhoea … I'm like Ghandi, with no hope of getting back any fat on my bones on that diet. I'm always hungry.'[15]

Despite their desperate condition they trudged on and on until, after marches totalling hundreds of miles, they reached holding areas within Germany. Here they were gathered until transport could be arranged to their eventual destinations. From these camps the prisoners were marched to railway stations where they were crammed into railway trucks to continue their journey. At the German border one group of prisoners cheered when they saw the transport awaiting them – surely anything would be better than marching. Many would soon change their minds. All across Germany prisoners were crammed into closed wagons that bore the legend '8 horses or 40 men'. In spite of the notices

60 or more men were crammed inside, seldom able to sit down, never able to lie down. Some groups were even forced into wagons that had recently been used to transport horses, so recently that the floors were still covered in horse manure. In one case at least 80 men were forced into a single wagon. Desperate for a smoke men began pulling pages from their pay books and searching for shreds of tobacco in the depths of their pockets to roll cigarettes that helped them momentarily forget all they were enduring.

For what seemed like an eternity they travelled further into the heart of the newly expanded Reich. None knew where they were heading nor that their final destination would shape how they would live for the next five years. All thought of what lay ahead was submerged beneath the desperate desire to leave their transport and finally be allowed some peace. In wagons without toilet facilities, and without even a bucket provided for them to use, the POWs were forced to improvise. Desperate men used their boots or tin helmets as toilets and poured the contents out of the slits running along the sides of the wagons. Where excrement stained the floors they had nothing to wash it away with except their own urine and when they needed to wipe their backsides they simply tore pages from books or ripped the pockets from their uniforms. Gordon Barber recalled his journey:

> They loaded us into cattle trucks – like the ones they put the Jews in – and slammed the door. All you had were small slits either side of the door. Heaven forbid if you sat beside them, 'cause anybody who wanted the toilet would do it in their tin helmet and throw it out. Then you got the blowback. We were in them for about two or three days and that was the only time I remember falling asleep – sitting back to back with another bloke – and hearing the constant drum of the train wheels turning. I thought it was going to drive me mad. But deep down you knew it had to stop somewhere. They used to let us out, take the straw out 'cause that was a mess, so all you wanted to do was stretch your legs.[16]

Others were packed into barges where, deep in the dark recesses of the holds they travelled for days, sweating in the heat, the floor running with watery faeces courtesy of the men with diarrhoea. Few cared where they were heading, they simply wanted to be get out into the fresh air, away from the filth and the stench of shit, dirty uniforms and unwashed bodies.

For all the trials of their journey the morale of the prisoners remained relatively high. Many thought the war would be over quickly, expecting the British to reach a deal with the Germans – a deal that would see them soon heading home. Some of the younger men were buoyed by the words of old 'regulars' some of whom had already experienced captivity back in the Great War. Those maudlin souls, who despaired for the future, often attempted to 'pal up' with stronger men, men who they thought they would be able to rely on in the uncertain times ahead.

Eventually the trains and barges stopped and the final march into captivity began. Many found themselves in East Prussia or areas of Poland and Czechoslovakia annexed by the Reich. Their humiliation began in front of a cowed population:

> They marched us into a town. It was Danzig. There were young Jerry soldiers in the streets flicking their fag ends to our blokes and some of our blokes were grabbing them. The Jerries were laughing. Some of them flicked the fags then trod on them when our blokes went to grab them. I said to my mate 'The bastards, I won't pick 'em up. I'll never let them see they've got the upper hand.' And we were both smokers. [17]

This final humiliation was the perfect preparation for what they were soon to suffer in the German Stalags. The shock defeat of the BEF and its allies had left the Germans unprepared for such a vast influx of prisoners and there were seldom enough facilities to house them all. Some were sent to temporary accommodation in tented camps whilst others found themselves without beds and were forced to sleep on the cold concrete or wooden floors of their huts. Others were sent to former Polish army forts where they spent their days enclosed within thick concrete walls. Toilet facilities in some camps consisted of open tubs kept in the middle of huts which had to be carried outside to be emptied. Although for many of the prisoners the conditions would improve, for others their life was hardly to change until the long-awaited return to Europe of the Allied armies.

But before this could happen many more men would join the remnants of the BEF behind the barbed wire fences of the Stalags. The defeats suffered during the dark years of the war, up until the defeat of the Afrika Korps at El Alamein in October 1942, had seen waves of prisoners make their way into captivity. Norway, Greece, Crete and North Africa all saw thousands of men captured. Britons, Canadians, Indians, South Africans, New Zealanders, Australians, Cypriots and Palestinians were all destined for captivity.

Each defeat brought more men into the clutches of the enemy. Many were embittered by the defeats, blaming their officers for battlefield failures, feeling their defeats were the cause of somebody's ineptitude rather than any military failing on their behalf. Some vented their anger by booing officers trying to address them in the POW enclosures. Many of those captured in North Africa or Greece experienced even worse conditions in their first days of captivity than those taken prisoner in France. Just as prisoners in France had been forced to spend the night in flooded fields, some in North Africa were made to stand for hours in swamps. They too paid the price with months of rheumatic pain following them through their incarceration. If that was not burden enough the extreme heat left them dry-mouthed and exhausted. Flies swarmed over what little food they had – the same flies that were feasting on the pools of excrement filling the festering open latrines within the concentration areas. Worse came as mosquitoes fed on their sun ravaged skin, leaving many to suffer the inevitable effects of malaria. Even when moved into indoor accommodation they seldom had beds, instead sleeping on bare floors or rush mats. One group of men were kept in a warehouse, the floor of which was already soiled with the excrement of the previous batch of prisoners who had passed through. Such were the extreme conditions endured by one group of South African prisoners that it reached the point where 14 men a day were being admitted to hospital.

In face of such conditions it was little wonder that tempers grew short as the men divided themselves along national grounds. Whereas in France the British had been hostile towards the French, in North Africa there were many fights against prisoners from South Africa. In the aftermath of such fights, some of the offenders were publicly flogged by their Italian captors. In particular the British blamed the South Africans for the fall of Tobruk – it was an argument that would follow the prisoners through the POW camps of Italy and on into the Stalags and work camps of Germany.

Even when they had been transferred from North Africa to Italy, conditions didn't improve much with prisoners crowded into tented transit camps for weeks on end, still suffering the extremes of weather. Not all even reached Italy in safety. One Italian transport ship was torpedoed on its journey from Tripoli. Of the 500 British and Indian prisoners on board just 57 were saved. When another ship was torpedoed the crew abandoned ship leaving the prisoners to their fate. The ship stayed afloat for long enough to allow most of the prisoners to escape from the hold, but with no lifeboats available there was nowhere for them to go. After two uncertain hours the stricken ship finally slid beneath the waters, taking with it 160 of the 300 POWs on board.

Once in Italian camps few of the prisoners tasted the fabled local cuisine, instead they made do with starvation rations of weak macaroni stews and biscuits described as looking and tasting like kitchen tiles. Others fought each other to get hold of biscuits that were already green with mould or crawling with maggots. Even in the cold of the Italian winter they survived on a bowl of stew and two bite-sized bread rolls for a whole day. Hunger reached such a level that some men considered frying pieces of cardboard to sate their cravings, and others happily ignored the maggots they found living in biscuits. In desperation prisoners willingly swapped their wedding rings for pots of jam, or exchanged their watches for chunks of bread. Others used boxes to make sparrow traps, their prey being plucked and thrown into the pot. Within months their health tumbled to a state where prisoners had to be careful about standing up too quickly for fear they might pass out. At one camp built on a hillside the starving men could only make their way uphill by crawling on their hands and knees. As one prisoner later wrote: 'Is it any wonder that we do not love the Italians?'[18] They soon realised the benefits of Red Cross parcels, as one later wrote: 'The greatest event in the life of a prisoner of war was the distribution of Red Cross parcels. Without them many of us would not be alive to tell the tale.'[19]

The situation was much the same for the men captured on Crete. For weeks many were kept on the island clearing up in the aftermath of battle. They worked all day under the blistering Cretan sun, filling in bomb craters, clearing rubble, preparing runways for the Luftwaffe, and burying the dead of both sides. Stinking and clad in rags their dry mouths craved for liquid refreshment, their stomachs yearned for hot food. As they toiled they watched their guards smoking British cigarettes, eating British rations and wearing British khaki drill uniforms. Each time local civilians attempted to give them food or water the guards chased them away, hitting them with rifle butts or firing over their heads. Some noted how they were taken prisoner in early June but were not registered as POWs until late August. In the intervening period they faced treatment that had serious repercussions for their health. It was little wonder the British doctors reported that many among the wounded were found to have infections in their wounds. Conditions soon became desperate and an Australian POW, Sergeant Maurice Kelk, later recorded the shocking treatment they were subjected to: 'When I say no food, I mean no food.'[20] He also noted how hundreds of the British and Australian prisoners died from dysentery, malaria or starvation. Describing his own skin as looking like parchment, Kelk noted how he dropped from 13 stone to just 7 stone in two-and-a-half months of captivity.

As hunger bit, the prisoners scrounged whatever they could find to eat. When one group of men found a sack of flour they mixed it with olive oil and locally grown sultanas to bake a cake. When the cooking was complete, much to their surprise they found the cake was rock solid. On closer inspection they discovered the 'flour' had actually been plaster of Paris. Some among the prisoners noted that the 'lentil' soup given to them was actually hot water with dirt mixed into it.

Eventually, their work complete, the prisoners began the long haul to the Stalags of Germany. Exhausted from the weeks of hard labour, clad in filthy rags, their humiliation was almost complete. For some among them the final sign of how low they had fallen came when Italian soldiers emptied chamber pots over them from the upstairs window of a house. Marched to a port they were crammed into the deep holds of cargo ships where they were locked into the darkness. Exhausted they lay down, squashed like sardines against the men next to them, only to feel rats scampering over their faces as they attempted to sleep. The floors ran with urine and faeces as they awaited their arrival in port. It was a fitting prelude to life in captivity.

Once ashore they were transferred to rat-infested barracks at Salonika on the Greek mainland where they endured more disease and degradation before they were eventually moved north through the Balkans into Germany. Night by night they heard shots and cries as the guards opened fire on those going outside to use the stinking latrines. No mercy was shown to these men wracked by dysentery and in the morning the bodies of the dead were laid out as a warning to their fellow prisoners. Even during the day the guards had a habit of tossing hand grenades into the latrines to force the prisoners out. As a result the prisoners began to use the parade ground as their toilet. Yet again the prisoners faced a daily routine of boredom and starvation rations. They lived on weak stews and soups, and noticed how the only meat arriving at the cookhouse seemed to be horses' heads. When they were called out to parade some dropped dead, others collapsed from exhaustion. Those who stood up too quickly found themselves blacking out. The wretched men were forced to walk sideways up stairs, one step at a time gripping the handrail, for fear of falling. Others were reduced to crawling. One group of ravenous prisoners were able to steal a donkey that was cut up and divided between them. Nothing was wasted, with one desperate

Australian cutting off the animal's genitals, saying he would boil them for three hours and then eat them.

The raids on Dieppe and St Nazaire in 1942 brought many more soldiers trudging wearily into the Stalags of Germany. The campaigns in Italy and north-west Europe also brought more prisoners although with no major defeats their numbers were fewer than in the preceding years. Even in the opening hours of D-Day some men were left to the mercy of the enemy. The parachute drops of the morning of 6 June left many of the airborne soldiers isolated. Eric 'Bill' Sykes of the 7th Parachute Battalion was among them. He and his comrades were dropped far to the east of their target, the Orne river. He recalled how his plane's crew had told them they 'knew the exact field', however: 'They may have known the exact field but they sure as hell didn't know the right river.'[21] Teaming up with other stranded men he attempted to make his way back to his unit. After a number of days wandering, with occasional encounters with the enemy, they were eventually apprehended:

Finally on the thirteenth day, unlucky for some, the group of seven that I was with, eventually got ourselves into a predicament where we were pinned down in a ditch by machine gun fire and suffered the ignominy of capture. To our questionable credit, I must say that we were some of the first of the all-conquering liberation army to enter the city of Paris, albeit under armed guard with a German tour director. The German guards were very proud to show us their recent real estate acquisitions, the Eiffel Tower, the Arc De Triomphe, etc.[22]

Like so many of those taken prisoner in northern France four years earlier Sykes would suffer much before his final liberation:

At the Gare du Nord railway station in Paris where we were stood outside on display to the French people before being locked in box cars in the railway siding. Two days and two nights we were locked up in a boxcar before we got under steam and started our journey to far away places. The reason for this fright was that the siding was bombed each night by Allied aircraft and as we were locked in the box cars with no means of escape we were sitting targets and a hit would have meant our immediate demise. A large sliding door, which was locked at all times, was the only means of entry into, or exit from, our less than luxury accommodation and this could cause much alarm especially during the periods of strafing by Allied aircraft whilst we were en route to our final destination. The box cars had one small window about nine inches deep by 18 inches long situated near the roof and secured by strands of barbed wire, and during the heat of the day, it was a personal struggle to avoid suffocation by getting air from under the sliding door by rotation of people. I believe that there were about 30 prisoners to each car and we slept whenever possible on the bare floor boards. The only toilet was a bucket in one corner, which was not the most hygienic or the most fragrant aspects of creature comfort but, after all, we were prisoners. There were many times when we were locked in the car for several days on end without food, water, or sanitation, and in our particular luxury coach we had several walking wounded who did not survive the hazardous journey due to lack of medical treatment for the gangrenous infections in festering wounds which they had sustained in battle.[23]

Three complete months elapsed between capture and the moment Sykes finally entered the working camp that would become his home until liberation.

For soldiers captured after D-Day there was one further burden they had to endure, something that had not been a factor for the men captured in the early years of the war. By 1945 the Allied airforces had almost total command of the skies. Often able to patrol above the battlefields of Europe with impunity, they were entrusted with destroying the transport and supply infrastructure that brought German troops and supplies to the front. This involved daylight attacks on individual trains by fighter-bombers and heavy bombing raids on railway yards. For the newly captured men being transported on the trains that were the targets of their countrymen it became a fraught time. Unlikely to escape from the wagons and unable to see what was happening the prisoners listened in horror to the whooshing of rockets, the rattle of machine gun fire or the scream of bombs as they came under attack. Hearts beat fast and men prayed as they waited for the deadly impact of explosives. Bill Sykes remembered: 'the fear of the potential horror of imminent death during one of the constant strafing by Allied aircraft, took its toll and many of the "unfortunates" never reached the promised land where "Arbeit macht frei".' He watched the reactions of the men around him as his train became the unwitting target of aerial attack:

I was with a group of POWs of different nationalities locked in a railroad cattle car which was located for some days and nights in a siding of the Gare De Nord railway station in Paris, mid June 1944, during the nightly bombings and strafings of the sidings by Allied aircraft there was a tendency for a few believers, mostly American, to pray out loud for salvation. The British POWs kept a stiff upper lip and chastised the 'offenders' for their doom and gloom attitude. Those couple of nights locked in the railway siding were the most frightening that I have ever experienced.[24]

The last great influx to the Stalags came in the aftermath of the defeat of the 1st Airborne Division at Arnhem when over 6,000 airborne troops were taken prisoner. This last large-scale defeat came in the aftermath of a bitter and intense battle in which both sides fought with a fervour seldom seen on the western front. Bryan Willoughby was among the paratroopers spearheading the drive to the bridge. Like so many of his comrades it was a journey he would not complete:

> We ran right into the Germans in the woods. Straight away we were into one hell of a battle – no messing about. We lost half the company before we started. That was rough. I don't think I was scared – you didn't have time to be. I knew everything was going wrong. It was chaos. We didn't know what to do next because we were cut off and the wireless didn't work. Then on the Monday we headed into Arnhem. We just rambled along doing our own thing, getting shot at by snipers and so on. It wasn't too bad. At four o'clock in the morning they said we'd go for the bridge. We were being shot at from all over the place – blokes were going down right, left and centre. Eventually we had about a 1000 yards to go but the company was down to about 20 men. The CO said 'Right, make for the bridge'. There was none of this 'Go! Go! Go!' like you see in the Yankee films. There was hardly a sound. We were pinned down straight away. We realised we would be hit eventually but there really wasn't any alternative. You couldn't go backwards or sideways, so there only one place to go – forwards. We just kept shooting and running – and hoping to get away with it. Our chances of getting to the bridge were nil. I saw the company commander outside a house about 150 yards away, shouting 'C'mon'. We were down to about half a dozen by then. I dived off to make for the house and got fairly near it. The next thing I felt a thump in the back and I'd been hit by a hand grenade. I span around and saw a dark object sailing towards me, I knew it was another grenade, I jumped back but it got me in the legs.[25]

Realising his role in the battle was over Willoughby knew he had to find help:

I was getting a bit 'slap happy'. I joined a group of wounded with a Red Cross made from blood on a white shirt and we were taken prisoner. How did I feel? I was highly relieved to still be alive. Nothing else matters when you're in a situation like that. Then this tank comes up and I was taken to a casualty clearing station in a café. Then they got behind the bar and started serving us drinks. They were quite sociable. There was no real animosity towards the Germans, they treated us like we treated their men.[26]

In the aftermath of the battle there were many prisoners, like Willoughby, treated with kindness by the enemy – a kindness that saved their lives. For others the experience was very different. Those who resisted as their captors robbed them of personal possessions were shot without compunction, the actions of the guards ensuring compliance from the rest of the prisoners. When others escaped from a truck the guards opened fire on the remaining men causing many fatalities. A shadow of fear was cast over the prisoners by the conflicting behaviour of their captors. At one moment they were being well treated, at the next they were being executed without warning. To deepen the confusion some even watched as Germans who had executed prisoners were themselves executed by their own officers.

For all the POWs, wherever and whenever they were taken prisoner, many of the experiences were the same. Sitting in fields among crowds of fellow prisoners as they awaited their fate. Forced marches with little food or water. Day upon day crammed into railway wagons, or locked into the holds of ships. Fear and hunger, deprivation and despair. What was common for all these men – from those captured during the retreat to Dunkirk to those taken prisoner in the fields of Normandy – was a shared sense of bewilderment upon capture. Few had any clear idea of what their fate might be. Receiving a punch, kick or rifle butt across the head was the least of their worries. The theft of personal possessions, whilst frustrating them by their inability to take action, was little more than an inconvenience. They could also be used as human shields by the Germans, who knew men would be unwilling to fire on their comrades. Like Gordon Barber at St Valery, many expected to be shot – indeed some were. During the retreat to Dunkirk over one hundred men of the Royal Warwickshire Regiment were executed by SS troops, as were a similar number of men from the Norfolks.

Though lucky to be alive most felt disappointed to have failed to perform their allotted tasks on the battlefield, aggrieved at being lost in the chaos of war. The emotional turmoil caused by capture was explained by John Mercer. Though only in captivity for a matter of hours, upon release he realised the impact such an experience could have:

> I did suffer a mild form of hysteria. I was introduced to some press people. Captain Thompson said 'You, have a chat to this guy, something interesting for you.' And they all gathered around me and talked to me, and do you know, I could not tell them where I lived. I mean I wanted to but I just couldn't. I couldn't tell them how old I was, I could get my name out that's all. They went away and came back about half an hour later and I still couldn't. I was traumatised. But it passed, I slept it off. I just couldn't articulate, it wouldn't come out. I thought to myself that was very strange.[27]

Yet despite the mental stress, not all the feelings of surrendering soldiers were negative. Jim Sims, captured at Arnhem, explained: 'I have often been asked what my feelings were on being captured and my answer seems to upset those asking that question. I felt relief that I was still alive, although badly wounded, and with a bit of luck would see my parents again.'[28]

Men like Sims really were lucky, like so many of the men captured earlier in the war, he went 'into the bag' in the company of his fellow soldiers. Although wounded he was fortunate to be in the company of his comrades, men he knew and could rely on – men who could help share the burdens of what lay ahead. They retained much of the comradeship that had made life in the army bearable – indeed, the men captured at Arnhem even had the staff of their own field hospitals on hand to assist them.

Others were not so fortunate. Many of those captured in minor battlefield actions found themselves lost and alone, and at the mercy of their captors. Sometimes the experiences of the first hours of captivity set a precedent for what was to follow. George Marsden, a private in the Duke of Wellington's Regiment, captured in the Netherlands in late 1944, explained the beginnings of his ordeal: 'A small number of our Company were ordered to move forward to a very deep and wide anti-tank ditch, and capture the position. This we did, surprising the enemy, causing little casualties, capturing all the German unit. We dug in outside a farmhouse and were attacked by a large force. After losing some men we were ordered back to our lines.' At nightfall they successfully recaptured the ditch but once again came under counterattack:

> A lot of the lads were shot. I was blasted through the arm and shoulder
> by a machine gun. I regained consciousness some time after and was
> carried away on a door by two Germans. I didn't feel fear and certainly
> not relief. I had lost a lot of blood and was in and out of consciousness.
> I appeared to be the last of our group, the others killed or taken pris-
> oner. I was carried into a coal cellar. When I got used to the dim light
> from the grate above me I saw two Germans in the far corner. They were
> wounded and had their heads bandaged. When they realised who I was
> they crawled towards me and started shouting and punching my head. I
> shouted out and they were dragged away, then they attacked me again.
> I was then carried down a street to a house where a lady tried to wash
> the blood off me, before the street further down was attacked by an RAF
> plane firing rockets.

Refused admittance to a civilian hospital by his captors, Marsden was
dumped on a footpath until eventually taken to a makeshift hospital
where he was operated on and then spent the night drifting in and out
of consciousness:

> I never had my trousers removed at all, my underpants were stiff with
> dried blood, these I never removed until the war was nearly over. I was
> taken to a hospital train and put in a bed near a big iron stove where
> food was being prepared by the Germans. I soon realised I had a couple
> of hand grenades in my pocket, I managed to hide these under the mat-
> tress I was on. I was taken to a big hospital which housed a number of
> German wounded. The doctor used to poke his fingers in my wounds
> saying 'Pain! Pain!'[29]

Eventually sent by train to a POW camp hospital, Marsden finally met
up with fellow prisoners and began life behind the wire. It was a life that
would mirror much of the loneliness, pain and terror he had known in
those first uncertain days of captivity – a life familiar to so many of his
fellow prisoners.

TWO

Abandon Hope
All Ye Who Enter Here

'The atmosphere in the POW camp was dog eat dog, and one soon adapted'[1]

'Horrible. The bed bunks in the sheds at XXb were four or five high with no room to move at all.'[2]

With their journeys finally over the weary POWs stepped down from the goods wagons to begin the final march into the Stammlagers – or Stalags as they were most commonly known – that would become temporary homes for most until they were sent out into industry. Few had travelled in comfort and most had endured extreme hardship but, as 18-year-old paratrooper Bill Sykes noted of his arrival: 'Not a pleasant experience, but we'd survived.'[3] Wearily moving forward, step after step – often dizzy from the physical deprivations of the journey – the prisoners had no idea of what awaited them. Would they be moved into barracks not unlike those they had known back in 'Blighty' or would a more uncomfortable fate await them?

As they approached the camps many had a deceptively pleasant look. As Bill Sykes put it:

My first impression upon entering the camp was – I hate to say this, as I believe that I'm leaving myself wide open to a great deal of criticism – that it appeared on the surface to have a sort of Butlin's holiday camp type environment with a soccer pitch, garden allotments, and many other features which included classes on a varied assortment of subjects. There were bands, instruments, an orchestra, a choir, a small theatre, all of which I really hadn't expected. If I remember correctly after all these years the camp was sectioned off into three sectors, British/American, French, and Russian. The British/American sector was to the best of my knowledge commanded by a senior British officer who, amongst other duties, controlled the actions of various committees which had been formed in order to try in someway to relieve the inmates of the everyday boredom of being caged up like animals behind barbed wire and get them to pursue active social lives.[4]

Despite initially noticing how well organised the camp seemed to be he also spotted the barbed wire fences that seemed to run for miles. Two fences, filled with coils of barbed wire, seemed to offer no prospect of exit.

To compound the misery of incoming prisoners were high wooden towers containing searchlights and machine gun posts, another sign that the enemy took the business of detaining them seriously. And beyond the wire they saw what would be their 'homes' – long lines of charmless, wooden huts. It was a chilling prospect for the incoming prisoners. Most camps had an unfinished and unpromising look about them. The huts were basic, laundry was often spread around the compound – hanging from windows or strung between huts – bored looking men wandered around within the wire, there were few real paths or roadways and mud seemed an almost permanent feature for long periods of the year. As one man later wrote, the Stalags should have carried the slogan 'Abandon Hope All Ye Who Enter Here'.[5]

Before they could enter the main camps the incoming men had another port of call. Their first stop was usually a transit barracks separated from the main enclosure, in which they waited to be processed by the camp authorities. Crammed into vast huts, usually with never ending rows of bunks, with bare boards and often devoid of any furniture, they awaited their turn. At Stalag XXa at Thorn the prisoners passed through Camp 13a. Here many among the first batches of prisoners arriving in 1940 were beaten with rifle butts for refusing to comply during interrogation. In the camp up to 1,000 men were housed in three vast huts where they slept in triple-tiered bunks. Conditions were so cramped there was no space for tables and chairs between the bunks. When their time came they were photographed, fingerprinted, sometimes given chest x-rays, then given a small piece of metal with their POW number stamped on it. Although oblong in shape the prisoners always referred to this as their 'disc'. This was to be worn around their necks on a length of string, a symbol that they were no longer a free man but instead just a number in the Reich's vast new labour force. Once they had been processed the new prisoners were sent for delousing. They were stripped and their uniforms sent to be boiled. Entering the showers the prisoners had no realisation of what lay ahead. Then the taps turned on and their naked forms were assaulted by scalding hot water. After what was little more than seconds, but which seemed like hours, the hot water was turned off to be replaced by freezing cold water. With no towels to dry themselves they were then rushed out to where their now clean clothes awaited them. They struggled to dress themselves, some finding their uniforms shrunk by the heat of the wash, others unable to find their own uniforms as groups of men scrambled around trying to find what was theirs. One man re-dressed only to find a sock had been lost and, knowing the importance of protecting his feet, the lost sock was replaced with a mitten. Washed and clothed, they were finally let loose into the main compound to find themselves a bunk. Now they were *Kriegsgefangene*, or 'Kriegies' as they called themselves, men whose fate rested in the hands of the enemy.

At well-organised camps they were greeted by senior NCOs who allotted bunks to them, at less well-organised ones they were simply left to find themselves a suitable sleeping place. For men arriving at Thorn in the early days of the war an even worse fate awaited them – there were no bunks. Ken Wilats arrived at Fort 17, in Thorn, after three days and nights packed into a cattle truck from Trier. He stepped down from the train to see the Napoleonic Fort in front of him:

Our feelings were mixed when we arrived. The train journey had been so horrendous we were pleased for any change and any situation that didn't stress you too much. Although the conditions in those days were horrendous. Everybody had lice. We slept in rows on the floor on straw in a big open room, there were no bunks. The toilet arrangements were a deep trench with a tree trunk across it. You sat on the tree trunk and held on and hoped for the best. The conditions were primitive but everybody was so worn out you just lay there. The food was inadequate, just a bowl of barley and potato soap and five men to a loaf. You were just existing in those early days. It was absolutely degrading, especially the diarrhoea. It was frightful. There was no organisation, it was every man for himself. There were some NCOs there from my regiment but they all fell to the level of the private soldiers. We became quite equal, because everybody was in the same boat. The NCOs ate the same food as us and had the same diarrhoea as us, so it was a great leveller. I never had a bed at Fort 17. So the first thing I wanted to do was get on a working party.[6]

Fort 8 at Poznan was another relic of the Napoleonic wars. Here too the prisoners slept on the cold stone floors of underground cells and queued for hours just to collect a mugful of water from the single handpump available for washing and drinking. It was not just water that was in short supply, many of the necessary basics of life were unknown to POWs in the early days of captivity. At their first meals in the Stalags many prisoners felt lost. Those still in possession of their mess tins or enamel mugs were lucky, they could collect the soup or stews they queued for. Others were less fortunate, arriving with nothing to hold food they simply had to improvise. For some it was a situation that would change little in the years ahead. At one work camp it was discovered that more than half the prisoners had no cups or bowls in which to take their meals, and just two men out of 89 had eating utensils. One prisoner, desperate for food, was forced to collect his first meal in his boot. Another stole a dog bowl whilst on a working detail and used that. Others held out their upturned helmets or empty food tins they had scavenged from rubbish dumps. It was humiliating, but food was a precious commodity – food was life.

One group of men arriving at Stalag XVIIIa in Wolfsberg received their first proper meal since their capture in Crete. It was a mixture of cabbage and mashed potato. They marvelled at the fare, excited at the prospect of two hot, filling meals each day. They were soon to be disappointed. As one later recorded it would be one of only two solid meals given to him during four long years of captivity, the rest would be soup or watery stews. In the summer of 1940 prisoners experienced frighteningly little food. Unable to cope with the influx of men the Germans had given them little more than a bowl of thin watery soup each day, with maybe a little bread or a handful of vegetables. In the following months their bodies had grown thin and their eyes sank deep into their skulls. The once proud prisoners walked, or shuffled, with stooped backs, their eyes fixed on the ground ahead of them, their minds full of thoughts of the meals they might one day enjoy. Day upon day their misery continued as they lost weight and grew weak, hardly able to motivate themselves to rise from their beds in the morning.

Then came salvation. The arrival of Red Cross parcels in late 1940 changed the world for the prisoners. The food parcels, each in a cardboard box about the size of a shoebox, were designed to give supplementary food for the prisoners. Using charitable donations, branches of the Red Cross from around the Empire purchased tinned foodstuffs and basic necessities such as soap, toothpaste and toilet paper. They also contained one luxury – cigarettes. These were then packaged together to provide a box considered enough for one prisoner per week. Although the contents varied, the basics were tinned butter, cheese, fish, apple puddings, jam, margarine, curried mutton, peas, corned beef and condensed milk, sugar, as well as packets of tea, sugar and cocoa. Some parcels were more popular than others, with Canadian parcels being particularly favoured for the quality of the foods contained within, whilst American parcels were prized for their ever-popular brands of cigarettes. Such was the high standard of the Canadian parcels that the Canadian military believed they played a vital role in the high morale maintained by the 'Canucks' in the Stalags and at work camps. Canadian reports on returning POWs suggested the quality of their parcels meant they were better able to withstand the mental rigours of captivity than their British, New Zealand or Australian counterparts who often felt forgotten by their governments when they looked at the contents of their parcels. It was little wonder since some British parcels included bizarre provisions such as pots of Coleman's mustard for which the POWs could find little use, apart from using them to make cold compresses.

Regardless of nationality, the parcels were sent by sea to neutral Portugal, from where they were transported by railway to Switzerland. Vast stores were accumulated in Red Cross warehouses then sent by train and truck to be distributed around Stalags throughout the Reich. Once within the Stalags the parcels were put into stores under the control of senior NCOs among the prisoners whose task was to ensure their fair and consistent distribution. It was a thankless task. If they thought stocks were running short and cut the distribution to one parcel between two they were accused of cheating the prisoners. If they continued with one per man, per week, then ran out they were often accused of having stolen the rest of the parcels.

Whatever the truth in such accusations one thing was certain, suddenly they had enough food to survive. No longer were they slowly starving to death. Instead they began to recover. Energy returned to their muscles courtesy of the sugar and chocolate within the hallowed boxes. Fat returned to cover their muscles, the old spring returned to their steps and once more they stood proud – soldiers rather than starving drudges. Yet as they slowly recovered their health, and became strong enough to face work without fear of collapsing at the slightest exertion, their minds remained fixed on one important thing. They were at the mercy of the Germans, the Red Cross may have been their saviour but the Germans retained the power to prevent the distribution of parcels. With this in the back of their minds, the very real fear of starvation hung over the prisoners for every day of their lives in the Stalags – even as late as 1942 some prisoners noted how their daily rations were little more than soup made from mushrooms floating in hot water.

The provision of food was not the only role played by the Red Cross. From their offices in Switzerland they kept in regular contact with both London and Berlin with regard to the welfare of prisoners. Their representatives made regular visits both to the Stalags and to work camps and compiled reports on conditions, in particular channelling complaints back to the War Office in London. Through these means the British were able to protest about conditions and sometimes the combined weight of government indignation and Red Cross pressure ensured the Germans would actually make changes. Yet their work did not stop there. They also provided a framework for clothing parcels to be sent to prisoners from their families and for spare uniforms to be provided by the British army. Sports equipment, books and costumes for camp theatres – all came courtesy of the Red Cross. Yet it was for the food parcels they would always be remembered.

The misery of poor rations was not the only burden prisoners would endure and living conditions within the Stalags were seldom anything more than barely tolerable. Some camps were better than others but even the best offered little comfort. Not all of the Stalags were the traditional hutted POW camps later portrayed in films. Some consisted of solid, if rather dilapidated buildings such as the stables of former cavalry barracks. Others saw prisoners sleeping in tents as the Wehrmacht struggled to build enough accommodation for the vast influx of POWs.

By 1942 many of the POW camps were overcrowded and unhealthy. At Lamsdorf, which had appeared a well-organised and tidy camp when the first of the post-Dunkirk prisoners arrived back in 1940, the camp had to be closed to visitors after an outbreak of typhus – little wonder in a camp where POWs slept 128 men to a room. By late 1943 there were almost 13,000 POWs living in quarters that the Red Cross believed should house no more than 6,000 men. After the influx of prisoners in the aftermath of the surrender of Italy the newcomers were forced to share straw mattresses on the cold floor of huts and it was believed that over 1,500 of them were without a blanket. Among the worst camps was Stalag XXb at Marienburg which housed a total of 25,000 men, 10,000 of them British. Within the camp all the ground was mud where thousands of men stood for up to 2 hours a day as the Germans carried out innumerable intolerable roll calls. The single room barracks were dark, the gloomy atmosphere heightened by damp laundry hanging in room after room as the inmates desperately searched for space to dry their clothes. The three-tier bunks were crowded closely together with the men in the lowest level sleeping close to the ground.

These conditions were replicated at camps throughout the Reich. One common feature experienced by POWs was discomfort at night. The insanitary conditions in most of the Stalags ensured they were a breeding ground for all manner of insects. POWs may have been de-loused before entering the camps but the insects always seemed to reap-pear. The prisoners were plagued by fleas, lice, cockroaches and bed bugs, all combining to make their lives a misery. Such was the prolifera-tion of bed bugs that prisoners dismantled their beds and passed each piece of the frame through a flame in a desperate attempt to eradicate the bugs. It worked for a short time but just days later they would be back. By night, prisoners in the lower bunks could feel the bugs falling from the bunk above as the man above moved in his sleep. It was awful for them to feel the bugs landing on their faces, a feeling reinforced by the terrible smell of bugs when they were crushed by the men trying to sleep. They were also supposed to sleep on straw filled palliases but in-sects living in the straw made them impractical. They tried filling them with sawdust but the dust merely escaped through holes in the fabric. So they resorted to sleeping on bare boards. Long hours were spent sit-ting on bunks searching the seams of their clothing for insects, squash-ing them between finger and thumbnails, searching each other's hair for bugs – only to restart the next day.

It was not only fleas, lice and bed bugs that tormented the prisoners in their beds at night – there were other creatures roaming freely within many of the Stalags. As one inmate at Stalag XXb recalled:

> You'd feel something touching your leg and you'd turn to the bloke next to you and say 'Do you mind? Keep your fucking leg out of the way.' He'd say 'It ain't me'. You'd look down and there'd be a rat on you. They were all over the camp. There was rubbish all over the place. Not that much food got thrown away, but what did the rats had.[7]

Covers had to be kept over the latrines to try to keep rats from climb-ing out from the open pits and the prisoners were constantly aware of the vermin that scuttled across the piles of excrement beneath them as they sat down to empty their bowels. There was little they could do to prevent the infestations of rats.

Though heated by small stoves there was seldom enough fuel to keep the stoves burning at night; at Stalag VIIIb the daily ration in the middle years of the war was just 25kgs of coal per hut, per day. This was supposed to heat a room for over one hundred men. Unsurprisingly the prisoners awoke cold and damp day after day, month after month. Even the heat of summer hardly penetrated the damp atmosphere, the foetid air heavy with the sickly aroma rising from the buckets they were forced to use as toilets during the night. At Marienburg no recreation rooms were available and each barrack room of 75 bunks provided tables and chairs for less than a third of that number. At night those without seats were forced into their bunks purely by lack of space. Even the men with a seat at a table could not relax with a meal. For all the food they received in Red Cross parcels there were no facilities for cooking. Not that it mattered too much, in June 1942 13,000 Canadian parcels destined for the camp were reported to have gone missing. Indeed, one detachment from the camp reported receiving no parcels between November 1941 and March 1942. Yet these were the lucky ones. Almost half the prisoners at Stalag XXb lived a semi subterranean existence in turf roofed earthen huts with just one small window for light. From a distance the shelters appeared as folds in the land rather than homes for soldiers.

For the inhabitants of these huts even when they returned above ground there was plenty more misery for them to endure. The toilets in the camp were open pits with bare boards above them where the men squatted to empty their bowels. By early 1942 one of two toilet huts had been abandoned since the conditions had deteriorated so much as to make it unusable. The Red Cross reported:

> The latrines are also most inadequate. A hutment of old boards has been constructed over a cement trench, through which a current of water passes at regular intervals. The seats are merely a very narrow plank which runs the length of the trench and a vertical partition separates the men using the latrines. They are extremely dirty and can be smelt from a long distance away.[8]

There were no showers for the prisoners, instead the whole camp shared one washroom of stone troughs, each with a single cold tap. By June of 1942 most inmates reported they had not had a hot shower in many months and only those on work details where showers were available had been able to wash properly. An even worse fate befell prisoners at Stalag XIA who found their camp was built on such flat ground there was nowhere for the latrines to drain away to. The only solution was to dig long ditches to act as overspill areas, which soon left a disgusting smell hanging over the camp. It was little wonder the Red Cross requested the number of inhabitants in the camp should be cut by 50 per cent.

In such barely tolerable conditions POWs across Germany settled down to a routine of mind numbing boredom. In a pattern followed at camps throughout the Reich one prisoner noted his daily routine at Stalag XXIa. They rose at 6.30 a.m. for a breakfast of coffee. After the 8 a.m. *Appell*, or roll call, they washed in the very basic ablutions facilities, then spent the morning sitting around chatting about food, or walking around the perimeter fence. At 12.30 they were issued with soup and spent the rest of the afternoon anxiously awaiting the 5 p.m. daily issue of bread, which they sliced with the edge of their POW identity disc since no knives were allowed in the camp. After that they had the evening roll call and retired to their beds. And so it went on, day after day after day.

At first there was little scope for recreation. In the period before the arrival of Red Cross parcels few had sufficient spirit to do anything except lie on their bunks scratching at insect bites, reading any available books or dreaming of meals to be consumed in the future. Alternatively they used what little reserves of energy they had to walk ceaselessly around inside the perimeter wire chatting idly to their mates, their ragged uniforms hanging limply from their malnourished frames.

Of course, not all among the new prisoners were able to take their place immediately within the Stalag system. The nature of defeat on the battlefield resulted in many among the POWs needing extensive hospital treatment. It was a strange experience for them, first the enemy had tried to kill them and now they were desperately trying to keep them alive and return them to health. Not only that but many lay in hospital wards beside the very men whom they had previously faced on the battlefields. Side by side they shared the attentions of doctors and nurses who, in general, remained dedicated to the treatment of the wounded regardless of nationality. Bryan Willoughby, captured in the streets of Arnhem, was among those to benefit from the attentions of his captors:

We were moved to the St Elizabeth's hospital. It was so crowded. One of the nurses came along and said 'Would you like a drink?' I said 'Yes, please.' She offered me punch or something else. I said 'punch will be fine' she came along with a mug and it was bloody lethal. It was great. What was worrying me was my back injury. I was in great pain and couldn't breathe properly. I don't know if there was any real damage, I got one of the chaps to take a few bits of metal out. That evening a German ambulance came along and took us out. I got in the front with the driver. We hadn't got very far and the driver got his Luger out. He didn't point it at me but was showing it off. Then I realised he was trying to sell it to me! He put it away and got out his waterbottle. The ambulance was hurtling from side to side and the bottle was half full of the most lethal booze I'd ever tasted. I thought the only sensible thing to do was not let him have any more so I finished it off.[9]

Upon arrival at Appledorn hospital he was taken by stretcher to the ward where he stayed for a week:

We'd had injections at the café, at St Elizabeth's hospital, and again at Appledorn. I think I had about ten times more than I should have done. And I couldn't care less. They looked after us. The food was great, the beds were more comfortable than any I'd been in for years. Then we moved to Enschede, where I had my operations. There were four or five Brits among the Germans. We were all chatting, we were all fed up. The German and British soldiers were just the same when it comes to a situation like that – telling crude jokes here and there. After the operation I woke up in the corridor in a bed with a frame over it. In the ward we were amongst the Germans, all mixed. The German soldiers would come in and sit on the bed and have a chat. One of the airborne fellows was a regimental type, he said 'No fraternising' but we didn't take any notice.[10]

After recovering from their treatment the wounded men were released from hospital and once more thrown back into the system where few would experience the same standards of care that they had known in hospital.

Even after they had regained their health, and leisure activities had begun, few could escape the sense of claustrophobia that prevailed. Most did their best to ignore their problems, and did their utmost to rise above reality. Bryan Willoughby was among those who tried his utmost to remain optimistic during his imprisonment, despite the knowledge that his wounds posed a very serious threat to his health and future well-being: 'I can honestly say I was too interested in the situation to despair about it. It was something new, a new part of war for me. I wouldn't say I was relishing it, but I was too busy taking it all in and seeing what was going on around me to be worried about anything else. I just took it as a new experience. That was my feeling all the time.'[11]

Despite such optimism most within the Stalags felt they were cut off from the real world. Some among them retreated into a mental shell, spending their days sullen and silent, ignoring their fellow prisoners, their hearts gripped by despair and their thoughts unspoken. Even the most optimistic men realised that somewhere, far away, a war was being fought – but they were not in it. Somewhere children were growing up or wives growing lonely – but they did not see it. Somewhere the world was still turning – but they could not feel it. Instead they were cocooned into a world of roll calls, hanging around, meals, more hanging around, more roll calls and sleep. Tied into this routine they craved contact with outsiders and the chance to see what lay beyond the barbed wire – in short, an opportunity to experience life again in whatever form it might take.

With boredom clawing at their minds it was little wonder many prisoners were desperate to find any way out of POW camps. But it would not be the ingenuity and intrigue of escape committees that offered them the chance. Instead the break in the monotony came courtesy of Article 27 of the Geneva Convention which stated that all able-bodied prisoners below the rank of corporal were obliged to work. The Convention made clear such work should offer no military benefit to the host nation, but for many of the captive labour force this made little difference. It soon became clear they had little choice, as prisoners they would merely have to do as they were told.

The system for employing POWs outside the camps was relatively simple. They were in effect the property of the camp commandant and could be loaned out to any firm bearing the necessary credentials. There were three types of work detail they might expect to be sent on. The first were the Landwirtschaft Arbeitskommandos or farm details. Next came the Gewerbe Arbeitskommandos where the men toiled in industrial concerns. The third possibility were the *Bau und Arbeitsbataillons* – or Building and Work battalions These were pioneer units which were not administered by individual Stalags but which were available to be transferred around the Reich wherever men were needed for heavy building work, commonly referred to as 'pick and shovel' duties. The German authorities kept lists of the types of work POWs could be asked to undertake, including general agricultural work, forestry, agricultural development, mining, railway construction, shunting and loading, construction of hydrogenation plants, cellulose or artificial wool factories, building of roads or housing, construction of dams, quarrying, brick

making and peat production. Most importantly the official list concluded with the sweeping statement 'any other work of national importance'.[12] In time the assessment of 'national importance' would have a
dangerously wide brief.

Any employer wishing to use prisoners could get a form from the local labour office granting them a permit to utilise captured labour. The
labour office of the local POW camp could then be approached and a
contract drawn up between the employer and the commandant. This
contract meant the prisoners would never in the future be able to make
individual claims against the company concerned. All detachments were
supposed to be of around 20 men but in practice many were much larger. Groups of less than ten men were only permitted if they could be
lodged with other prisoners in their locality and if sufficient guards were
available. Within each detachment a 'Man of Confidence' was elected.
Usually an NCO who had volunteered for a work detachment, this was
the individual responsible for the well-being of the prisoners and whose
task it was to liaise between the POWs and their captors.

The lodging of the POWs was the responsibility of the employer,
although the government compensated them for the expense of preparing accommodation. All lodgings needed windows to be covered with
grates, a fence around the camp area, safety locks on the doors, lighting, heating, drinking water, washing facilities and toilets. Within their
lodgings the prisoners were entitled to one straw mattress, a pillow,
two woollen blankets, one towel, a wooden stool, a bowl, a spoon and
a drinking cup. Additionally, lodgings should also provide tables and
racks for clothes.

However, not all working parties were lodged in outside facilities.
At Stalags near to major towns the men were transported to work on a
daily basis, returning to the main camps at the end of their shifts. For
those remaining in the main camps the return of the working men was a
great bonus since they seldom arrived without some form of contraband
concealed about them.

For meals the prisoners were to be given the same rations as civilian workers with supplementary food for those engaged in heavy work.
They would also have to work the same hours as the local labour force
with the proviso that they receive at least one full day without work
each week. In return for their labour they would receive 60 per cent of
the German wage for the job, minus a reduction for board and lodging. Some were shocked to hear they would have deductions made for
income tax. At one work camp prisoners were even forced to pay for the

transit of their own mail and parcels from the Stalag to their place of work.

However the payment of wages was not the great benefit it might have been. Whilst the Reichsmark was becoming Europe's dominant currency, spent and traded throughout the ever expanding Third Reich, the prisoners were given no access to its purchasing power. Instead payments were made in 'Lagergeld' – camp money – that had no value in the outside world. The prisoners laughed about it, this was monopoly money, OK for use in a game but of no real value. All it could be used for was making purchases in the canteens and shops set up for prisoners, enterprises that offered little to the men except beer, lemonade or the occasional supply of razor blades. It was little wonder many of the prisoners shaved little more than once a week since a single pack of razors could cost as much as a month's wages. A few canteens had fresh vegetables for sale, but only if they were lucky. Where canteens were not available they were forced to rely on local shops, where one prisoner would be escorted by guards or would give his parole in order to go shopping. Ignoring the rules stating the prisoners should be allowed to spend their wages, many shopkeepers failed to accept the 'lagergeld' offered by the prisoners, regardless of assurances they would be reimbursed by the Stalag commandants.

An indication of how poorly the prisoners were paid is shown by the price of the beer on sale to them in camp canteens. For 30 pfennigs they could buy half a litre of beer. Yet their daily wage was just 70 pfennigs, or the price of two pints of beer. Translated into modern terms they were working as much as 12 hours a day for a wage of just £5. Frustratingly for men whose clothes grew filthy during the course of their labours, and who often had few spare clothes to use outside work hours, the cost of having their uniforms laundered was prohibitive since almost two days' wages were needed to pay for a weekly wash. Nor could the POWs always benefit from the wages they earned. Men at Bau und Arbeitsbattaillon No 21 found they could earn supplementary wages of up to 2 reichsmarks a day. However they received no more than 70 pfennigs each day since any surplus was retained to pay for camp improvements.

Yet in many ways these were the lucky ones since not all prisoners ever received the full allotment of cash. Rules were introduced to decree that any man not working a full day would not receive his full wage. The short working day could be a result of many factors – poor weather, accidents in workplaces, or simply that a factory had little work to do. This may have been a respite from their labours but it hit their pockets.

At a wage of just 30 or 50 pfennigs a day their somewhat limited purchasing power was further reduced.

Even on the 70 pfennigs a day wage rate they were not rich, especially
since the Germans made them pay for many facilities that the prisoners
might have expected would be provided for free. At one work camp men
wishing to play football were forced to hire a pitch from their employers.
The rate was so high it cost more than the combined daily wages of the
entire 661-man detachment to afford a single game of football. Yet these
were not the most unfortunate of prisoners. Thousands toiled for five
long years for their captors yet never received a penny in wages.

For all the failings of the system there were some commandants who
adhered strictly to the rules, even if this led to some bizarre situations.
Bill Sykes who had parachuted into Normandy on the early hours of
D-Day, found the Geneva Convention was sometimes enforced a little
too stringently:

> During my stay as a guest of the German government I never experienced
> any degree of psychological or physical abuse tantamount to extreme
> brutality, except perhaps for the initial day of our capture when we were
> ordered to strip naked and placed in front of what appeared to be a fir-
> ing squad. The Germans that I came into contact with in my particular
> case always strictly adhered to the Geneva Convention – so much so that
> during one period of our incarceration, the Germans found that there
> was a stipulation somewhere in the convention that all prisoners must
> be deloused on, or at, three monthly intervals – seeing that we hadn't
> been deloused for some considerable period of time and the huts that
> we occupied were louse infested, we were then deloused three consecu-
> tive days in a row in order to conform to the Geneva Convention rules. It
> was a time consuming procedure where you entered a four or five cham-
> ber structure. The first chamber was the disrobing chamber where all
> clothing, including boots, belts, and other apparel were placed in wire
> baskets and fed on a conveyor belt through a very hot duct. The second
> chamber was the body delousing chamber where buckets of disinfectant
> and large brushes, handled by German employees, distributed a very
> caustic substance onto all locations containing hair – head, underarms,
> and genitals. I can assure you that the brushing of the substance on the
> genital area was not a pleasant experience and the genitalia didn't like it
> either and tried their best to escape by receding into the body cavity. The
> third chamber was the washhouse where very strong jets of water, lo-
> cated close to the ceiling structure, sprayed extremely hot, near scalding,

water on the unfortunate participants below in this cleansing exercise. The fourth chamber was the drying chamber where a large four/six foot cold air fan, placed in one corner of the chamber, did its best to blow all and sundry into a state of blue coloured inanimate objects. The last chamber was the hurry up and dress chamber, and seeing that all British uniform trousers had brass buttons on the inside for the attachment of 'braces soldier' in order to keep one's trousers up, you can imagine the discomfort that extremely hot brass buttons can do to the adjacent body skin.[13]

As the new prisoners became aware they would have to work they spent hours sitting around talking about what their employment might be. Although few desired to work for the enemy most were realistic and simply hoped the work would not be too tough. Farmers hoped for agricultural work and civilian miners, though seldom welcoming a return to the coalface, at least knew what to expect. Former cavalrymen from the regiments still mounted during the inter-war years yearned for the opportunity to once more work with horses. It was a difficult time for the prisoners, as they discussed the relative merits of Stalags and work camps: 'The conversation did touch on the subject of either staying in Stalag and be bored to death, or go out to a working camp and be worked to death .... We didn't really have much choice, work it was to be.'[14]

Not all among the prisoners were without a choice. Some of the men wounded before capture were given papers showing them as exempt from labour, however some among them chose to join work parties rather than languish behind the fences of the Stalags. Bryan Willoughby was initially sent from hospital to the *lazaret* at Stalag VIIa in Moosburg. Whilst recuperating from the wounds he had sustained at Arnhem he realised the Stalag was somewhere he wanted to get away from:

We arrived at VIIa, Moosburg, and life changed. It was tough. I was put in the lazaret – the hospital – and I stayed there until the end of February. The food was very, very scarce. The lads in the main compound were able to get out on working parties and there was a system of rackets where they exchanged Red Cross cigarettes for bread. I thought if I could get out of hospital I can get into that very quickly. You couldn't trade in the hospital because everything was counted. But eventually the German doctor came round and I persuaded him to let me out. He said '*Nix Arbeit*', no work. He gave me a piece of paper saying I was exempt.

So I got into the main compound and the first thing I did was to sign up for a working party.[15]

Although NCOs above the rank of lance corporal were officially exempt from work the issue forced a dilemma for many among them. They knew how life within Stalags would offer less personal freedom than on work details. It was easy to recognise how labour would keep both their minds and bodies active and that men on work details had a greater access to comforts such as food and women. Another question vexed the NCOs. Was it more responsible to refuse to work and thus offer no assistance to the enemy or should they volunteer to go on work details to offer leadership and guidance to their men? The answer to this moral dilemma was a personal decision that no outsider could fully understand or criticise. It was little wonder that many elected to join working parties only to leave once they discovered the labour could be intensely hard or deadly dull.

Those who did volunteer to join working parties often found they were tricked by the Germans. When they agreed to work they signed a six-month contract. Under this they would be free to return to the Stalag once their allotted time had passed. Many found it was not that simple. The contracts included a clause in the 'small print' that meant the NCOs had to resign officially, in writing, one month before the contract terminated otherwise the contract was extended for a further six months. Others found themselves tricked into going on work parties. Some NCOs signed what they were informed were insurance contracts only to find they had actually waived their right to exemption from labour. In some cases NCOs were simply told they had no choice, Convention or no Convention, and in 1944 one group of NCOs who questioned being ordered to work were simply told that the Germans no longer recognised Article 27 of the Geneva Convention. Similarly, a group of 200 NCOs and warrant officers at Stalag XIIIc were deprived of all their personal effects and separated from the rest of the prisoners. Their guards informed them they would be detained until they volunteered for work. For 12 months they were locked into a barrack hut, unable to go outside to exercise. Eventually they relented and agreed to join working parties.

The issue of NCOs working was also an irritant to some of the private soldiers on working parties. Once at work camps the NCOs were usually given the role of administering the camp, in effect meaning the NCOs got all the cushy jobs. As a result fewer of the private soldiers were able to avoid the drudgery of heavy labour. It was not only the NCOs whose exemption from work was ignored by the Germans. All medical staff should officially have been protected personnel and only allowed to work in a medical capacity. This group included all Royal Army Medical Corps staff, regimental stretcher-bearers and orderlies, and men from other units attached to the RAMC as drivers. However the enemy often failed to recognise their credentials. Upon capture many regimental medics and bearers had lost the typewritten forms identifying them as such and, since the Germans only accepted as 'protected personnel' those whose capacity as a medic was marked in their paybooks, they were forced into industry. The War Office attempted to remedy this by sending out the correct documentation but this was not always successful. In June 1943 it was reported that 200 RAMC personnel unrecognised by the enemy were employed in a single labour detachment. Complaining or insisting that the Germans allow medics not to work was not simple. When a Private Bull of the RAMC protested that he was a 'protected person' and refused to work he was shot and killed by his guards. As a result some of the trained medics, whose work could have helped alleviate the misery of so many men in POW hospitals, found themselves pressed into service as miners, wasting their talents at the coalface. Even those recognised as medics were sometimes forced to work. At Stalag IVa staff from the camp lazaret were taken at bayonet point and informed that they had to build new barracks for the enemy. They had choice but to comply – none wished to become patients in their own hospital.

The medical staff had learned the one vital rule for all employed in the industries of the Reich. They were possessions of the Wehrmacht and could be loaned out anywhere to do as instructed. Despite the relative freedom possible on some work details most prisoners only had to watch their guards to know they could expect little lenience. They did not need to read the rules on how they should be treated to know to expect no indulgence. As the regulations on foreign workers in Germany stated:

> Every prisoner of war liable for work and able bodied is expected to exert himself to the full. Should he fail to do so the guards or auxiliary guards are entitled to take rigorous action. Guards who fail to take such action will themselves be held responsible and severely punished. They are entitled to enforce their orders by force of arms .... When a POW is not attaining normal efficiency it is the duty of the guard to take action

... he is entitled to make use of his weapons.[16]

'Normal efficiency' was a term that was liberally interpreted by the Germans. Many kept their prisoners working despite failing health and in one instance sick prisoners were forced to carry railway sleepers and sent to work breaking stones. This matter was complicated since the prisoners were often left under the guard of civilians. Although a breach of the Geneva Convention, many of these civilians used force against the prisoners, some even using guns against them.

Despite these dangers, the system of work parties had both positive and detrimental effects on the men behind the wire. For many the thought of staying in the dismal Stalags, with their crowded huts, lice and boredom, was too much. They relished the freedom of being out in the countryside or in factories, mixing with civilians and, most importantly, meeting women. Yet there was a downside. Allocation to work details was arbitrary. Men were suddenly split from their mates and sent away, sometimes never to meet again. They might return to the Stalag but not necessarily at the same time. There were even fathers and sons who fought long and hard to be transferred to the same camps, yet even they could not guarantee being sent on the same work details. For soldiers who found the camaraderie shared with their mates was the only thing that made army life tolerable, to be constantly split up from mates was a burden few enjoyed. Yet there was little choice. As the inmates of the Stalags soon learnt – it was adapt or die.

In face of the dirt and discomfort within the main camps most of the POWs not on work details attempted to make the best of a bad situation. Musical instruments were begged, borrowed or stolen and bands set up to entertain their mates during the long hours of inactivity. Theatres were established where all manner of plays and revues were performed and in which men in drag became the only sight of 'female' flesh the 'Kriegies' ever had. Bands formed using musical instruments sent from home, singers entertained the prisoners and all manner of men were recruited to appear in variety shows. Books arrived via charities allowing men a large amount of reading matter, with some camp libraries believed to have as many as ten thousand books. Card games, chess, draughts, backgammon and any number of board games were played.

Not all the activities were so cerebral and all manner of activities were used to pass the time. Home made tattoos were popular in some camps, with amateur artists adorning the skin of their friends with writing ink and the needles from their sewing kits. Amateur jewellery designers made skull and crossbones rings out of scrap metal and pieces of leather that became fashionable in some camps. Other men developed strange games that helped keep the prisoners entertained, placing bets on anything that could pass the time. Some sat outside barracks and took bets on the hair colour of the next man to walk around a corner. In extreme cases prisoners organised séances and played with Ouija boards. At Stalag XXb they improvised some highly unusual entertainments, as Gordon Barber recalled: 'We had a big cock contest. It was won by a little sergeant in the Rifle Brigade. He couldn't get his knob into a tin for 50 cigarettes. We also had a contest to see who had the most lice on their blankets.'[17] The diet of unfamiliar vegetables soon provided another source of basic entertainment, as Thomas Crawcour recalled:

> One night I mentioned to one our chaps that human intestinal gas was combustible. Surprisingly they refused to accept this as a fact, so I suggested that it could be proved by experiment. Lights went out and the fun began. It should be recorded that a diet of cabbage, potatoes and German ration bread were an ideal combination to provide an abundant and ready supply of the appropriate gas. One man bravely announced he was ready with a box of matches, another said he was ready to provide the gas. The seat of his pyjamas protruded over the edge of his bed and glowed in an eerie green light as gas and match came together, which caused great hilarity in our room. Another chap announced his readiness to participate, so a match was struck and a bare bottom could be seen hanging over the edge of the bed. The match drew close and a fart released of such force that it blew the match out! We shrieked with laughter and my stomach hurt with the continued hilarity. It was a wonder the guards did not investigate what was going on.[18]

To keep their bodies active they took up sports. In summer cricket was played and throughout the year, wherever the men could gather in a suitable place, they played football. They even played international matches – England against Scotland, England against France or Belgium and so on. At Stalag IVb 'Bill' Sykes attended a lecture given by a padre that revealed an interesting history to their football pitch: 'I was horrified to learn that in a previous extremely harsh winter, that due to the small amount of rations given to the Russian prisoners that acts of cannibalism took place and 2,000 Russian prisoners died of starvation and were buried under the football pitch.'[19] Regardless of such stories there was little that could stop the prisoners from joining in with sports.

It was not only the sportsmen and spectators who stood to benefit from sports. As vast crowds gathered in the recreation areas 'wide boys' among the camp populations opened books on the result, taking bets in food or cigarettes. These same 'wide boys' were often behind many of the scams in the camp. They grew legendary among their fellow prisoners – such as Harry Don at Stalag XXB who was described by a mate as a 'whiz kid' who could 'charm the birds out of the trees'.[20] These were the men who somehow knew when deliveries of food were arriving and where it could be pinched from. Often the efforts of such men made the difference between subsistence and starvation. One of those in the thick of the rackets explained: 'We became self sufficient. If there was anyone who was a little "Artful Dodger" I was. If there anything going on I was always in the thick of it. If I knew something was going to be brought into the camp I'd be there, at the front.'[21]

These were the men who became the wheeler-dealers within the camps. Whatever they could swap was swapped, if someone had something to sell they would find a buyer, when extra food came into the camps they would trade it for a profit. Watches and jewellery were soon traded by men who were desperate for a full belly or a smoke. The Stalag market, like all markets, was prone to fluctuation. When mail deliveries from home or Red Cross parcels arrived there was a sudden surplus in goods, particularly cigarettes. For a short period prices dropped as the smokers enjoyed their fill of tobacco. Yet once the supplies began to fall, prices began to rise. In response to the ever-changing prices, lists were pinned up on doors indicating the new rates of exchange.

The 'tobacco barons' became vital figures within the camps, buying and selling cigarettes and ensuring a widespread distribution. Their efforts ensured heavy smokers were still able to keep up their habit. Only through the exchange of goods were those with surplus fags prevented from smoking more than they really wanted just to whittle away the hours of boredom. During the latter stages of the war the shortages of tobacco were such that many of the heavy smokers became noticeably irritable as the withdrawal from nicotine began to affect them. James Witte, captured in North Africa in 1941, became a 'tobacco baron', continuing his trade from the first days of captivity until his liberation. It started when he found a haversack full of cigarettes in an abandoned lorry after he was captured: 'I was launched on a racketeering career which lasted four years. I was determined to make things as easy as I could for myself.' Yet as he soon found out, the dealers had to take care: 'Tobacco barons had hard lives in POW camps, lives of tension, unable to trust anyone.'[22] They couldn't leave the fags alone for a moment, knowing full well the second their back was turned they would be pinched. At one camp Sergeant Major James of the Sherwood Foresters was able to corner the market in tobacco. He was reported to have stolen 200 parcels of tea from Red Cross packets within the Stalag store. For each packet of tea he was able to buy three packets of tobacco from the guards. From the deal he kept a third of the profits – 200 packets of tobacco – for himself.

This dark side to the rackets ensured that arguments frequently boiled over into fights between prisoners. Often these were trivial – petty arguments over habits that irritated men living dull lives where the smallest incident could be the notable event of the day – but sometimes there was real menace behind the violence. Whilst for many of the prisoners, adversity had brought out the best in them – giving up their valuables to buy food to share with their mates – others were not so charitably minded. In the close confines of the Stalags there was one activity guaranteed to ensure a violent reaction – theft. All the prisoners knew that it wasn't counted as theft when they stole from the Germans, that was just 'appropriation', but stealing from among fellow prisoners was another matter. 'Wide boys' in the Stalags were known to sell or swap packets of tea they had opened, emptied and half filled with sawdust. Others siphoned out the milk from tins then refilled them with water before selling them to unsuspecting fellow prisoners. As Gordon Barber explained:

The worst thing you ever done was steal from your mates. If you ever got found out you were in trouble. In Marienburg they had a bloke called Charlie MacDowell, he was our 'Man of Confidence', if you had any problems you went to him. So if anybody got caught stealing and you couldn't handle him then Charlie would sort him out. He was good. He came from Glasgow. He'd start with his fists but if he found a bloke was a boxer or was a tough fighter he'd go for their knees. He would wack 'em. He'd give 'em a good hiding. I never had to call on him 'cause I was handy myself. But I never used to pick on someone I couldn't handle. You didn't want to do that in them days. I've seen blokes go to bed with a loaf of bread under their heads, wake up and both ends are gone. I remember a bloke stole my mate Paddy's overcoat. I said 'How are you going to find it?' He said 'When we go to *Appel* I'll go down the lines and have a look'. So when the guards had passed us I moved over and he went down the rows. I was watching him and all of a sudden I saw him drag a bloke out. He ripped the coat off him. He recognized it, it had his name in it.'[23]

When fights broke out – usually over the theft of food or winter clothing – they were bitter brawls. Seldom were punches pulled, instead the men waded into each other, knowing that in the 'dog eat dog' world of the prison camp they could afford to show no mercy. Trading blow for blow they would keep punching until one man was down and the last man standing could claim the spoils of victory.

For some thieves retribution was swift – they were dragged to the latrines and dumped unceremoniously into the foul-smelling pits of excrement. As they attempted to claw their way out men stood on their hands or kicked at them, forcing them back into the filth until their humiliation was complete. For others the punishment was more drawn out. Some of those caught stealing were taken before 'kangaroo' courts. Trials were held and the sentences read out. In some cases the perpetrators of the crimes were tied across tabletops and flogged. Sometimes whole groups of men joined in the beatings and prisoners reported hearing terrifying screams as the gangs exacted revenge for having condemned fellow prisoners to hunger. Yet not all the retribution was so overt. When one man suffered the attentions of bread thieves on a number of occasions he decided to exact punishment on the offenders. He hid a razor blade inside the loaf ensuring a bloody revenge upon the culprit.

Some attempted to make public their disdain for the thieves. Describing theft as 'a crime second only to murder' the editor of the handwritten 'Snips' newsletter, produced by prisoners at a copper mine during 1944, set out his opinion of those who were responsible for this 'base, sordid stealing'. In the December issue he wrote:

He is considerably worse than the ordinary common thief, who steals from strangers for one thing, and does not reduce his victims to extreme want which cannot be relieved for another. No, our bright fellow walks and talks with his victims, they are his comrades in misfortune, and he leaves them no remedy: nothing can replace that bread or those cigarettes – the victim, a man living under exactly the same conditions as the unprincipled wretch who has robbed him, is quite unable to make up his loss.

In his conclusion the writer almost seemed to extend pity towards those among them who had fallen so low as to commit such crimes: 'there are individuals here so devoid of all sense of decency and honour, so lacking in every honest and manly feeling, that they stoop to acts which must take away whatever self respect they have forever'.[24]

Yet justice was not always done and some of the victims of crime dared not claim what was rightfully theirs in the face of the violent reputations of some of their fellow prisoners. In some Stalags vicious gangs were formed who exerted their authority with the slash of the cut-throat razor. They terrorised their fellow prisoners, taking food and clothing as they wanted, knowing the NCOs were almost powerless to control them. Weaker men were forced to submit as the gangs took anything they wanted. It was little wonder the prisoners soon learned they should carry any treasured possessions with them at all times, never leaving anything unattended for even a second for fear it would be pinched. Only those with a mate they felt certain they could trust would ever let their food or fags out of their sight. Clothing was also a target for thieves, resulting in many POWs walking around in summer carrying their greatcoats. It was depressing for them. As they carried their coats day after day, they realised time was passing them by and the summer was being wasted as they awaited a winter that would inevitably see them still in captivity.

In the atmosphere of fear and uncertainty it didn't take long for most men to adapt. There was nothing like the fear of losing food and clothing to thieves to ensure the prisoners grew tough. It was no longer the discipline of the army that counted, rather it was the discipline and comradeship among small groups of men who banded together to protect themselves. Les Allan remembered life in the Stalags:

> Discipline was non-existent. Just self-discipline. You had your groups of mates, it was usually four who mucked in together, because contrary to popular belief you didn't get one Red Cross parcel per man it was shared between groups of us. After a couple of weeks the average POW became very tough. He would never allow anyone to bully him unless he had a rifle. Discipline was for self-preservation. If a man was caught stealing he'd be very severely thrashed by the people he was stealing from.[25]

There was another dark side to activities within the Stalags. Some men accused their fellow prisoners of being overfriendly towards the enemy. This was more serious. Indian POWs at Stalag XIId reported their 'Man of Confidence' for encouraging recruitment to the Indian Legion, the unit recruited from among prisoners to fight against the British Empire with the aim of securing independence for India. This individual was also accused of causing friction among his men by favouring those of his own religion. At one camp where members of the Legion turned up on a recruitment drive, they were stoned by fellow Indians disgusted by their treachery.

It was not just soldiers from the Empire who changed sides. There were also a number of British POWs suspected of working for the Nazis and they, along with English-speaking Germans masquerading as POWs, were infiltrated into the Stalags. Some were pre-war fascists whilst others were simply opportunists who, certain the Germans would be victorious, decided cooperation would make their lives easier. Men in Salonika found themselves under the command of CSM Storer. He ate, slept and drank with the guards. He also spoke fluent German and was reported to be assisting them in every respect, whilst offering no help to the prisoners. Instead he spent his time telling them Germany would win the war. Later he was reported to have been issued with a revolver for his own protection and eventually it was rumoured he had joined the German army. Whenever possible the treatment such men received was swift and bloody. Some were killed by their fellow prisoners, their bodies being dismembered and dumped piece by piece into the foetid mess of the latrine pits. One prisoner recalled the process: 'We did have a method of exacting punishment if it was deserved. If they were caught their life was in danger. Punishment was extreme and quick. On one oc-casion, I know for a fact, one was caught and condemned and he ended up face down in the water tank where he was found the next morning. Discipline to that extent was most severe.'[26] At Lamsdorf prisoners fish-ing in the pool found both a complete corpse and a dismembered hu-man thumb, despite no one having been reported missing. In all such cases the Germans failed to make any effort to find the killers for fear of revealing how they used informers within the camps.

One of the collaborators who survived the violence was Sergeant Styles. Styles had been captured in France in 1940 and appeared in vari-ous guises at a number of camps. He was known to report both on the activities of his fellow prisoners and on any guards who were considered friendly towards them. He was also seen wearing a German uniform and on one occasion he was forced to draw his revolver to defend himself from prisoners. One prisoner later reported that Styles was thought to be a bit 'simple' and how he was invariably discovered and beaten up.

The social strata that existed among prisoners led to a degree of displeasure for some. Since the NCOs were not forced to work they became important figures within the Stalags, able to use the system to their advantage. Most of the senior NCOs did a solid job in protecting prisoners and representing their complaints. When asked about their experiences in post-war debriefing questionnaires thousands of prisoners replied how their NCOs had played a vital role in sustaining them during the darkest hours in captivity. One of these highly valued leaders was Sergeant Arthur Mills who was seen coolly taking a rifle from a German who was about to shoot a prisoner. Yet the respect of the men was something that had to be earned. Among the NCOs were some who did little for those they should have been helping. These were men whose self-serving deeds never became part of the POW myth. There were plenty of prisoners, especially in the period immediately following the defeat of the BEF, who had no intention of continuing to follow military discipline. These were often men who had been called up, had just a few weeks of training, then witnessed the appalling shambles of a defeated army. To them, playing any continuing part in what had seemed such a farce was an anathema. Why should those who had led them to defeat continue to lead them once they were behind wire? It was a simplistic argument, but one that suited the minds of men who had experienced the humiliation of an army in disarray. To such men saluting or standing to attention seemed totally out of place, as one explained: 'We did everything we could to make sure there was no discipline. There were no officers, just NCOs and us. We had no thoughts about the NCOs. Everyone was equal – we were all just prisoners – we weren't soldiers. We would do our duty with regard to sabotage, but that was it. I think we'd have told a general to shove off if he'd asked us to do something we didn't like.'[27] For their defiance they were often greeted by displays of military authority where their NCOs called in the German guards to deal with offenders. At Stalag VIIIb the situation deteriorated to such a degree that the camp leader admitted he had 'some difficulty' upholding his authority over the 6,500 POWs nominally under his command. Theft and violence were rife with the razor gangs reportedly terrorising the weaker prisoners. To combat the gangs vigilante groups were formed to beat up anyone attempting to steal from vegetable plots. Finally the problems within the camp were only solved by the formation of a camp police force consisting of senior NCOs.

In some cases such actions helped to deepen the divisions. Why, some among the prisoners asked themselves, were British soldiers joining with the enemy in disciplining fellow Britons? The answer was simple. Senior

NCOs could only control the activities of the more violent prisoners with the help of the guards, yet this relationship between captors and captives caused resentment. Many of the prisoners at Lamsdorf were annoyed that the NCOs of the 'police force' were accepting extra rations from the Germans in exchange for their efforts at subduing the prisoners. The situation was mirrored at Marienburg where a sergeant major took charge of a squad that enforced punishments on fellow prisoners. Offenders were given starvation rations and forced to march double time under the watchful eye of senior NCOs. Those prisoners hostile to the continuation of military discipline were mistrustful of such behaviour and hated to see their NCOs hand in hand with the Germans, despite their undoubted success in controlling the more wayward elements.

Though the majority of prisoners soldiers didn't hold their NCOs in such disregard there was certainly recognition of how some appeared to be living a life far better than those prisoners who were shunted around farms and factories. Prisoners heard rumours about senior NCOs who were given extra food and access to women within Stalags, which stirred up resentment. Some watched the NCOs doling out food from behind the safety of windows and became convinced that the barrier between themselves and the NCO with the ladle was a sure sign he must be stealing their rations. However, in the most part the men envied their NCOs rather than felt animosity towards them. Like all among the prisoners they did not choose their role, rather the Germans had allotted it to them. Many prisoners later realised their animosity towards the NCOs was generated as much by confusion and the enforced deprivations within the Stalags as by any real misdeeds by their NCOs.

That NCOs were at times able to carve a 'cushier' life for themselves was therefore something most among the prisoners could accept. What really mattered to them were obvious abuses of privilege. One man recalled his experiences: 'At the end of the shed – where about 300 of us slept – was a kitchen. Our daily ration was potato and barley soup with a tiny bit of horsemeat. You'd lay there at night and you could smell our cooks cooking the meat for themselves in the kitchen. They were stealing our rations, which were poor enough anyway. So that didn't go down too well.'[28]

The divisions were even evident between the senior NCOs and their more junior comrades. At Stalag VIIIb Philip Simon, a South African NCO, considered the behaviour of the senior NCOs as collaboration. He reported how he and his fellow prisoners were denied access to stores of new clothing unless they volunteered for working parties. Another South African, Hugh Glynn Baker, was blunt in his appraisal of the NCOs: 'The British prisoners put in charge of the camp refused to give clothing to men who refused to work for the Germans and generally made things unpleasant for the men who would not work.'[29] Similarly, a New Zealander POW reported on poor management at Lamsdorf. NCOs were discovered trading German issued supplies for cigarettes. These were supplies supposedly issued for the comfort of prisoners, instead they were being used to ensure the NCOs could control the tobacco market. Worse than that, the inmates found the contents of Red Cross parcels were being openly traded before they were issued.

Such offences were seen throughout the camps. A group of men from one Stalag were sent on a three day train journey with just two-thirds of a loaf each as rations. This was despite CSM Allen, in charge of the Red Cross store, having plenty of spare parcels. At Stalag XXIb Sergeant Major McLeod was repeatedly accused of stealing food. He also used the Germans to punish prisoners and reported a Private Vine, who was caught in the middle of an escape attempt. In some camps there appeared to be a conspiracy among the senior NCOs. At Stalag IIIa RSM Tracey of the clothing store and Sergeant Lindsay and Bombardier Short of the camp post office were all suspected of theft. Lindsay and Short were believed to have stolen from personal parcels destined for the men. When prisoners insisted the post office be put in charge of men with postal experience Lindsay intervened to frustrate their plans. He went to the commandant and asked to be put back in charge. The plan worked and he was able to return to the job, once more continuing to exploit the prisoners.

Another prisoner remembered the life he saw when he returned to Stalag XXb from work detachments: 'The sergeant-major and his little clique had a good life. It's like anything in life – human nature. You couldn't do nothing about it, you could only join them – if they'd allow you. I didn't like the sergeant-major's attitude. He always looked smart and clean, as if he'd had enough to eat. They did get enough to eat. They had all the know how to get food. There was the "Man of Confidence", that you'd go to with any problems. But if it was going to do them any harm they wouldn't do it.'[30] At Stalag IIIa a similar situation was found, with men reporting how BSM Henderson was never around when there were problems over the issue of Red Cross parcels. Another accusation was that he never kept records of how many parcels were available. Furthermore when the Red Cross sent leather to the camp, to be used to resole boots, it soon ran out. Whilst British and Commonwealth troops were forced to wear clogs the leather itself soon became available on the blackmarket, being sold openly by a Serbian prisoner. In the words of another prisoner who referred to the privileged NCOs as 'The Golden Circle', some among them displayed the attitude of 'Fuck you Jack, I'm alright'.[31]

A prime example of the petty and domineering attitude of some senior NCOs was shown by RSM Read, the 'Man of Confidence' at Stalag VIIIb. In January 1945, irritated that prisoners were exchanging their clothing for food, he contacted the British government via the Red Cross and asked permission to punish the offenders by refusing them access to the dwindling stocks of Red Cross parcels. His request was denied and the prisoners were allowed to continue with the trade that was the only thing standing between them and starvation. At Stalag IVb new prisoners entered the camp to be greeted by a sergeant major seemingly eager to help the incoming men. He informed them that since all money was worthless to them they should hand it over for safekeeping. Trusting the NCO and hardly understanding the reality of their situation many handed over all they had. They soon realised they would never see their money again.

These conflicts and conditions endured within the Stalags were a drain on morale and spending day after day sitting around with nothing to do sapped the POWs' physical and mental strength. It was easy to grow bored with walking around inside the perimeter wire, having the same conversations with the same people, day in day out. Their world was limited to the sight of the horizon, anything beyond might as well have been on another planet. The resulting mix of boredom and discomfort, teamed with theft, violence and the behaviour of some NCOs, meant it was little wonder many prisoners were happy to be put to work. It was an enthusiasm many would soon learn was misplaced.

THREE

Industry

The majority of British prisoners of war in German hands are employed in work detachments.[1]

The amount of work enforced on English personnel in comparison to the amount of food was inhuman. *Trooper Vincent Silverthorne at Gruba Erika Arbeitskommando.*[2]

Coal, salt, iron, copper, lignite, graphite and potassium mining. Road building. Sugar mills. Lime factories. Welding. Riveting. Brick kilns. Potassium mines. Barge repairing. Pipe laying. Ground levelling. Gravel pits. Quarrying stone. Repairing trains. Smelting. Laying railway lines. Cutting ice from frozen rivers. Boot and clog factories. Paper mills. Post offices. Goods yards. Demolition. Clearing bomb sites. Shunting. Unloading goods wagons. Street sweeping and refuse collection. Breweries and distilleries. Timber yards. Gravel pits. Building sites. Cigarette factories. Woollen mills. Print shops. Cutting firewood. Gardening. Dam construction. Bridge building. Dyke building. Cement works. Oil refineries. Glassworks. Seed factories. Fish farms.

So reads a bewildering list of employments spread across factories the length and breadth of the Reich. Yet such a list can only give a taste of what was on offer to the thousands of POWs who made up Hitler's new workforce. Yet whether they were emptying the dustbins of hotels in the major cities of Germany or were harnessed to a grinding wheel like slaves in the Old Testament, all suffered a common indignity – knowing they were nothing but the servants of the enemy. It was little wonder they complained to the Red Cross that they were being: 'slave driven like the Jews'.[3]

Upon arrival at Gewerbe Arbeitskommandos the new workforce had little idea of what awaited them. Indeed, many who had eagerly volunteered for work in food processing plants would soon be disappointed, few of the promised factories ever materialised. Instead appealing work details were often a ruse designed to find volunteers for the worst jobs. At some Stalags prisoners were specifically chosen for work in industry after they were made to fill in their professions on Red Cross forms. All the tradesmen were then separated from their comrades and sent to the appropriate industry.

Yet the use of prisoners as specialised labourers, directed to where their skills might best be utilised, was seldom achieved within the network of work camps. Instead most among the captive labour force were simply picked at random to work wherever they were needed. At a cement factory in Silesia one prisoner made a list of the men of his detachment, a list that reflected the mixture of men in the vast army of 'civilian soldiers': industrial labourers, office clerks, regular soldiers, territorials, a travel agent, an architect, a commercial artist, a bank clerk, a farmer and a carpet layer. Such varied groups meant there were many thousands of men who quickly had to learn the realities of heavy labour carried out hour after hour, day after day and year upon year.

Throughout the journey to their new homes the men speculated as to their fate, a fate that for many would mean years of unrelenting toil in conditions few had previously experienced. As they were once more crammed into trains for the journey to their new homes rumours flew around as to what the work might be, some good some bad. There were men pleased to be leaving the drudgery of the Stalags and others who knew their physical condition would make heavy labour an intolerable burden. Some thought work camps might offer a chance to escape whilst for others the escape from the boredom of the Stalags was enough.

The question of health was important for many of the labourers. Among those captured in the summer of 1940 were plenty of men with little experience of manual labour. Among them were volunteers and conscripts whose working lives had been spent in offices. There were shopkeepers and chefs, clerks and college students, and all manner of men who had never previously seen the interior of factories or mines. Furthermore, plenty of the prisoners were experienced regular soldiers, many of whose age counted against them.

Upon arrival for their first day at work all these men would have to embark on a harsh lesson on the realities within German industry. These were lessons they had to learn in order to adapt to life within a regime that had little time for shirkers and skivers. Although some prisoners were fortunate to be allocated to work camps where life could be easy, plenty more were detailed to live and work in conditions unfit for animals, enduring a burden of labour that would exhaust them both physically and mentally in the years ahead.

One of the first lessons to be learnt was that the language barrier between POWs and their bosses had to be overcome. In some camps interpreters were provided, but in others there was no assistance. Some arrived to find civilian overseers who refused to speak anything but German. They shouted their orders at the prisoners, giving them a brief demonstration of the work they were to do and then leaving them to it. The prisoners soon realised they would need to understand as much of the language as possible if they hoped to survive in any degree of comfort. Most soon learned the most important words, they'd heard the shout of 'Raus!' – meaning out – a thousand times. Now they learnt new words 'arbeit' – work – all too often followed by the instruction 'Schnell' – or fast – which needed little explanation. One German word did however bring a measure of comfort. Some among this new labour force were designated as *Schwerarbeiter*, a classification that meant their heavy labours entitled them to extra rations. It was a bonus that could mean the difference between existence and starvation.

Another thing the POWs learned as they were shunted around German industry was that no two camps were alike. Some were vast enterprises such as factories belonging to the industrial giant Siemens, or synthetic oil plants run by I.G. Farben. Others were small local sawmills, or factories with just handfuls of men employed. Conditions within depended on the attitudes of the employers, the guards, the foremen and the fellow workers. On some work detachments the POWs were kept working throughout the day – their labours were never ending. For others the labour was less gruelling. Some were offered *Akkord Arbeit* that meant they were allotted tasks and would be free to return to barracks as soon as the tasks were completed. Some reasonable employers decreed that prisoners who worked late into the night due to the immediate requirements of the factory should be allowed to start late the next morning. As a result of these differences for some POWs it was an easy life where, as long as they kept working, they were untroubled by their guards, but for others it grew into a life of drudgery where they were forced to work ever harder with constantly decreasing rewards.

Of all the tasks to which the prisoners were detailed nothing struck dread into the hearts of the prisoners like the mention of mining. When rumours went around the Stalags that men were being detailed for mining the rooms fell silent. Even for those prisoners with experience of mining the thought of spending the war years in pits was something few had contemplated. Had Alec Reynolds wished to spend the war underground he could simply have remained at home in the pit where he had worked since leaving school. Instead he had given up his reserved occupation to join the army: 'I didn't have to go to war. I had five brothers, we were all miners, we all went to war and we all came back. They told me to go home and look after my mother, because my dad had been in the Boer war and then in the First World War. He was gassed and never did another day's work in his life.'[4] Finding himself a prisoner, after having been captured on Kos in 1943, Reynolds had little idea of what was in store for him:

> Someone said to me 'Watch what you say if the Germans ask what you did before the war'. So I was in this room, naked, in front of six of them and they asked me what my job was. I said I was unemployed. They looked at my body and said 'Miner'. They knew right away I'd worked in a mine. So that was it. But I had no worries about anything. I was very fit. I looked after myself. I didn't worry about what would happen.[5]

The knowledge of men like Reynolds was of great benefit to the rest of the prisoners, as knowledgeable miners were able to offer advice that would help many survive in the treacherous conditions underground.

Whether for coal, salt, iron ore, copper or lignite the basic rules were the same. The work was heavy, the hours long and the conditions almost unbearable. For one group their introduction to the mine was daunting. When they claimed that coal mining would qualify as war work and that they would not go down the pit, the German reaction was swift. The men were beaten with rifle butts and kicked by their jack-booted guards. Then they were starved for 24 hours.

Not all had such a violent introduction to their new homes, yet as the POWs arrived at camps in mining villages few could fail to miss the scarred landscape of winding gear, slag heaps, coal dust and chimneys. As one man later recorded, it was: 'an oasis of industrial sordidness in a sea of cultivated land'.[6] This was a world that would engulf many among them and at most camps the prisoners could look out from their huts and see little but the mine buildings from which they would descend into the earth. At one salt mine the winding gear was just 60 yards from their accommodation, with both huts and mines enclosed within the same barbed wire fence. It stood as a constant reminder of the unrelenting nature of their employment.

Left: British Paratroopers of the 6th Airborne Division going 'into the bag' under the watchful eye of a German soldier.

Below: A mixed group of British and Commonwealth troops assembled in Cyrencia, North Africa, ready for transport to Italy (Red Cross)

A boxing match for prisoners at Stalag XXa at Thorn. In the background is the entrance to the underground dwellings of the Napoleonic forts in which the prisoners lived. (Red Cross)

A group of British prisoners of war. Their tattooed arms present an image of POWs far removed from the middle class officers so often portrayed in post-war books and films. (Red Cross)

A group of British prisoners on 'pick and shovel duties' at a 'Bau und Abeitsbataillion'. Their motley clothing shows the wide mix of captured uniforms issued to prisoners in the early years of the war. (Red Cross)

Prisoners collecting Red Cross parcels at Stalag XXb in the winter of 1940. 'The greatest event in the life of POW was the distribution of Red Cross parcels. Without them many of us would not be alive to tell the tale.' (Imperial War Museum HU5710)

Red Cross parcels in storage at a warehouse in Portugal, ready to be delivered to POWs within occupied Europe. (Imperial War Museum AP14800B)

Prisoners washing outdoors at a camp in Germany. At Fallingbostel George Marsden remembered: 'there was just a cold water tap at the back of the hut somewhere, no towel so no wash.'(Imperial War Museum HU23387)

The squalid conditions within overcrowded huts that were home to Indian POWS at a working camp in Germany. The triple tier bunks were a common feature for men on working parties. (National Archive)

For men with no previous experience of mining the work was an intolerable burden, and few were ever given any proper instructions over their duties. Instead they had to pick up what they could from watching the civilian miners. Nor was any serious check made over the physical suitability of men chosen to descend into the forbidding darkness. Even men with glasses were included in the work details, the gloomy conditions only serving to further damage their eyesight. Those men who were inspected by German doctors found there was seldom an interpreter available to assist and that any examinations were superficial. As a result prisoners who had caught malaria in North Africa were forced down the mines. Even some of obvious poor health could not escape the mines. Red Cross inspectors found men classed as fit for light duties working at the coalface, and one man with active TB, who had originally been classed suitable for repatriation, was sent to work underground.

By late 1940 over 600 men from Stalag VIIIb in Upper Silesia were employed in four coal mines and 136 men from Stalag IXc were employed down salt mines. By 1944 the figure had risen to 4,000 POWs from Stalag VIIIb employed on fifteen mining detachments. Few were prepared to hide their feelings, as Private Deakin of the Leicestershire Regiment wrote home in early 1943: 'I have been forced down the mines here. Our own RSMs are partly to blame, but I repay them when I return. I am not fit for this work, but either you go down or else.'[7]

If the prisoners thought working conditions in coal mines were bad it was soon discovered there were even worse places they could be sent to. Many discovered that copper mining involved working in even more cramped conditions. At the huge Eisleben complex prisoners were called for the early morning shift at 3.50 a.m., which was followed by a second call at midday for the next shift to get ready. They soon collected their equipment and entered the cage, a cold draught whistling past them as the lift slowly made its way underground. Among them a few of the lucky ones were issued kneepads, but most worked with no protection. Nor were they issued helmets to protect themselves from falling rocks. Instead they simply fixed their lamps to their army caps, the weight often pulling the caps over their eyes, and the heat of the lamps burning their foreheads. From the base of the lifts they had to walk as far as 2 kilometres to reach a second lift which descended even further into the bowels of the earth. Then they began a nightmare walk downhill over rough paths. Hardly able to see through the gloom, and bent double in the tiny passages, they bumped their heads on the low ceilings, often arriving at their workplace with bloodstained faces. It would not take long for the sweat of their exertions to wash away the blood.

In the depths of the mine there was a main roadway with seams leading off from each side. The prisoners looked around themselves to see pit props straining under the weight of the rocks above them. All knew if these were to give way there would be no escape. At the end of each side tunnel were the workfaces where miners blasted and bored into the rock, pushing it behind them to be loaded into the wagons. Rails were laid in the side tunnels along which the miners had to push carts laden with copper ore. These tunnels were sometimes no taller than 39 inches and the prisoners shuffled along on their knees, pushing the heavy carts. In these conditions they worked for as much as 12 hours a day. For those at the face there was seldom an opportunity to stand up for hours upon end. Alongside the German miners and French or Russian prisoners, they lay down to eat their meagre lunches.

Though an experienced coal miner, Alec Reynolds found himself sent from Stalag IVb to a copper mine. Familiar as he was with life beneath ground, the conditions there were far from what he had known:

> A copper mine and a coal mine are two very different places. In a copper mine they only work at very shallow faces, just three or so foot. You only find copper in thin strips in the rock. So you sit down at the face with a hydraulic drill and just work the thin seam. They keep it as low as possible. Though I was a miner it was still hard work. I had this long handled shovel. My job was to lay on my back where they were working and shovel the ore into these wagons. Then we pushed them down the incline on rails. I wore shoes made from pulp. You could ride the wagons down the slopes. You could judge the corners and turn the wagons. But at speed it would blow your lamp out and leave you in darkness. Then blokes would push the wagons along to where they were tipped out. We didn't have knee pads or any protective clothing. No helmets. We worked anything up to 12 hours a day. It was heavy going. It was hard work for me, so what must it have been like for the other blokes? I found one bloke sitting there crying in the mine. The Germans were all laughing at him, so I told him not to cry in front of the Germans. That time I walked off the job.[8]

Within any mine the worst place was the face. These were usually narrow galleries little more than 6 feet high and running for as much as 100 yards. At the face teams of men cut, drilled and blasted into the seams of coal, then shovelled the ore into tubs on conveyor belts or the wagons of the small underground railways. In many locations gases built up causing men to collapse from carbon monoxide poisoning. Some also worked in mines where iron pit props were used. Though supposedly stronger than wooden props they gave no warning when they were under pressure and a roof fall was likely. As the prisoners learnt about life within a mine they learnt to recognize the signs that a collapse was due. Alec Reynolds spotted the familiar sounds:

> When you're down a mine you hear thumping, and that's rocks falling down from the ceiling. That's alright, you know it's holding. But when you're in a place and you hear the thin fall of dust you know it's all coming down and you get out of the way. One time we were working – it was just a few feet high – I felt the dust coming down on me. I said 'Out!' so we sat outside. Along came the foreman and he asked me what we were doing. I told him. So he must have guessed I was a miner. And that night, after we'd finished, the roof caved in. So the other chaps down there were very frightened, but they got used to it. Most learnt to cope with it. A few people got downhearted, they'd come back from the mine and just lay on their bed. They'd never wash, you couldn't help them. But one thing that made us feel better was that we lived downstairs and the Ruskies lived upstairs. And they had everything worse than us.[9]

One of the most terrifying experiences came when the coalface had to be moved forward. To prevent too large an area of supported roof in one area the overhead rock would be deliberately collapsed. This entailed new supports being put in place at the foremost parts of the face and then pulling the supports out from the previously worked area. This had to be done carefully and quickly to avoid the inevitable rockfall. It was a tense moment as miners pulled away the supports and then jumped aside into the supported area – it was also a moment accompanied by an almost inevitable number of casualties.

Conditions may have varied from mine to mine but they were, more often than not, appalling and even experienced miners found them intolerable. As Frederick Williams, who had been an insurance clerk when called up for service, later wrote: 'Had we been adequately fed it would have been, in the most cases, heavy and unpleasant, however in the circumstances it was deadly.'[10] In the words of another man, the conditions were such that it took just one shift to realize the mine was being worked: 'with a complete disregard for human life'.[11] After their first day's work underground some men were found prostrate and had to be carried to the surface, their exhausted bodies too weak to move. In time their finger joints grew permanently stiff from gripping picks and shovels for hours on end. Cuts and bruises became a part of life, something that could not be avoided, but which had to be kept clean in an attempt to ward off infection. In time most displayed the dark scars where coal dust had got into their wounds leaving a permanent black mark on their skin. Since few could really keep themselves clean blood poisoning grew increasingly common among the injured miners. Shuffling along over the sharp rocks in tiny tunnels, whose depth was measured in inches, left many prisoners with cut knees. If these became infected they were simply transferred to 'light duties', which in a mine could mean pushing wagons full of copper ore and tipping them into larger wagons by hand. The only benefit was that at least they were working standing up. When wagons came off the rails the prisoners would have to lift them back by hand. They soon learned to line up with their backs against the wagons and use what little strength they had to force them back onto the rails. Many found themselves losing fingernails to the clips that held the wagons to the cables that pulled them along the tunnels. More injuries followed when the prisoners found themselves slipping on the rails, their hobnailed army boots unable to grip on the shiny surface.

Even in salt mines, which in peacetime were used as cure centres for the sick, there was no respite for the prisoners. The salt may have prevented their wounds getting infected but it was of little benefit – they still faced much discomfort. One of the worst jobs endured by those working at salt mines was the cleaning of the drying machine. This was a barrel-like container into which wet salt was fed and then dried by having coal dust ignited within the drum. All day long hammers pounded the sides of the drum to loosen the dried salt. Periodically the prisoners had to enter the drum to hack away at the compacted salt. They had to wait for the drum to cool before they could enter, although the temperature was never allowed to drop far enough for them to remain within the drum for more than a few minutes. There was little respite for the workers. For 12 hours a day they toiled deep inside these mountains, where salt icicles hung from the rock walls, their mouths getting uncomfortably dry and unbearably thirsty courtesy of the salty dust that hung in the air. Travelling to and from work on miniature trains passing along narrow rock tunnels, they spent nearly all the daylight hours far below ground, breaking the salt walls with pick axes, then shovelling the salt into a truck. Unseen by sunshine, their skin turned white and they found their fat falling off them, until all weighed less than 10 stone.

In some areas men were forced down the mines with just one day off in three weeks – one such group endured this relentless work inside a mine that was constantly flooded. At Klausberg the prisoners found themselves working seams just 2 feet deep. Yet in other mines ex-miners among the prisoners were shocked to see seams twice the depth of the ones they had been used to back home. This complicated their work since though they were used to listening out for the coal 'working' above them, with ceilings at such heights, their ears couldn't pick out the sound of movement, making it difficult to predict falls. Furthermore, many Silesian mines were found to have steep seams which made work difficult. In these steeply sloping areas they were at increased danger since when coal or rock fell from the ceiling it bounced and rolled towards the unsuspecting miners, often causing serious injury. Even worse were the seams within the Pfeiler mine. Here the coal seam, worked by the prisoners, was vertical. As they drilled and dug into the coalface they were working with the ceiling up to 20 feet above them. The risks from falling rocks were great but still they worked on, knowing that their exposed skulls would be crushed by any major fall.

The conditions meant that wherever possible the miners contrived to ensure they worked in the safest places within the mines, although of course this was not always possible and many found themselves working the coalface. Most tried to make sure they could work on the underground railways, pushing or pulling carts full of rock through areas least likely to see falls. The easiest way to ensure they got the safest jobs was to show a complete inability to do the dangerous jobs, to the extent that local workers didn't want them on their teams. This was not a major concern where the prisoners worked alongside Germans, who were, at least in theory, the enemy. The problems arose when the prisoners worked alongside Poles. With the prisoners avoiding work it was the Poles who suffered causing an antagonism between the supposed allies – a difficult situation when the same Poles were also the source of black market food enjoyed by the POWs.

At the Brandfeld mine conditions were so bad that even the commandant of Stalag VIIIb complained to the German High Command that the managers 'abuse and exploit' the prisoners and even forced them to buy their own Red Cross parcels. Regardless of what was contained within the parcels the POWs were forbidden to purchase more than three bars of soap a month, and even when they had a chance to wash few had towels to dry themselves with. Those that did found the Germans charged the prisoners to get the towels laundered. Additionally they had to pay for any repairs to their lamps and claimed that on the weekend double shift there seemed to be higher levels of prisoners working compared to civilians. But that was not the worst of it. The mine was situated alongside a disused mine that was burning. Such was the heat that spread into the Brandfeld mine that the civilian miners did just 15 minutes work and then rested for 15 minutes. For the prisoners no such breaks were allowed, instead they had to keep working through.

It was not just the breaks that separated civilian workers from the prisoners. At one mine the prisoners recorded how at the end of their day's labours they were forced to remain underground for up to an hour until all the civilians had returned to the surface. For men already spending as much as 12 hours a day working the loss of what little leisure time remained was a serious blow.

Recognising these concerns the Foreign Office made attempts, via the Swiss government, to ensure the Germans were careful over those men employed underground. In July they wrote:

> the employment in a mine of a man who is without previous experience in mine working is likely to be injurious to the health of any but those of above average fitness and physique ..... I am accordingly to request that enquiries may be instituted as to the manner in which, if at all, prisoners are medically examined in Germany before being sent into the mines and in particular to what extent enquiry is made into the past medical history of those whom the Germans intend to employ upon this work.[12]

Their protestations had little effect and the Red Cross continued to report 'clerks, students and professional men'[13] working down the mines.

Undergound mines were not the only places where the prisoners were to face the prospect of unceasing toil in exhausting conditions. At the Grube Erika work camp the prisoners mined lignite, a soft brown coal similar to peat, used for fuel. The men worked in open cast pits:

> in immense wide excavations of several hundred metres. The beds of lignite are found at a level which varies from 30 to 80 metres below the level of the ground. Dredger buckets remove the sandy soil which carries the lignite and the latter is loaded into panniers on trams which transport it to the neighbouring briquette factory. The lignite is impregnated with water and the men who work at the loading and unloading of the panniers work practically in the water. The work is done under the open

sky and is very laborious because the lignite, being full of water, is very heavy. The workmen are not provided with rubber boots.[14]

In these conditions leather boots lasted no more than three months. Standing hour upon hour up to their ankles in water the prisoners' decrepit boots became waterlogged, their feet grew soft and puffy, the flesh weakened and fell prey to infections.

Hundreds of men also laboured at open iron ore mines, including the forbiddingly named Eisenerz – 'Iron Mountain'. Such mines were usually vast awe-inspiring complexes, layer upon layer of terracing carved into mountainsides by dynamite and pickaxes, visible for miles around. Here the prisoners stood on the exposed hillsides hewing at the rockfaces that scarred the landscape. They swung their picks for hour upon hour, breaking off the mixtures of rock and ore, loading it into the trucks mounted upon rails that lined each of the terraces. In the rain and wind of autumn the POWs continued swinging their picks, as they had done all summer when many among them collapsed with heat exhaustion. Not only was the work dirty, dusty and exhausting, it was also dangerous. Men were crushed and killed by falling rocks, others lost fingers or had their toes smashed by stones tumbling down the hillsides.

Others laid new rails to carry the ore away from the rockfaces, unloaded machinery, or dug trenches and laid pipes. Once the iron ore had been hewn from the mountainside prisoners worked to sort it, taking it from the wagons and separating the ore from the stones. They stood all day dropping the ore down a hole into a wagon ready for smelting. As one man described it, the work was: 'agonizing in the extreme'.[15] They stood all day at the benches, their backs grew stiff, their legs ached and their feet went numb.

Those working at quarries found much the same conditions. Men were sent out with sledgehammers that they wielded all day to break rocks. Other prisoners spent hour after hour, shovel in hand, filling wagons with the broken stones. They were ordered to load seven wagons a day, each carrying one-and-a-half tons of stones. Others filled the tubs of suspension railways, the procession of baskets hanging from the overhead cables reminding them of the never-ending nature of their labour. Ken Wilats was among a working party sent from Stalag XXa:

I went on the night shift at a gravel quarry. It was cold. It was hard work for me, I wasn't a labourer. I was a chef, before the war I'd been working in the Savoy. So it was a shock to suddenly find myself in a gravel pit.

Physically it was a strain, but it's amazing what you can work yourself up to. I remember saying to someone 'I really can't do this'. But as you have no alternative you have to knuckle down and do the best you can. It toughens you up – mentally and physically. Eventually you gradually get fit. That was despite rations being meagre and Red Cross parcels not having started. Conditions were dire. The pit was open 24 hours, with shifts on all the time. You stood in front of a wall of gravel with a skip behind you. And you shovelled gravel over your shoulder until the skip was full and it was pulled away. Then another one came up. So you worked for eight hours a day, without stopping. It was good for the muscles, but not good for the soul. You just stared at a gravel wall for most of the day. It was boring.[16]

Throughout these mines and quarries the work was intensive, hour after hour, day after day the routine was the same – work all day, sleep for a few hours then begin again. Come rain or shine most worked outdoors, soaked to the skin or tormented by the sun they had no choice but to keep on. Their bodies covered in openly festering septic sores, their hands blistered, their feet stuffed into clogs they struggled to maintain health and morale. Men collapsed from exhaustion no longer able to hold their sledgehammers, picks or shovels, but as they fell to the ground their mates had to keep working, knowing their guards would tolerate no slacking. Only when the snows of winter came were they offered a respite from the hacking and loading, instead they were sent out to shovel snow. Still their work continued for hour upon weary hour, the cold so great it froze their gloves to the handles of their shovels – if they were lucky enough to have gloves. At one iron ore mine the prisoners could hear the chiming of the local church clock. Every 15 minutes its sound rang out across the mine, making the prisoners aware of how slowly the time was passing – making them realize how as they toiled time was passing them by. But for some among them time stood still for ever – in their first winter at the mine five men would die from a combination of cold, hunger and exhaustion.

AK1231 at Roemhild was used as a Sonderlager, or punishment camp. The German authorities insisted it was not actually a punishment camp, rather it was a centre for 're-education' where prisoners who had been caught escaping could be sent to learn the error of their ways. They faced all the usual harsh conditions of working parties with a few extra deprivations heaped on top. They were placed in the camp without trial and allowed a warm shower just twice a month. They received no wages for the work and were made to remain in the quarry for 11 hours a day. Unlike conventional criminals they faced one final hurdle – they had no fixed sentence and thus had no idea when their ordeal might be over. Instead they had to remain at the punishment camp until the commandant was convinced their will had been broken and they had been sufficiently 're-educated'.

Among the working prisoners were hundreds of men employed to load or unload trains. Some had volunteered for 'railway work' in the mistaken belief they might be detailed to drive locomotives or shunt wagons around goods yards – the dream of every schoolboy who'd ever owned a model railway. Yet few among them were fortunate to get the jobs of riding in engines or switching the points as wagons were shunted around. Instead they were mainly employed for heavy labouring. The POWs hung around the sidings awaiting goods trains, then unloaded the contents before refilling the wagons ready to continue their journey. The work could be light – even for men existing on minimal rations mail sacks were not too great a burden – but it could also be heavy and unpleasant. Some carried sacks of lime, covering their faces with handkerchiefs to prevent the dangerous dust getting into their lungs.

Another important concern for the prisoners was that the railways never closed. Trains ran day and night, seven days a week. As a result the prisoners' work had to match the timetables and there was no definite day off on Sundays. When one prisoner insisted he should not work Sundays the reaction was immediate – the guard beat him with his rifle butt and stabbed the protester in the arm with his bayonet. The message was clear, there was no point resisting. Other concerns had implications for morale. One of the worst features of the goods yards was that they had to endure the sight of troop trains passing through on their way to the front. Often the German soldiers shouted insults at the toiling prisoners, comments that were replied to with profanities. One group of POWs, clearing bomb damage at a station, simply waited until the train had began to move off and then started pelting the carriages with bricks.

However 'railway work' could also include heavy maintenance work. Gangs of labourers carried lengths of track by hand, each man clutching an oversized pair of tongs as they struggled to move the rails into place. Once they had been carried to the correct spot the prisoners had to lay them in place and fix them to the sleepers. They then hammered ballast stones beneath the rails. Others used hand drills to bore holes into the rails to fix them together, each hole taking at least an hour to drill. Even in heavy frost, when the cold made the naked flesh of their hands stick to the metal, they kept working. Many of the track labourers found themselves working through every hour of daylight as the Germans desperately tried to keep the railways running in face of almost constant Allied air attacks. One group of prisoners even spent two days jacking up a derailed locomotive, forcing it back onto the tracks – all without the assistance of machinery. They were also sent to repair or construct sheds alongside civilian workers and prisoners from across the occupied countries of Europe. Men were given files and shown how to file down sheets of metal ready to be used to make the boilers for the locomotives. Others hammered rivets into place, or were detailed to work as welders, where they operated the equipment without gloves or safety goggles. Much of the railway work could be dangerous, with many fingers and toes being crushed by falling sleepers or tracks. Even those on loading duties found themselves in danger, working as they did in goods yards where giant steel engines rolled past them, often under the control of people with no concern for the well-being of prisoners. At a working camp near Klagenfurt, Colin Brodie from Wandsworth was killed when he fell from a train the controller had moved without warning. As the train lurched forward Brodie tumbled from the wagon, falling to his death under the rolling wheels.

All across the Reich small detachments of men were sent out to maintain the railways. They worked in cities, towns and villages – even down to the smallest country stations. In the winter their job was to sweep snow from platforms or scrape ice from the points to stop them freezing. They often spent hours hanging around waiting for major snowfalls then trudged along miles of track clearing the rails. In the spring and summer they searched mile after mile looking for any damage caused during the winter, then replaced damaged rails or decayed sleepers and reinforced eroded embankments. In the summer and autumn they cut back trees from beside the tracks and cleared paths through the undergrowth alongside the railways.

Work on other major transport construction projects could be even more onerous. The men detailed to construct the autobahn between Berlin and Danzig, a project that remains incomplete even 60 years later, faced harsh working conditions. They worked all year round in all weather, with frostbitten POWs continuing to toil with their toes sticking through their boots. Despite the frozen ground they slaved under the direction of their guards, breaking the solid ground with their picks. Whilst they worked inland, other POWs were employed on the Baltic coast laying paths along the shore. With the wind whipping across a frozen sea the prisoners endured freezing temperatures as they walked along the beaches collecting pebbles to be laid on the paths.

Of course, there were a few industrial work details that were popular with the prisoners. Since they knew they had to work they just hoped their labour would have some benefits. In particular the men sent to breweries and distilleries realized they would be able to sample the fruits of their labour. Although much of the work involved shovelling hops and barley, or piling up barrels, there was always the hope that a few bottles could be pinched or traded with civilian workers. For all the benefits of the work, the prisoners always got the worst jobs, as one remembered:

> It was a three story building. On the top floor you had the hops and barley, we had to go up there and keep turning it over. When you did that all the husks and the dry bits would filter down through the floorboards and eventually landed up in the cellar. Every week the maintenance man and one of the prisoners would go down to check the machines and sweep the floor. The husks were a wonderful food for the rats. They had the finest colony in the world! They were huge. But in that cellar they also had a colony of wild cats. The prisoner was given a hammer to bang on the pipes as soon as the rats got too curious. Bang! Away they went. Then you would sweep up around the machines. Then when you saw their eyes shining and getting close you'd bang the pipe again to scare them off. When I tell people they have a laugh about it, but it was serious stuff.[17]

The onerous conditions led to much conflict between prisoners and their guards. For many of the POWs the notion that they should withdraw their labour in extreme conditions was obvious – many had experienced industrial strife through the lean years of the 1920s and 1930s and wondered if the same tactics could be used. For most their defiance of the authorities was nothing more than a refusal to carry out certain tasks, or simply staring blankly at their overseers when ordered to do a job. Playing dumb was a simple tactic, pretending not to understand could buy the prisoners a few minutes' rest, a chance to recuperate before restarting work. When faced by small groups of strikers the solution was simple. Guards unslung their rifles or drew their pistols and told the men what would happen if they refused to keep working – seldom did the POWs ignore such threats. With bigger groups of men the reaction tended to be different. Few guards wanted to open fire on a large group of men for fear of being lynched. Though few prisoners would have dared to react violently the guards could never be certain. Instead the usual German reaction to large groups of strikers was to threaten them with violence, promise to cut their rations and deny all privileges. Even the vital Red Cross parcels could be stopped. If that didn't work the guards had a simple solution – the ringleaders were separated and returned to the Stalags. Without the leaders it was easy to force the rest of the men back to work.

Though an extreme and dangerous course of action, the men at the Eisenerz mine dared to organize a strike. They had seen wagons leaving the yard with the name 'Krupps' emblazoned on the side. These were destined for the infamous German industrial plant in the Ruhr known for its production of heavy weapons. To the prisoners this was forbidden war work, something they were not obliged to continue with, and they simply downed tools. When the striking prisoners were hauled before the commandant they reiterated their position. However he presented them with his version of reality – all the iron ore would be used for making civilian goods such as forks and spoons. Inevitably one joker piped up: 'Tell him to get his shit plaited, we believe they are making knives as well.'[18] For all the attempts at making light of the situation the prisoners were trapped, knowing if they did not work they would not be fed. Facing the stark reality of starvation they had no choice – they returned to work.

When British prisoners were sent to a woodworking company near Danzig they found an ideal solution to being made to do war work. At first they had no idea what they were making, they were simply nailing together pieces of wood to make large frames. Then they discovered these were moulds for concrete anti-tank traps. Knowing any attempt to stop work would only be met by violence they decided to take direct action. They had discovered their barrack huts were only separated from the factory by a single barbed wire fence that could easily be passed through in the dark. One night a prisoner was able to sneak out, enter the factory and start a fire that destroyed the entire building. The Germans must have suspected the prisoners but could take no action since once the fire was noticed the culprit was safely back in his bunk.

They were not alone in being forced to do such work. Inevitably many questions were raised over the nature of POW labour and how much it was benefiting the Nazi war machine. Though banned from doing any work of military value, as in the Krupps case the lines between civilian and military work were often blurred – and only became more so as the war progressed. Early in the war prisoners complained they were forced to construct brick barracks for the Wehrmacht, whilst in Greece troops cleared wrecked planes from airfields or were made to sandbag gun emplacements. It seemed the Germans were even breaching their own rules which stated POWs should not be employed anywhere they might be able to carry out espionage.

The real military benefit of much of this work was debatable – it was certainly a technical breach of the Geneva Convention but was of little consequence to the progress of the war. Others found themselves more directly involved in the aiding of the enemy, as Sergeant Perry of the Royal Artillery reported of his experiences in Greece:

> Reveille was at 4.45, parade for work at 5.30 a.m. Prisoners were then taken to the aerodrome to load bombs into Stukas, they also had to load olive oil and maize which was flown to Germany … Work finished at 6p.m. After returning to the camp prisoners are confined to their billets which are lousy with lice and every imaginable insect … So life goes on for the British prisoners. From what I experienced in Salonika the English were treated like pigs and they were made to live like them.[19]

It was not just the nature of the work that troubled this group of prisoners. Seventy per cent of them worked on through severe attacks of dysentery and one man was forced to work with appendicitis. When he was eventually released to go to hospital he survived for just two days. They also had to endure witnessing their guards abusing Greek civilians who attempted to aid them, watching one teenage girl hit with a rifle butt for throwing food to them. She too died in hospital.

As the war went on more and more reports of illegal work reached London via complaints made to the Red Cross by prisoners. Work detachments reportedly worked in munitions factories filling shells for the Siemens company. Prisoners from Stalag VIIIb complained they were made to operate blast furnaces in a munitions works, they had been in the factory for some months working in the coking plant but when the enterprise was reorganized they found themselves making munitions. They downed tools and were returned to the Stalag. Despite their complaints later reports found 450 men from the camp forced to work in a munitions plant. Another group of 80 men were found to be working in a stove factory, closer examination uncovered that it had been converted to be an armaments plant. Others made bombs, loaded army trucks headed for the Russian front, constructed ammunition boxes, built army trucks and manufactured engine parts for tanks and planes. At one detachment prisoners were even made to construct what were obviously aircraft fuselages. The thought that they were constructing machines that might soon be heading off to bomb their homes hung heavy over the unfortunate prisoners.

And so the list went on. POWs operating furnaces in Friedenshutte discovered they were melting scrap metal to produce artillery shells, whilst at Ohlau hundreds of prisoners were employed to load trains headed to the Russian front. At Farge, near Bremen, 31 captured merchant seamen were employed to build underground submarine repair shops. One 55-year-old seaman who refused received 25 blows with a rubber truncheon for his disobedience. Some were detailed to build, camouflage and maintain anti-aircraft sites, unload transport planes at Luftwaffe bases in North Africa or load bombs onto planes in Yugoslavia. Indian prisoners were sent from Germany to Genoa to load ammunition into ships and those who refused were beaten with rifle butts, with 50 men taken to hospital, whilst other Indians at Mainz were detailed to load artillery shells onto trains. In France another group of Indian POWs, who refused to build runways for the Germans, were sent from Rennes to Fort Bismarck in Strasbourg. There they were detained in underground rooms in an attempt to break their spirit. After a month most found their dark skin had turned pale, whilst two among them had been driven insane.

In July 1943 280 British POWs were asked to volunteer for agricultural work at Foggia in Italy. When they arrived they discovered their true employment was as labourers building runways for German bombers. When they refused the Germans informed the prisoners that such work was legal as long as it was at least 200 kilometres from the front line. Four South Africans and nine Indians from the same camp were killed in a bombing raid whilst employed in what the Germans described as 'agricultural work' near an airfield.

A group of captured Palestinian troops were firstly employed as stevedores unloading German supply ships in North African ports, then sent to Berlin to manufacture machinery – with many suffering acid burns in the course of their work – then sent to Palermo to load petrol onto German ships heading to North Africa. They were eventually released by the advancing Allies whilst working as stevedores in Tunis. In one particularly appalling case Australian troops on working parties from Stalag XXa were reported to have been handling mustard gas shells.

It seemed those troops captured in North Africa were among those facing the worst breaches of the Geneva Convention. A Sergeant Small-combe later wrote of the conditions faced by him and his comrades, as they worked 18-hour days with their guards firing at them at the slightest provocation: 'The work consisted of the handling of bombs, ammunition, tanks, guns, petrol and food destined for use by the German forces ... Protests against this only met with punishment and some of the men were badly manhandled.'[20] They spent 10 months in these conditions with no change of clothes or chance to repair their footwear. Despite Sergeant Smallcombe's protests there were other British NCOs in North Africa who were implicated in the forcing of prisoners to work. One mixed group of South African and Indian POWs reported how an RSM Gibson had made a great effort to force them to unload ammunition for the Germans, threatening to withhold their rations if they did not follow his orders.

Yet whilst the prisoners were engaged in this illegal and degrading work, the War Office seemed uncertain as to the truth of such stories. Although serious investigations were made via the Swiss government there seems to have been a willingness to accept the German explanations of the work. Despite the reports one official wrote in late 1941: 'Have we sufficient evidence to show that the Germans are using our prisoners of war for work or in ways which is or are in contravention of the Geneva convention?'[21] This remained a serious issue that vexed officers back in London. Whilst British and Commonwealth prisoners of war were defusing bombs, loading ships and building runways, the War Office was agonizing over whether German and Italian POWs in Britain could be employed to build air raid shelters or repair military uniforms.

Yet for all these arguments there were some prisoners who had no protection or representation, and there were some among the king's men who disappeared into German industry, bound into the misery of slavery. A group of 30 coloured soldiers from South Africa were taken into captivity by the Luftwaffe who failed to report them to the authorities. Instead they were kept in Italy as slaves and forced to work for the Germans. They received neither Red Cross parcels nor mail, indeed they could receive no mail since officially they didn't exist. This continued for months before they were finally given POW status, even then their misery was not over. Six of them were forced at gunpoint to drive lorries to the eastern front. After their departure they were never heard of again.

It was not just labour related to the war effort that vexed the prisoners. There were other duties with which they were less than comfortable. In the early days of captivity some prisoners were taken to a park. Here they were forced to break paving stones and obliterate all traces of the park. Its crime was to have been Polish, and the Germans were intent on humiliating the prisoners by using them to help eradicate all traces of Polish culture. As they worked the prisoners watched as Poles were forced to walk in the gutter when they passed Germans, and were made to show their nationality in the form of a letter 'P' displayed prominently on their clothes. Some among the group of prisoners who had been forced to destroy the Polish park were later ordered to destroy gravestones in a Jewish cemetery. To a man they refused, even when the guards threatened to shoot them. They were lucky, their guards relented and the work was cancelled. Later in the war POWs at Maxthal were more personally involved in German efforts to wipe out evidence of the Jewish community, when they were detailed to clean out train wagons. What they discovered shocked them. These were the cattle wagons used to transport what the Germans referred to 'refugees' and 'deportees' – in other words those destined for concentration or extermination camps. By the time the men had finished their work their bodies and uniforms were alive with lice and fleas, their hands and clothes soiled with the filth left behind on the trains by their unfortunate occupants. It was not a task they would soon forget. In the final days of the war prisoners who had been marched all the way from Poland were made to dig pits for the Germans to bury concentration camp victims, in a desperate attempt to hide the evidence of their crimes.

Whilst arguments raged about what work was suitable for POWs the men themselves had more pressing concerns – their own physical well-being. Thousands of those on work detachments found conditions an almost intolerable burden. The Red Cross did their best to get some harsh work camps closed down, knowing the men could not continue to work in industry with insufficient food. The Red Cross representatives returned to camps month after month and watched as the POWs got thinner – it was only a question of how long they could survive before disease and death took control.

It was not just the burden of physical exertion that took its toll on the prisoners. They were also made to work long hours. For most the notion of an 8-hour working day was a long forgotten memory. The old idea of dividing the day between 8 hours' labour, 8 hours' recreation and 8 hours' sleep was something few knew the luxury of. Instead, across the

Reich, many found themselves working up to 12 hours a day. Without warning the Germans could simply change the hours of the working day. One man working a 9-and-a-half-hour day in a coal mine was caught resting when he should have been working. His punishment was to be kept working for an extra 4 hours. By the time he finally got to eat his evening meal it was 14-and-a-half hours since he had begun his shift in the morning. For some men such impositions became the norm. Repair teams at some mines were kept on duty for as long as there remained work to do and were forced onto double shifts without food or drink. One of the repairmen was kept at his post continuously for 23 hours. At one work camp announcements were made stressing that the men had to do 2 hours 'overtime' each day on top of the 9-and-a-quarter hours they were already working. Even when the men thought they were about to rest they were sometimes told they should keep working. One group of copper miners finished a 12-hour shift only to be told they would have to spend the night clearing snow. When the Red Cross inspected the work camps they discovered work details nearly always working for at least 10 hours a day, seldom with a day off. As they reported to London, the conditions were: 'extremely bad ..... such as might be expected of slave labour being used'.[22]

On top of such excessive hours the prisoners also had the time spent travelling to and from work, which for most meant walking. One arbeitskommando, recorded rising at 5 a.m., walking for an hour to reach their workplace, toiling to level ground for 12 hours and then marching back to camp where they arrived at 9 p.m. – just 8 hours before they would rise the next morning to restart the routine. Another detachment was woken at 3 a.m. to depart for work at 4 a.m. and not return to camp until after 7 in the evening. For some the walk to work was even longer, as much as 4 hours each day. Others found themselves finishing work but being forced to remain in the factory until the guard decided to march them back. Salt miners at Kaliwerke found themselves in a similar situation. They worked a 10-and-a-half-hour shift but were forced to remain below ground until the civilian workers finished an hour and a half later.

Even with these extreme hours some men found themselves forced to work beyond the norm. In many factories the shift system ensured that when shifts were swapped over at the end of the working week those men on the final shift would be forced to remain at their posts continuously for up to 18 hours. Their only consolation was that they could look forward to a straight 18 hours of rest at the end of the following week when they could recuperate.

On occasions the Germans offered the prisoners some respite from their labours, promising that if they worked hard and got a task completed they would be allowed to finish work early. For many this was ideal, they were working at less than a breakneck pace and could easily pick up the pace to make sure they would get plenty of time off. However the offers were not always what they seemed. When one detachment were offered Boxing Day as a holiday in return for extra work on Christmas Eve they jumped at the chance. It would allow them a chance to celebrate Christmas and then have a lie in the next morning. Yet when the morning came they heard the usual shouts of 'Raus' and were roused from their beds, denied their one day of peace.

The very real depths of exhaustion felt by the men working in heavy industry was poetically described by Cyril Baddock working in a copper mine, when he wrote in the camp's newsletter, secretly pinned up within their huts for the prisoners to read:

> She was the most desirable thing in the world. God knows how I needed her – what eternal bliss just to rest in her arms, what unalloyed happiness I could find in the ecstasy of her kiss. At times she seemed as far away as the sun, and others just within my eager reach, but when I tried to draw her close she would slide laughingly out of my embrace. …. She would not come to me at night when I most needed her. But whilst I was at work she took me into her loving arms and I gave myself to her absolutely. I was caught of course and the chief did not like it. He avowed that the mine was no place for that sort of thing and he reported me. You see, 'she' was the daughter of Morpheus and her name is 'Sleep'.[23]

The burden of work became intolerable for some, as they found themselves forced to carry enormous weights. Men on 'light duties' found themselves sent to be bricklayers, the problem was that the 'bricks' each weighed 18 pounds. Some labours seem designed to exhaust them, forcing them into heavy manual work more normally carried out by machines. At one industrial complex prisoners were forced to carry out pile driving by hand. Using a platform, they strained to pull the ropes that lifted the pile that they dropped to drive lengths of tree trunks into the ground. It was heavy, monotonous and seemingly needless work. Some worked in damp conditions without suitable protective clothing and soon found themselves suffering from rheumatism. One extremely damp mine was kept open until eventually all the German foremen had been conscripted into the Wehrmacht, only then were the prisoners offered any respite. At some industrial concerns the prisoners held the directors personally responsible for their sufferings. At the Vietscher magnesium works at Trieben in Austria the workers blamed the director, Herr Koenig, for their being forced to work in the most dangerous part of the factory where the magnesium was burnt.

Men sent to a brickworks were dismayed to find their part of the process kept them far from the heat of the kilns. Instead their work involved standing in the waters at the edge of a lake cutting clay and carrying it to skips in relays. Each day they worked in sodden uniforms that they tried desperately to dry overnight. Yearn they might for the heat of the kilns but men working at them also found their situation unhealthy. They found their noses and throats being clogged with dust from the drying clay and without proper face masks they only had rags tied across their faces. Likewise for men employed in cement works it seemed there could be no escape from the dust. They were without protective clothing, the dust attacked their airways, settled in their already matted hair and stained their skin and clothes.

Even in winter men laboured in mountain tunnels where the wind whipped through and water dripped from the ceiling. Those prisoners working outdoors without gloves often found their skin sticking to the metal of the tools they used. POWs in flax factories were forced to buy their own goggles and make their own face masks in order to keep their eyes and lungs clear of the dust and loose fibres. In one stove factory all among the working POWs suffered burns to their feet since their footwear offered little protection, whilst miners reported new boots lasting just six weeks as their leather soles cracked making them impossible to repair. Such complaints became a common feature of Red Cross reports, as the lack of protective clothing meant there were many accidents, in particular causing the amputations of fingers of men working in mines and quarries.

The prisoners placed the blame for such incidents on their guards and foremen, and anyone involved in the process of sending them to work without suitable protective clothing. As one man later wrote there were 'numerous accidents through their neglect'.[24] One of the victims of this wilful negligence was Frederick Keast, killed in April 1943 at an Arbeitskommando in Stiermark, when he was run over by a passenger train. Even when such serious accidents took place the prisoners were seldom allowed to stop work. Instead they continued to work as the injured and dead were removed from the workplace.

Although a few work camps issued all the POWs with overalls conditions varied from place to place. At one camp, of the 1,166 British POWs only 20 per cent were issued with overalls, the remainder worked in whatever clothes were available. Without overalls these were soon stained with dirt and oil and stiff with sweat. In time they would be reduced to rags. Once their work clothes were worn out they utilized their spare clothing, which in turn became threadbare. Reduced to just one set of clothes, many of the men on working details were a pitiful sight, as one recalled of the mine he worked at: 'majority of the prisoners are dressed like tatters'.[25] Some toiled for day after day, month after month, year upon year, without washing or changing their uniforms. Even when infested with fleas and lice the prisoners had to continue wearing the same clothes through good weather and bad. The heat of summer just added more perspiration to the fabric, the cloth becoming stiff with dried sweat, the smell becoming overpowering for outsiders. Then in the cold of winter men working outdoors were soaked to the skin with little chance of drying their clothes before they dressed again for the next day.

Of course, not all the prisoners were employed in large industrial concerns. Nor were they necessarily sent to work in gangs along with their mates. Plenty found themselves all but alone, maybe in small gangs of two or three, in locations that only served to enforce the notion of servility. Many were sent daily into towns and cities near to their Stalags and employed to build air raid shelters for use by civilians, where they often deliberately reduced the levels of cement in the concrete to ensure the shelters would be useless. It was their simple way of playing a small part in the war effort. Others were employed to sweep the streets of German towns and cities, spending 8 hours a day picking up the rubbish dropped by their new masters. Shuffling along in their clogs, broom in hand, there was no greater sign that they were the members of a defeated army. In the eyes of the Germans their humiliation would be complete, but for the prisoners there were still plenty of perks. They searched for cigarette butts that could be split open to be re-rolled and smoked, they also picked up sheets of paper that could substitute for the toilet paper often in such short supply within the camps.

Les Allan, was one of those prisoners sent out to do menial work for the Germans. In the middle of the winter of 1940, wearing a mixture of the wretched scraps of his uniform and the old French and Polish uniforms the guards had thrown into the compound, he was chosen to work on the frozen River Vistula:

It was the first time I was made to work. I was taken down to the river that was thick with ice – that shows how cold it was. I had to bang a hole in the ice, then they gave me a two-handled tree saw. On one end was a lead weight, you had to put that through into the river. Then I had to saw two-foot blocks of ice. These then had to be carried to the river bank where they were built into a pyramid, which was then covered in leaves. I assume it was for the German officers to have nice iced drinks.[26]

It was not only the conditions of labour and imprisonment that weighed heavy on the minds of the prisoners. There was also the question of who they toiled alongside. Many of the larger industrial concerns used prisoners from across Europe – Poles, Belgians, Russians, Frenchmen, Yugoslavs – indeed, from all the defeated nations. Even when they saw the appalling treatment of the Russians, who were starved and beaten mercilessly, it could not prepare them for the sight of some of their fellow labourers. On some work details the prisoners worked alongside the most wretched of all Hitler's slaves – the concentration camp inmates. Unlike the prisoners they had no Red Cross parcels and no one to complain to. Theirs was not just a life of heavy labour, boredom and discomfort, indeed theirs was not a life at all. Their existence was a living death, the sight of which drove many of the POWs to despair. They watched the concentration camp inmates in their striped pyjamas grow weaker day by day. They watched them be beaten and killed. They had no choice but to stand aside and watch the physical abuse of the old and weak, knowing they could do nothing to save them. Intervening to stop a beating would not save the victim, but it might cost the life of the POW. Even Jewish children worked alongside the prisoners, scurrying around in their ragged oversized prison uniforms, their bare feet filthy, their eyes old before their time. All the prisoners could do was pass them scraps of food from their own rations. When Red Cross parcels arrived they would save their midday meals, waiting for an opportunity to hand over whatever could be spared to those even more desperate than they were themselves.

Australian Private John McInerney, detached from Stalag VIIIb to a tea factory, witnessed the brutality of the Germans towards Jewish men and women. Towards the end of the war a column of 2,000 concentration camp inmates were marched into the Australian's camp. The next morning he counted 25 bodies lying dead on the ground. As the column departed the SS rounded up any who had attempted to hide. McInerney watched in horror as 20 of them – both men and women – were executed in cold blood. He even saw civilians he worked alongside in the factory bringing in Jews to be executed. Of the nine recaptured by the civilians five were executed by pistol shot to the back of the head in full view of the POWs.

Of all the work details to which the prisoners were sent none would have the lasting emotional impact of one particular camp. A number of work camps, initially known by their simple Arbeitskommando numbers, might have been just some of the many work details dependent on Stalag VIIIb at Lamsdorf. Yet these were not just any work camps, for they were housed in the small Polish town of Oswiecim or, as it would soon be known, Auschwitz. Here the unfortunate prisoners were forced to witness some of the horror of the Nazis' attempt to purge Europe of its Jews. When working prisoners at this camp were made to carry rifles to the repair shops they were not merely playing a part in the German war effort they were being forced into playing an unwitting role in the extermination of millions of innocent civilians. It was an experience few would ever forget, and which fewer still ever wanted to remember.

The British POWs were housed in Camp Three, or Monowitz. Though few came in direct contact with the gas chambers and crematoria of Camp Two, or Birkenau, none were unaware of the horrific scenes being played out around them. Up to 140,000 slave labourers, mostly civilians, were housed in the complex of camps around Auschwitz, a complex that in total covered an area of 25 square miles. Among the German companies employing prisoners was Buna who used them as labourers on the building of a synthetic rubber factory. Others among the elite of German industry had plants within the complex, including IG Farben, Krupps and Siemens. Day by day the POWs watched the ceaseless toil and never-ending violence inflicted on the inmates of the camp, who shuffled around in their striped pyjamas under the watchful gaze of SS guards. It soon became a common sight for the prisoners to witness beatings or to see corpses left on the ground awaiting collection for cremation. Sometimes they would see the bodies of inmates left swinging from the gallows, their corpses a chilling reminder of the price of disobedience. In a moment of pure horror one British soldier, Arthur Dodds, witnessed Jewish children being burned alive in a pit. It was hours before he was able to speak and it would be many years before he was able to tell anyone what he had seen. Such was the scale of evil experienced by the soldiers that few could really believe what was going on around them – nothing could have prepared them for such scenes.

What made it worse was that they knew they were powerless. With the SS in charge of the camp they could expect little mercy; when one man tried to intervene to assist a young girl carrying a container of soup the guard simply ran him through with his bayonet.

The prisoners carried another burden. Many were certain they would never be allowed to live to tell the tale. Surely the cruel slavery and brutal extermination of Europe's Jews would have to be kept hidden from the world? Surely the Germans had no intention of letting the POWs live to tell the tale? Thus they spent their days almost certain they too would be exterminated before they would be allowed to leave. In their desperation they did all they could to try to undermine the efforts of the Nazis. They sabotaged machinery, fitting the wrong parts into the networks of pipes in the chemical plants, or forcing stones into them. In the railway sidings prisoners swapped destination plates, filled axle boxes with sand and broke holes into the roofs of wagons, hoping the rain might damage whatever was carried within. They slipped morsels of food to fellow inmates in the desperate hope it might keep them alive for just one more day. The surrendering of food in such a manner was a moral dilemma for the prisoners since they had little enough to sustain themselves. Was it worthwhile to risk one's own health at the expense of helping someone who would surely be dead within weeks anyway? It was a personal decision that could not be taken lightly, nor could the individual be criticized for the choice he made. A handful took their resistance to another level. A few of the prisoners were courageous enough to team up with the Polish underground who operated within the camp. They helped smuggle weapons and explosives into Auschwitz, aiding the locals in their attempts to make sure the factories would never operate. Bravest of all were the prisoners who helped the Jewish inmates to hide from the Nazis and were even able to smuggle a handful of them out of the camp.

For the POWs at Auschwitz, the living conditions they endured were much the same as in many of the other work camps across the Reich. Their accommodation huts were basic and their food often appalling. When one group arrived to start work at the camp – as punishment for having previously refused to work – they were given a meal of fish that many among them refused. They were right to do so. Those that ate the fish were immediately sick. Yet this meal that included meat had been a luxury, albeit an inedible one. Most meals consisted of simple soups, often made from chestnuts and what seemed to be sawdust. The soup, which the prisoners mockingly compared to dishwater, was served from 25-gallon containers, which contained enough – in the view of the Germans – to feed hundreds of workers. Alongside it they were served a small slice of black bread, apart from that they relied on the contents of Red Cross parcels. With parcels growing increasingly scarce in the latter stages of the war the prisoners saw their own failing health mirror that of the concentration camp inmates. They too grew thin, their bones protruding through pale skin, their bellies yearning for something – anything – to quell the pangs of hunger. By the time the camp was finally evacuated some among them weighed as little as 6 stone. Most grew certain that even if they survived the attentions of the guards they would surely never survive if salvation did not come soon.

Food was not the only thing on their minds and it was not just the sight of inmates being abused and murdered that affected them. They also had to endure the sickly sweet smell of burning flesh that hung over the area. With this smell engulfing their senses the prisoners had to carry on with their daily labours. Whether they were constructing walls, digging ditches and laying pipes or unloading railway wagons, they worked with the knowledge that death was never far away. In some parts of the camp their ears were constantly assailed by the screams of inmates as they were beaten by the sadistic guards. With life so cheap it was little wonder imprisonment in Auschwitz took its toll. Some found solace in the dangerously cheap alcohol they were able to trade for the contents of their Red Cross parcels. Others retreated into themselves whilst some, unhinged by what they saw around them, made hopelessly suicidal attempts to escape.

It was not only as labourers that some among the POWs found themselves within concentration camps, some were unfortunate enough to be thrown in amidst the mass of inmates. One group of two British sailors and an army NCO who were evacuated from Italy in August 1943 were sent to Dachau, one of the first concentration camps to be established by the Nazis. In this living hell, situated outside Munich, the POWs were subjected to senselessly brutal beatings by guards. With their POW status an irrelevance, they were punched and kicked for no reason other than for being there. After four months they were finally transferred from the camp, although one man – Sergeant Edwards – was left behind due to an attack of malaria. Any hopes the men had of being returned to a Stalag were dashed when they found themselves hustled behind the wire of Buchenwald, yet another concentration camp. The treatment they faced was much the same as at Dachau, with one of the men severely beaten for the simple crime of having his hands in his pockets.

After two months a courageous Czech interpreter on the camp staff intervened, they were then finally released and sent to Stalag XIIIc. Just two weeks after leaving Buchenwald the two sailors were classed as fit enough to be sent to a work camp. After just one day's labour one of the sailors, W. Holt, went straight to bed where he remained until he died a week later. Though the cause of his death was given as influenza it was clear that Holt had never been fit enough to work. As a protest his former concentration camp colleague, Stoker Robertson, refused to do any further work.

The visible mistreatment of concentration camp inmates was a sobering thought for all the prisoners who witnessed it, or even heard rumours of the evil perpetrated by the Nazis. The possibility of being worked to death by their guards hung over all the prisoners like a dark cloud. For some it was made all the more ominous by the knowledge that the protection of the Red Cross would not be enough to save them if the Germans decided to take action. There were many Jewish soldiers among the prisoners. Many were born and raised in cities throughout the British Isles. Others were Jewish exiles from Europe who had adopted British names and officially changed their religion so as to avoid identification if they were captured. Such concealment of their identity was not so simple. There were also large numbers of Palestinian Jews, captured during the campaign in North Africa, for whom the spectre of German abuse was very real. Of the 234 Arbeitskommandos formed from Stalag VIIIb at Lamsdorf 16 were exclusively for Jewish POWs, many of whom were assigned to mines where they experienced conditions far removed from that of their homeland. At E86, in which one of these detachments was based, they were subjected to many reprisals by their guards. In protest 30 men went on hunger strike. Yet surprisingly, despite their fears, most discovered they were treated little differently from prisoners of other religious denominations and were able to work through the hardships until their liberation.

Jewish prisoners were not the only ones segregated into their own work camps. Black British and Commonwealth troops were often sent to segregated work camps, despite being integrated within the Stalags. At AK1740, a work camp dependent on Stalag XIIIc, a group of 48 black soldiers were not allowed to take walks outside their camp. This was a privilege often extended to men at work camps since their guards knew they would not try to escape. The German authorities gave very definite reasons why the men should not be allowed out into the streets. They thought the sight of negroes would 'cause a sensation'[27] and thus confined the unfortunate men to the camp.

Segregation was also used for political purposes. The German authorities were confident they would be able to turn some among their captives against the British. As a result the Irish were singled out for special attention. It was hoped that they would find Irish nationalists among the captured men and be able to turn them against their supposed oppressors. However, the Germans were in for a shock. They established Arbeitskommando 961 at Friesack, which came under the jurisdiction of Stalag IIIc. Here 120 'Irishmen' were assembled into a working party that was kept away from the influence of the 'English'. The plan had numerous drawbacks that undermined their intentions. Though the camp had both hot and cold running water, with showers described by inmates as 'excellent' and with 'perfect' latrines, the prisoners were not satisfied. Nor did the fact that they seldom worked for more than 3 hours a day, or the fact that they were given days off when the weather was bad, help to sway their minds. The problem was the 'Irishmen' were from a wide mix of backgrounds. There were men from both Ulster and from the Free State. Some were simply men from England of Irish heritage and others were men born in Ireland yet brought up in towns across the United Kingdom, or simply Englishmen serving in units like the Irish Guards. Even those from the south of Ireland were men who had happily joined the British Army, either out of a determination to fight the Nazis or from a sense of adventure. Many among them simply considered themselves British despite their heritage. Whatever their cause or their backgrounds the Germans failed to raise any significant interest among the prisoners. Despite initial efforts to bombard the men with anti-British propaganda there was no question of an Irish legion being raised to fight for Irish independence. Indeed most among them questioned why they had been forced into the camps and argued for their reintegration into the camps from which they had originally come. For some Irishmen segregated in working parties just for the 'Irish' the situation was made worse by the widespread belief that they were receiving preferential treatment and extra Red Cross food and clothing. One 'Irishman' later reported how they actually received no Red Cross parcels and no spare clothing. At work they would be handed one of two coloured tickets, according to how hard the foreman believed they had worked. Men with red tickets could draw full rations, but those with green received just half the ration.

Whether at segregated detachments or in work camps that simply picked men at random from the hordes within the Stalags, most of the working prisoners faced the same basic concerns. As the war progressed they faced questions over their future. What worried them was the heavy and debilitating nature of their work, the shortages of food and what the enemy intended for their fate when the Reich finally collapsed. Throughout the war – whether whilst the Third Reich was at the height of its power or descending into chaos – when questioned by the Red Cross about the conditions faced by the prisoners the Germans offered simple answers. They claimed working conditions endured by POWs matched those of civilian workers, hiding the fact that most civilians had suitable protective clothing. They also pointed to events that undermined their efforts to provide for the prisoners – most notably the Allied bombing raids that increasingly battered the Reich's infrastructure. In particular they highlighted the shortages of Red Cross parcels caused by the fact that the Allied advance had cut the normal supply lines via Portugal, France and Switzerland.

Though they made such claims about wartime conditions undermining their efforts and despite problems of infrastructure and inefficiency there was seldom a delay in sending newly captured men to work. A group of 80 paratroopers captured at Arnhem in late September 1944 had already been working in a sugar refinery for five weeks when they were visited by the Red Cross in early November. In those five weeks they had not been given a single day off, were working 12-hour shifts and had no cooking and washing facilities or sanitation. Nor were the prisoners given proper protective footwear despite often working with their feet submerged in water. The lack of access to cooking facilities was in many ways an irrelevance since they received no Red Cross parcels of food to be cooked. The discomfort of their immediate introduction to the rigours of working in German industry was a fitting precursor for the turmoil they and their fellow workers would endure in the final months of the war.

FOUR

The Land Army

'I knew all the places to get food ... If you walked in a barn and you saw a hen start moving and cackling then she'd laid an egg... You knew if a cow kicked out when you touched its udders then it wanted milking. I used to know when the pig was going to have babies, then I'd wait a couple of weeks and go down and knock one off... There were lots of things you could use, it was like fieldcraft.'[1]

Whilst those prisoners forced to labour in heavy industry endured appalling conditions and bemoaned their fate, many of those sent to work on farms praised their good fortune. Compared to some of the work on offer, the Landwirtschaft Arbeitskommandos were not a bad place to be sent. Whether they were working on small family farms high in the mountains of Austria or vast state farms in the newly acquired lands of the east, the prisoners enjoyed a relatively comfortable life. It was not that their work was not heavy – indeed like all prisoners they endured much during their captivity – yet the countryside offered a freedom that many were to enjoy to the utmost. As a result agricultural labouring became possibly the most favoured of all work details. The work was demanding, especially at harvest time, but they spent most of their days outside in the fresh air and compared to life down coal mines or in heavy industry, it was a blessing. There was usually enough food, even if it had to be stolen, there were plenty of women and in many cases little restriction was put on the prisoners, as one remembered: 'They sent me to a farm for three and a half years. It was a state farm in a little village not far from Marienburg, about 20 or 30 houses. Actually we ran the farm. We had two old guards, one of them spent most of his time with one of the women, getting his end away, so he never used to bother us much. So we ran the place.'[2] With many of the agricultural prisoners free to make their own way to and from work they found they had entered a world far removed from the unreal world of prisoner of war camps.

Ken Wilats recalled the first time he was called for work from Stalag XXa:

> I don't know how they decided who was going to go on a working party. But the Germans told farmers that if they wanted labour the Wehrmacht would supply them if they would provide board and lodging. Your name and POW number was called out from a list. The first one I was sent out on was to Bromberg on a project to strip large trees of their bark and then using a big machine to get the roots out of the ground.[3]

Working at an Arbeitskommando in a Polish forest was just one of the many jobs Wilats would have before he eventually settled down to spend almost three years on a state farm where labouring in all the jobs available he soon began to learn the ways of the countryside. For all he learnt in his new employment it could never erase the vivid memories of the world he came from – the same world he yearned to return to.

For some prisoners agricultural details were the perfect place to be sent. Those born and bred in the countryside were relieved to be somewhere where they could continue to practise their peacetime occupations. The livestock offered no shocks to them and the cycle of seasons and nature was what they expected of life – they had always risen with the sun and worked through the daylight hours. They had all the talents needed – they understood when animals were sick, they could predict what weather lay ahead and they could maximise their efficiency to minimise their workload. Whether crofters from the Scottish Islands or dairy herders from the pastures of England, whether cattle ranchers from the plains of Canada or shepherds from the rolling hills of New Zealand – all had talents they were eager to use. For such men to be detailed to stables to groom horses was no chore, merely a continuation of life under different circumstances.

Yet for thousands of the men, farm work came as a shock. Plenty of them had never been near a farm in their lives, never handled animals, nor indeed had much experience of the countryside. They had never been outside their home towns or cities prior to being called up for wartime service. Others knew little except what they'd seen in magazines or newsreels, or as the landscape passing the train windows during bank holiday trips to the seaside. They were to have a rude awakening. Life in the countryside was about more than leaning on a gate, chewing straw and wearing a smock. It was about long hours and hard work in all weathers.

One of the first things to be learnt by the prisoners was how different the landscape was from that of home. Since most of the soldiers were young men with little experience of the world, the landscape of central and eastern Europe was completely new to them. Indeed for many of the men from across the Empire this was their first visit to Europe. Used to the sun of South Africa or Australia, or the intense summer heat of India – and having been first introduced to Europe via the Mediterranean theatre – many among them struggled to adapt to a climate that was kind to them in the spring and summer yet savagely cruel through the winter.

There was a certain irony to what they were learning. Those POWs sent to work in the newly conquered Polish territories or in East Prussia, were labouring in the very lands that were the German focus of the struggle. The former included the fields and forests Hitler had taken his country to war to claim, the later were the German lands he sought to protect from the supposed attentions of his eastern enemies. This was the territory that the men from Britain and the Commonwealth had been conscripted to free from the clutch of the Germans. And now with an unconscious irony they slipped into the role of labourers bound to slave for the Nazis' expansionist dream.

Everything was different from the world they knew – from the crops to the livestock, from the houses to the wildlife. The POWs spotted small wooden houses with dark walls and forbidding windows, these were the homes of the Poles. Sharing the villages were more substantial buildings, one- or two-storey brick built homes, which housed the local German population. Yet the homes of the two nationalities shared some features. In the spring and summer their gardens were awash with colour, as daisies and poppies bloomed in the fertile earth. Enclosed within their short wooden fences these gardens and smallholdings were alive with the buzzing of insects and the chirping of crickets. They shared the common feature of wooden outhouses that perched above pits which were regularly emptied to feed the soil of the land they worked.

Fertilised by the human waste of generations of farmers, the fields of eastern Europe were bountiful. Crops thrived in these lands. Whether in the vast fields that fed the armies of the expanding Reich – or the gardens where the locals grew their peppers, cucumbers, tomatoes and dill, whose aroma filled the senses of all who walked through a village – nature was all around the prisoners as they slipped into a rural existence. Perched atop almost every chimney, church tower, or telegraph pole were the nests of storks. Every village had a pond from which ducks and geese waddled to quack at the prisoners as they marched to work. Every home seemed to have a chained dog, roaming the garden, protecting the livestock from the attentions of the foxes that emerged each night. Other animals crept out from the woods into the fields. As the sun set, deer and boar slipped from the woods, marching through the crops ignoring the careful lines laid out by the POW ploughmen, and treading a course their forebears had trod long before man had chosen to fight over the ownership of these fields.

It was not just the look of the houses or the layout of the fields that opened the eyes of the men. The very scale of things was a revelation. After the relatively crowded British Isles the Polish countryside seemed a vast expanse of field and forest, dotted with farms or small villages and almost swamped by lakes. Fields rolled for mile after mile, connected by pitted tracks or rough tree-lined roads, whilst rivers seemed to be wider and wilder than those at home. Meadows full of sunflowers swayed in the wind, continuing for miles in places where it seemed no one lived near enough to tend them. Roads stretched forever towards the horizon, the roadside shrines and calvaries the only sign of human activity. And as the prisoners worked, like peasants from centuries past, the summer sky seemed to be an expanse of blue rolling ever onward above them. Even when covered in storm clouds, the sky seemed to have a startling blackness that hung over them as if to emphasise their predicament. This was the *lebensraum* Hitler had promised to his people.

The physical essence of this new world was not the only revelation for the prisoners. The very light around them seemed to have an intensity unseen in western Europe. The dust of the harvest, or that kicked up from beneath the horses' hooves, seemed to hang lazily in the air, glistening in the sunlight. Whether at sunrise or sunset, the colours thrown across the fields were outstandingly vivid. The yellowy orange of the summer and autumn sunset was unlike any they experienced at home. In the evenings they sat in the hazy shadows and watched as the sun set far away in the west. With the buzzing of insects and the crisp rustling of crops surrounding them, the weary prisoners settled down to rest, not knowing if they would ever follow the setting sun westwards to their own homes. Tied into this natural world, the prisoners slipped into a routine few could ever have dreamed would mark their wartime service.

The men sent to farms in the east were not alone in experiencing a world far removed from that they had known at home. Hundreds were sent to the farms of Bavaria and Austria where they worked land high up in the mountains. For many of the POW farm labourers they felt they had taken a step back in time. Many were delivered to farmhouses where they awaited the arrival of local farmers who came to view their prospective labourers. Like slaves at market the farmers looked the prisoners over before selecting which man they thought most suited their needs. Once working the men found almost medieval ways of working, there was little machinery and tractors were almost unknown. They ploughed with teams of horses and often reaped and sowed by hand, whilst hand-driven blowers were used to separate the grain from the chaff. The farmhouses also had a primitive quality unseen at home. The farmers lived on the upper levels of buildings where the ground floor was used to house their livestock through the winter, when the cattle bedded down on pieces of thinly cut pine branches. As the POWs ate their meals in the kitchens of the farmhouses, pigs and chickens wandered freely in, searching for scraps of food. The farms themselves were spread out around hills, valleys and mountainsides where the men worked small plots between forested areas and steep slopes where no crops could be planted. Thousands of feet above sea level the prisoners worked in the fields, breathing in the thin, clean air and enjoying the bright sunlight of the summer months.

Gordon Barber was among the new breed of farmers who stepped out into the farms of the Reich. Initially held at Stalag XXa, at Thorn, and then at Stalag XXb near Marienburg, he was soon sent on a work detail:

> I will always remember this farm. We didn't do bad in there, 'cause we got fairly good rations. It was a state farm and they realised if they didn't feed us we wouldn't be able to work. We were lucky. One bloke I knew, the Germans knew he was Jewish, they kept him in the Stalag and he died of malnutrition. They used to see him searching for potato peelings. But most of us were 'townies' we didn't know what a farm was. I didn't know how potatoes grew.[4]

Separated from his best mate Paddy who, as a pre-war regular in the Royal Horse Artillery, had been detailed to tend the farm horses, Barber was sent to the potato fields. It would be a sharp learning process for him, one which the German guards were prepared to ensure would not take too long. The prisoners soon realised their guards would not tolerate any insolence and their actions shattered any dreams the prisoners had of a rural idyll:

One afternoon in October, it was cold, we were digging up the last of the potato crop. The fields used to go for miles. We used to have a little three pronged fork and we'd get hold of the top of the potato plant, dig under and pull them all out. I was with a Scots bloke at the time, he had all boils on the back of his neck. This little bleedin' overseer came riding out on his horse. He'd got these packets of '*papierosa*' – Polish cigarettes – they were bloody horrible, but you'd smoke anything. He stuck them up on a stick at the end of the potato row. So the first one to finish would get them. I said to Jock 'This is what the Americans used to do to their slaves. Bollocks, I'd rather pack up smoking.' And the guard said 'Don't forget you'll be here until you're finished. You'll stop here until night time.' I still had a load of mouth so I said. 'Fuckin' hard luck. Then you'll still be here. You're not gonna leave us alone.'

Soon Barber and his mate were left far behind the rest of the workforce – both Polish labourers and fellow POWs – as they worked at a comfortable pace. Their efforts did not impress the foreman.

When it was time for them to go home – they'd all finished their rows – me and Jock still had a couple of miles to go. I wasn't worried, there was only one thing they could do – they could only shoot you. When the guards came back to us it was dark – they'd got torches. One was called Christian, he was a fucking evil man. They'd got these thin branches they'd cut from a sapling. I said to my mate 'We're going to get in trouble here.' I had a Polish hat on so I pulled it down over my face. They shone the torch at Jock and as he bent down they whacked him. The back of his neck was like a blood bath, they'd burst all his boils. He had a couple of false teeth and they were knocked out. They gave him a right going over. I thought 'You bastards, I'm gonna get it now.' So I pulled my collar up and bent down so I'd take it on my shoulders. They set on me and this Christian bloke loved it. He kept laughing when I cried out. Then when we finished they marched us back. The other blokes took our clothes off and washed us down. They said 'Look at your back!' It was covered in weals. I thought, if I ever meet that Christian again I'll kill him.[5]

It was little wonder men like Barber soon began to 'learn the ropes'. He and most of his comrades were on a steep learning curve. For young men from the cities it was difficult to adapt but the impetus was simple – by learning the ways of the countryside they would learn ways to keep their bellies full. Prisoners soon became proficient in catching chickens, and learnt that the best way to dispose of bones and feathers was to hide them in the manure pile. Born and bred around Crystal Palace in South London, Barber had no experience of rural life but he soon worked things out:

> I knew all the places to get food. I knew exactly where the chickens would lay their eggs. If you walked in a barn and you saw a hen start moving and cackling then she'd laid an egg. You learnt that. You knew if a cow kicked out when you touched its udders then it wanted milking. I used to know when the pig was going to have babies, then I'd wait a couple of weeks and go down and knock one off, 'cause the farmer didn't know whether it had been killed by the mother. There were lots of things you could use, it was like fieldcraft.[6]

Yet the trials of becoming farmers was about more than learning where to find food. They had to learn the twice daily routine of cow milking. They learnt when it was time to take bulls for breeding, or when to put horses for stud. They learnt to deliver lambs and calves, assisting the country vets or farmers when necessary until they could carry out the task unaided. They learnt how horses didn't like pigs and had to be kept apart for fear the horses would kick the pigs. Shepherding and shearing, milking and milling, all were part of the POWs' new life. Such was the amount they learned that even in the twilight of their lives the former POW farmers find themselves looking into fields and assessing the quality of the land – checking for weeds and nettles, or noting how many stones lie in the path of the ploughs.

Men who had only seen horses as something that pulled milk floats around the streets of their home towns were soon leading teams of working horses before the plough. William Hymers, formerly a London grocer, was part of a detachment of prisoners sent to a farm after they had disrupted a road building project with their almost constant acts of petty sabotage, such as breaking picks and shovels. He was already in his thirties by the time he found himself told to learn ploughing at an agricultural detachment from Stalag XXa. He later wrote of his labours:

> We paced out 50 strides from one end of the field and stuck in a stick.
> Then, going to the other side we did the same again. With two, some-

times three, horses abreast we ploughed a furrow as straight as possible from stick to stick. Then turning round we ploughed back again, which made a kind of ridge. After that we just went up and down with the ploughed area getting larger and larger until the end of the field was reached.[7]

At each turn Hymers had to throw the plough onto its side as the horses dragged it into position ready to start the next furrow.

Holding the plough with both hands Hymers was forced to put the reins around his neck and eventually learned to control the horses using his voice. He was taught Polish phrases that the animals, with years of ploughing experience, would respond to. He shouted 'Ho-com' to make them move forward and 'Ha-com' to make them turn right. At the command 'He-com' the team would turn left and 'Swick' would make them walk backwards. The command to make the horses stop was the sound 'Br-r-r-r', made by vibrating the tongue against the back of the teeth – it was a sound many were never able to master.

Working with horses, many among the POWs grew able to read their natures. They recognised the animals as having characters of their own. Some horses were clever, some were stupid, some were lazy, others hardworking or funny, and even lovable. Another important characteristic of the horses they worked with on Polish farms was that they were not the heavyweight carthorses they knew from home. Instead the ploughs and farmcarts were pulled by a breed of horse more suited to riding than working. The explanation was simple. Traditionally the farmers had been made to breed horses for use by the Polish cavalry who needed fast mounts rather than the heavy industrious beasts needed on farms. As they worked, the prisoners were clear about one thing – the Polish army would not be needing horses in the foreseeable future.

As the prisoners worked their teams of horses through the fields they had to keep watch for large stones that might be hit by the plough. In some areas superstition had it that the stones were so large because they grew underground. The ignorance of the locals was a joke to the prisoners, although the hazard caused by the stones was no laughing matter. At best a stone could cause damage to the blade, at worst it could cause the plough to jump out of the ground, at considerable risk to both man and horses. Some of the stones disgorged by the newly turned earth were so large they had to be dragged away with chains.

Once the fields were ploughed the POWs walked the fields with baskets around their necks, sowing the seeds that would grow into crops to fill the bellies of the German military. Once that was done there were many more days of walking the same fields, often in rows ten abreast, with metal trays hanging around their necks, spreading chemical fertiliser. Les Allan was among those men detailed to plant seeds on a farm in East Prussia. His attitude towards the work soon brought him into conflict with his captors:

> Captivity didn't deter us from anything we thought would help our side, but what I did was just plain stupid. It was a beet farm. A horse pulled a two-wheeled seed box and on the box were four tubes leading down to the ground. At the end of the tubes were these little star-wheels, these pushed the seeds into the ground. I waited till the guards weren't looking and stuffed a cloth down into one of the tubes, so the seeds didn't plant. Then I stopped, pulled the cloth out and stuffed another tube. I foolishly forgot that within weeks it would become obvious what I had been doing since whole rows of crops didn't grow. That resulted in a Court Martial. I was put in front of all these high ranking German officers, they asked me all about what I had done. Luckily I was defended by a Red Cross representative. He managed to get the case dismissed within an hour. He said to the Court 'What do you expect if you send an apprentice toolmaker to work on a farm?' So that was that. But as I came out afterwards the commandant took me aside and said 'For sabotage we shoot prisoners'. So I was lucky.[8]

And so the work continued. POWs spent day after day wielding scythes as they cleared pastureland of long grass to be laid aside for winter fodder. Their hands became blistered as they cleared weeds by hand or hacked at bushes with sickles. The blisters burst, then more formed until eventually their hands grew hard and calloused. The changes to their hands were not the only physical effects of their labours. Even many of the less physical men found their bodies changing. They grew lean and muscular, their strength increased, and their bodies grew hardy – it was a strength they would all need before the war was over.

Working outside in all weathers meant the prisoners endured almost ceaseless discomfort. They maintained their back-breaking schedule in the cold of winter, in the rains of spring and autumn, and in the blistering heat of summer. At harvest time they would rise early in the morning and work till dusk, hurrying to get the crops in before the weather turned. Others picked fruit, forever assaulted by the wasps and flies that swarmed around their heads as they worked. Under the late summer sun POWs worked till their skin was bronzed and their hands blistered – their bodies fit to drop by the end of each day. Hour upon hour was spent moving scythes through the corn, cutting the crops until the light faded and the day's work was ended. As the crops were threshed, often with nothing more than a horse to power the threshers, the POWs breathed in the clouds of dust from the stalks, then suffered again as the grain was milled. Men working at threshing looked on in dismay as cart followed cart, with seldom a break throughout the day. The only men who had breaks on some farms were those who waited for the grain to arrive at the stores. Yet despite the short breaks they enjoyed, their labours were an almost unbearable burden. The often poorly nourished men had to lift 70-kilogram sacks onto their shoulders then carry them up steep ladders to be loaded into the grain store.

Even with one harvest finished there was little respite for the prisoners on farms. When one crop was harvested another might be ready, with grain followed by the vegetables of the season, until eventually they were picking winter vegetables from frost-covered fields. The prisoners became part of the annual cycle of life known to farm labourers the world over – a cycle of endurance and endeavour where man plays but a bit part, forever under the direction of the seasons and the weather.

For many the restrictions placed upon them when doing their best to endure taxing conditions was too much to bear. At a farm in Wabsch two prisoners approached their guards requesting permission to enter their accommodation huts to change clothes after a heavy downpour. Why, they felt, should they endure hours of working in wet clothing when they had a dry uniform waiting for them? When the guards refused the men ignored them and went away to get changed. Their defiance cost them dear and both were badly beaten by their guards. When a third man also tried to get changed he too was beaten up. Following the incident all three men became targets for the guards, regularly being given all the worst jobs on the farm.

It was not just beatings used to get defiant prisoners back to work. Gordon Barber was among a group of prisoners harvesting winter crops:

> When we were out there it pissed with rain. We were soaked through. We came in so wet our clothes were stuck to us. We took all our clothes off but the only place you could dry them was in the kitchen – start the oven up. But with twenty sets of clothes? We had a meeting and decided to not go to work again until our clothes were dry. The guards said we

had to go to work in the fields. The foreman was out there shouting '*Arbeit*!', we thought 'Fuck you'. So we went out in our blankets. They didn't like that, since we'd have to go through the village. All of a sudden the guard fired over our heads. We went out! We went and put our wet clothing on. When they start firing you don't want to hang around, unless you're silly.[9]

For the agricultural labourers winter didn't mean quite the same misery as it did for some of the other men on labour detachments. In the eastern farms the snows seemed to arrive in October and lie on the ground until the following March. With the frost so deep they could hardly dig a fork into the ground, the POW farmers usually spent the winter months engaged on lighter tasks. Conditions were often so harsh that there were no winter vegetables to be harvested, if all the crops were not in by the time the snows came they would have to wait until spring. Many found there was little work to do on farms apart from looking after the animals. Maybe they would spend a few hours spreading dung onto the snow covered fields, maybe they might chop wood all day, ready to be burned in their fires and cooking stoves. To protect the animals from the weather they were kept inside throughout the worst of the winter. Twice a day the POWs would spread straw in the stalls to keep the livestock warm. By spring the floor of the stables and sheds had risen considerably. It was then left to the prisoners to fetch picks and pitchforks to dig out the compacted and frozen dung ready to be cast onto the manure pile. The depth of the frost was something few had ever previously experienced, as one POW farmer explained: 'We used to put the mangelwurzels and sugar beet out in containers. They used to pack them with straw all around. Then put a layer of earth, then more straw, then earth again. But when we used to get them out in the spring we had to break it open with pick axes.'[10]

Although most agricultural detachments found there was little heavy work to do during winter not all were so lucky. One group of men found themselves sent out into a lake in the middle of winter. Here they were forced to wade through the freezing water to cut reeds to be used to make mats. Others found that once the harvest was collected it was time to cut turf ready to be used for winter fuel. In the vast, sodden peat fields they dug away topsoil to the depth of a foot. Then began the task of cutting the peat. They had to dig drainage channels to bring water from old empty holes to flood the one they were working in. Working barefoot, the prisoners had to tramp down the peat in the water until it was the right consistency so it could be loaded into sledges then formed into bricks which were then left out to dry. As the pits grew deeper the work grew more strenuous, with the long-suffering men having to throw the peat higher and higher until they could hardly reach the top of the hole. As they attempted to throw the damp turf it slipped from their shovels, landing on their heads and bodies. By the end of a working day each man was covered from head to toe in thick, black soil.

Former chef Ken Wilats, who in 'civvy street' had spent his days preparing and cooking vegetables, explained the trials and tribulations experienced during the harvest:

> We did everything on the farm. It varied due to the seasons. The intensity of the harvest was the most difficult part. It was very hard. It was amazing what you discovered. You leant that a crop of barley was much heavier than oats. The crops were cut and placed into stooks. Then the big cart, pulled by four horses, would come down the rows and us prisoners with our two-pronged fork would throw the stooks up into the cart. There was a man on the back stacking it. Eventually it would be the size of a bus. If you were doing barley you'd find it very heavy, but if it was oats you'd just flick it on. Potatoes were also a bad one to be digging up. One way or another you'd have your back bent double from September to January. But we used to just tread a lot of the potatoes back into the ground. You'd each be assigned a patch of the field and a machine would come around throwing up the potatoes from the ground. So you'd have to have your patch clear by the time the machine came back. So if you were running slow you'd just push them back underground with your boots. You got used to plenty of little dodges. And there were plenty of them to put into your pockets.[11]

Probably the worst of all the agricultural details were those experienced by men engaged in the picking and processing of the sugar beet harvest. Such was the importance of the crop that the POWs were pushed to the very limit of their endurance. Starting in October the farms and factories became scenes of frenzied activity as the vital sugar beet was harvested, transported and refined. The period became known as 'The Battle of the Beet'. The prisoners would start work early in the morning, whilst the frost was still hard on the leaves. As they walked through the rows the frost got onto their trousers, soaking them as they worked up a sweat. Only when, and if, the sun came up was there any respite from the cold and damp. POWs walked the fields in long lines, each man carrying a 'ducker fork' to dig the beet from the ground, as one recalled: 'The worst thing was pulling it out of the ground. The leaves were high and you stuck a fork underneath and pulled it out – it was like a big turnip.'[12] The harvest was then laid out in rows on the frozen ground as the prisoners cut the leaves off with machetes. The beet was then ready to be loaded onto wagons. It was heavy, backbreaking work. The cold, damp weather made their situation worse since they were unable to wear gloves as the wool would become soaked within minutes of starting and their hands were left to suffer the ravages of the weather. It was little wonder one prisoner wrote in his diary that he would challenge any man to arrive from another job within German industry and endure even an hour on the beet harvest without sinking into exhaustion.

In that first gruelling winter of captivity the prisoners were introduced to the extremes of labouring for the Third Reich. For many of those drafted in to man the beet processing plants this was their first time out of the overcrowded tedium of the Stalags. It was an experience few would ever forget. For five long weeks the men on work detachment E253 worked 12 hours a day without a day off. For others the beet harvest lasted seven weeks. Within the factories that processed the beet the labour was as gruelling as in the fields. The beet was emptied into large rotating drums which shook the dried earth from their skins. This fell down a chute at the bottom of which waited queues of prisoners whose job it was to catch the dirt in sacks. As they worked they struggled to fill the sacks and clouds of dust swirled around them filling their nostrils and throats. As some prisoners struggled to clear up the dirt others loaded the beets into huge tanks in which they were boiled to begin the process of extracting the sugar from the beet. More prisoners worked the fires that kept the water boiling. They collected the ash that fell through grates beneath the fire, wheeling away the still smouldering embers to be piled up outside.

Few of the men thrown into the factories in the winter of 1940 had fully recovered from their exertions in the weeks that had followed their capture in France. The summer of forced marches and starvation rations had weakened their bodies and few felt ready for such extremes of labour. Les Allan was among them:

> According to the Geneva Convention we should have only worked certain hours, but in a sugar beet factory once the season starts it carries on until the last beet has been processed. It never stops, not even for a minute. I worked in two different factories. They were probably the

worst jobs I had. At the first factory we had two 12-hour shifts each day. Then on Friday we worked 18 hours to change over from day to night shift. We worked all winter and never got a penny for it. I was in the filtration room where all the processed liquid went through these cloth filters. When the pressure was getting too great we had to shut the machine off, open it up and shake the filters so all the impurities would fall off and through a hole in the floor. The temperatures were terrible, the room filled with steam and we worked stripped to the waist. Once the filters had been emptied you had to wrap yourself up in your clothes, go down to where the impurities had emptied, then push the wagon outside, where the temperature was −25°. You tipped it out then put it back under the machine. The worst thing was swapping between the extreme temperatures. At the end of a 12-hour shift you were knackered. The second sugar beet factory was even worse. I was unloading the trucks. As they came in on the railway lines we had to shovel them into a trough of running water so they could run down into the factory to be processed. The cold was extreme when you are working outside all day. [13]

Throughout the winter the decrepit prisoners endured the extreme temperatures. Those lucky enough to receive wages found they earned just 1.20 reichsmarks, just enough to buy them 4 pints of weak beer – if it was available. Few were allowed to report sick, even those with bad cases of piles were forced to keep working. Those men labouring within many factories were refused work clothes and instead worked in their own uniforms. Those without sturdy footwear were forced to buy shoes at the cost of over 8 reichsmarks – more than a week's wages. When their day's work was over they could do little but fall into their beds. For them the shortages of books and games were irrelevant. It was not just the prisoners who felt aggrieved by their treatment. At one Arbeitskommando fighting the 'battle of the beet' even the German civilian workers complained that the factory managers cared little for their staff – regardless of nationality or status.

However, the burden of labour was not only on a seasonal basis. Some of those who worked through the winter processing beet found themselves soon returning to work on farms, preparing the land ready for the planting of next year's beet crop. They became used to the weekly routines known to farm workers since the accepted use of prisoners was for them to work the same hours as local labourers. Despite rules about having days off this meant that prisoners had to work on Sundays. Cows still needed to be milked and animals needed feeding or eggs collecting. Nature did not stop nor did their employers allow them special treatment.

As the prisoners became accustomed to early rising, long hours and heavy work many grew strong and were able to handle the rigours of their labour. With both Red Cross parcels to fill their bellies and goods to trade onto the black market most did not endure quite the same physical debilitation as some of those in German industry. However, among this new breed of farmers were men who were simply not suited to the work. Their physical weaknesses, and the attempts of guards, foremen or other labourers to exploit this led to conflicts between the factions. Gordon Barber, who had quickly adapted to the heavy labour, watched the treatment of a fellow prisoner:

> My mate Fippo wasn't very strong. When we were unloading the harvest into the barn we had to pile it up then throw it up into the barn. There was one bloke unloading, then others passing it up and dropping it over the side. I was unloading, I liked that because the quicker I could do it the quicker I could get a break. But you had to work fast, you couldn't fuck about.

He soon noticed his work mate was not keeping pace. The problem was that the Polish labourer had built the stack so high he couldn't reach to throw the barley up. So they swapped jobs and he began quickly throwing the sheaves at the Pole:

> I was hitting this prat in the face with them. All of a sudden I got hit by a load of it. He'd piled it up and pushed it down on me. Down I went. I climbed up the ladder to where he was. He was a big gormless prat, looked like a simpleton. I brought him down and gave him a couple of whacks. I've never seen a look of hate like it on anybody's face. He got his pitchfork and was having a go at me. I ended up in the barley, and it was hard to get up. I got up and let him get up. I chased him backwards and hit him. He went over backwards into an empty bay and broke his arm. So I wasn't a very popular fellow with the farmer or the Poles.[14]

He began to realise the local labourers could be a serious problem for the prisoners:

> They were vicious, they didn't muck about, you had to fight their way. It wasn't just fighting hard, you had to have something in your hand. I

had a fight with the blacksmith and I was doing ok. All of a sudden his missus comes running down and hit me on the head with a fucking iron bucket. Bang! Next thing I know he pulls out a pair of bleedin' shears. I thought 'I'm not having that' so I ran behind the toilets and he started throwing bricks at me. He hit me in the ribs, and broke a rib. I got a day off work. One of our blokes strapped me up and I was put on chopping wood for the next day – to power their tractor – then when I was chopping wood a bloke gave me my mail and I chopped the top off my finger.[15]

Despite these conflicts the prisoners became part of the community – as much a part of village life as the housewives, farm manager or local priest. They took meals in the farmhouse sculleries, along with the rest of the farm hands and enjoyed a rough but relatively safe life. Prisoners working high in the Alps learnt the local customs. They attended all the seasonal dances, including one for men working on flax picking where they drank cider and indulged in a traditional game where the local girls slapped the men who would have to respond by kissing them. Gordon Barber recalled life on a state farm in East Prussia:

The Germans in that place didn't treat us bad. I was as fit as a fiddle, I used to box against Darkie Fenwick and this Brummie lad, we'd do press ups, and I was getting my end away – which wasn't bad. But it was boring, we used to have bets on when the war would end. We learnt Polish and could ask them when they thought the war would finish. The German women used to sit on their doorsteps and show us newspapers about the V1 bombs. We were friendly with them. We were part of the village. For three years we'd been part of the community, we'd speak to one another in the street. We could barter with them. Some of us were getting our ends away. It was like one little village.[16]

One of Barber's fellow workers at the farm, Ken Wilats, remembered how they spent their day off on a Sunday:

They had a sty with about 200 pigs in it and lots of outbuildings. They had a little dog called 'Footsie' and on Sundays it went rat hunting. I don't know what breed it was, but it was like a little terrier. He used to bite the rats on the back of the neck and then throw them up into the air. We watched 'Footsie' catch about 12 rats in one day. That was the only time I saw rats, they didn't have them in the Stalag. When I was in the Stalags there was no spare food so there was no incentive for a rat to be there.[17]

As thousands of POWs adapted to the ways of the countryside and were able to assimilate into the local communities, others were not so fortunate. Just as in the heavy industrial enterprises, some of the farmers were happy to work their new labourers to breaking point. At Marienau the POWs reported going 12 hours at a time without being fed. They would eat breakfast before starting work at 7.30 a.m. and toil in the fields continuously until 5.30 p.m. The farmer refused them any food and allowed them to eat only what was provided in their barracks. Prisoners at AK13, a farm in Gross Partenschir, were seriously exploited by their employer. He contravened the rules on employment of labour by loaning 'his' prisoners out to other farms in the locality, in return for payment from the owners. Once their unofficial labours were complete they were then forced to return to his farm and continue to work for him.

It was not just the actual farms that were staffed by prisoners. They took on all the duties found in the countryside. Some were detailed to maintain farm machinery, repairing tractors, ploughs and threshing machines. Others among them were employed to assist blacksmiths in their forges. They worked hour after hour in the heat of the forges, their hands grasping the tongs that held the metal over the anvil as smiths hammered it into shape. Trying to dodge the sparks the men kept working, often as the smiths laughed at their inexperience. Once they had mastered holding the tongs or operating the bellows the prisoners were able to progress to shoeing horses, as they slipped into the role of true countrymen.

Working parties were also sent into the countryside to work as foresters. For many it was a pleasant life. They worked in teams, operating the long, two-handled saws and felling trees. Others then stripped the bark from the timber and cut the trees into lengths ready to be taken to the sawmills. Most enjoyed the outdoor life, stripping to the waist as they worked under the summer sun. During rest periods they could collect wild fruit and berries from the woods, or search for mushrooms and nuts. For many it was as close to a rural idyll as anything else on offer within the system of camps and working parties.

There were plenty of other rural work details. Men in food processing plants often found the work to be arduous but these usually proved to be places where a certain standard of living could be maintained.

Men working in dairies, canning plants and the factories associated with food production were able to sustain themselves with the fruits of their labour. Just as on the farms, they found much of their labour had to be carried out by hand. At dairies the work began each morning with the arrival of horse-drawn carts bringing milk churns from the surrounding farms. Prisoners found themselves using machines to separate the milk from the cream but then having to do the rest of the work by hand. They learned how to make butter and cheese. These were manual arts that were dying out across much of the world as large scale industrialisation hit food production. They warmed milk in large vats, added the rennet, then waited for the milk to curdle before carving it up. then whisking and sieving it. Once the cheese was made it would be wrapped in muslin and left to drain. Then the prisoners would spend the rest of their day turning the cheeses over and cleaning up ready for the next day's milk.

With agriculture and industry geared up for the war effort the industrial-scale production of processed food for easy storage and transport meant that thousands of POWs were drafted in to work in processing plants. Some of these were vast modern plants using the latest technology to produce cheap and convenient foodstuffs. In some processing plants the prisoners were given overalls and pristine white hats and their feet were covered by smart white wooden-soled slippers. Former chef Ken Wilats was pleased to be transferred away from the exhaustion of labouring in a gravel pit to a cheese processing plant. It was a world away from the small country dairies employing some of the prisoners:

> In this factory they made dried and flaked cheese. It was quite a decent place. The man in charge was a Swiss German, he was quite generous with food. The division of labour was that cheese was brought in from a railway station nearby. It came into the sidings and a number of prisoners were detailed to unload it onto a lorry for the factory.

The incoming cheeses were initially stored in refrigerated rooms until needed for blending. The cheeses were then tested by cutting into them with a tool like an apple corer, to ensure the correct blend would be used to create the finished product:

> This was then put into vats and boiled. A little bit of good cheese and loads of rubbish stuff was all mixed together, melted and made into dried cheese. When I first went there I was in the cellar. These round flat cheeses were stored on boards and they had to be withdrawn from

the racks and wiped over with saline solution. Then they were inverted and put back on the racks. That had to be done every day. Latterly I was made the cook at this working party, which suited me, it was quite a nice job. And if we needed any extra food we acquired the 45 per cent fat cheese, we only took the best for ourselves. So we always had that as a standby. The only problem was that it gave you a bit of constipation. But it was a good detail to get on. He gave us a bit of pork and we had a vegetable garden and grew fresh vegetables. We also had a very good guard who used to take us up to a lake to go swimming. So we did alright. Added to that there were some beautiful Polish girls working there. Things were getting better. Compared to working night shifts in a gravel pit, it was 'chalk and cheese' – literally![18]

The cheesemakers were not the only prisoners to enjoy their work. Large numbers of Indian prisoners found themselves sent to detachments where the work had a number of benefits. They were sent to work in the vineyards of the Rhine and Moselle valleys. Here they planted and tended the vines, cleared weeds and eventually harvested the grapes for making into the local wines. Like all POWs employed to pick fruit they were able to supplement their meagre rations and Red Cross parcels with sufficient grapes to help keep up their strength.

For the POW farmers, like all farmers the world over, life was tough. Yet despite the rigours of countryside life most experienced an existence that showed them a world they had never previously experienced. Their lives were governed by the seasons not the petty dictates of politicians or army officers. Their boss was the rain and the sunlight – nature itself was both their friend and their enemy, their teacher and their taskmaster. They learned how the cycle of the natural world was unforgiving yet how life on farms offered prisoners a peace far removed from the drudgery experienced by their comrades forced into industry. It was an experience that changed them, both mentally and physically – a change that would help sustain many in the harsh days ahead as the Reich collapsed around them. As Ken Wilats recalled: 'We did all the manual labour. I learnt an awful lot. It was all new. I'd never been on a farm in my life. It was hard work but I grew fit and strong and was able to cope with it.'[19]

FIVE

A Place Not Called Home

'We were always billeted and quartered in the worst possible places i.e. wet cellars, converted barns, vermin ridden sheds and barracks, hopelessly overcrowded and always badly fed ...Geneva Convention was always under violation.' *Driver Alan Edwards, Royal Engineers.*

'The rats are not quite as numerous as they were last time.' *Red Cross report on Stalag IVa, February 1945.*

Having experienced defeat, degradation and discomfort between capture and their arrival at work camps the prisoners could at least hope for one thing – that their living conditions would be more comfortable than those within the Stalags. Like so many other parts of the POW experience, what they found on arrival at work camps was a lottery. Some looked up optimistically at the signs with the word '*Lager*' on them and thought they had arrived at a brewery. For most their destination was nowhere near so promising.

For men increasingly exhausted by the burden of labour it was important they be allowed to live with some measure of comfort. They yearned for somewhere comfortable to lay their heads after 12-hour shifts of mining, quarrying or harvesting. Yet for most comfort was a distant notion, a far off dream that few dared imagine and fewer still ever knew. With time their minds became shaped by all they had experienced – there was no real comfort, just varying degrees of discomfort.

Although the employers had control over their labour, it was decreed that camp commandants had the right to withdraw the prisoners if suitable housing conditions were not met. The importance of the role of the Stalag commandants cannot be overstated, the prisoners were their responsibility. It was their duty to ensure the men were treated in a manner befitting captured combatants. As the official German rules stated: 'The prisoner of war can expect to be treated with respect regarding his personage and his honour. Bad and degrading treatment is not compatible with German dignity.'[1] Time would prove few commandants remained true to this code. Although some were fastidious about following the rules, closing down work camps where prisoners faced arbitrary violence, others were less particular. The commandant of Stalag XIa at Altengrabow was one of those whose developed a reputation for caring little about the conditions of prisoners at Arbeitskommandos, making little effort to maintain contact with the work camps where his prisoners laboured. He was untroubled by the existence of camps where the employers showed no interest in the welfare of their working prisoners. It was little wonder his Stalag was latter described as: 'nothing but one big complaint'.[2]

Despite the differences between the behaviour of the various commandants certain trends emerged throughout the network of work camps. In general, conditions in the western regions of the Reich were better than in the east – with the occasional existence of flushing toilets – but that was by no means the rule, there were plenty of prisoners enduring unhygienic and unhealthy conditions throughout Germany. It became clear that few among the POWs were living a comfortable life. As the Foreign Office stressed to the Red Cross of the conditions endured by many labourers: 'To describe them as thoroughly bad is quite inadequate. Disgraceful is a more suitable word.'[3] As they rightly pointed out, how could one commandant keep watch over the conditions endured by 23,000 men distributed through 400 work details?

Few experienced anything more than basic comforts. They were housed in whatever accommodation was available near their workplace. Old school houses, stables, tourist hotels in mountain villages, former seminaries, Hitler Youth summer camps, empty beer halls, dance halls, disused factory buildings complete with abandoned machinery, purpose-built wooden huts, farm buildings, factory canteens, disused train wagons where prisoners slept on a straw covered floor – all became home to this vast new army of labour. One working party was even housed in an eighteenth-century riding school, and Cypriot prisoners were housed in an army barracks of similar vintage. Some lived amidst scenes of desolation, with their huts surrounded by a rubbish strewn wasteland. Most depressingly one working party was housed in huts hidden beneath a railway bridge. In an extreme case of POWs being forced to witness the overbearing pride of the Nazis, they were housed in the local dance hall. Each Sunday, on their only day of rest, the prisoners were marched out so that the local Nazi Party officials could hold rallies and political meetings.

Many of the POWs faced lodgings unsuited for use as housing. At AK35, a detachment from Stalag XXa, the prisoners lived in derelict buildings within the factory complex where they worked. In these depressing surroundings they slept 80 men to a room. At other Arbeitskommandos POWs lived in barrack huts sleeping up to 140 men. Not all rooms slept so many men, however one hut for just 36 men measured just 30 by 32 feet, hardly leaving the men any space to relax. The E3 workcamp, whose intake of POWs came from Stalag VIIIb, had over 700 men sleeping in just six huts. In these they spent their nights on palliases stuffed with straw that was changed just once in 18 months.

Certain basic conditions were common to most work details. Prisoners slept in wooden bunks, two or three tiers high, beneath rough woollen blankets that lay over straw filled palliases. They kept their possessions in small wooden cupboards and hung their clothing on wooden pegs fixed to the walls. Long tables ran along the middle of rooms, lined with stools upon which they sat to eat their meals, write letters home and play innumerable games of cards. Yet though such conditions could be expected at work camps, in reality the living conditions for prisoners were as varied as the jobs they did. Some POWs lived in clean comfortable conditions yet had no running water, whilst others lived in billets unfit for animals but had access to a tap. The whole system was a lottery. Whilst some men were given comfortable beds with three or four blankets to cover them, others didn't even have straw to sleep on. Even those fortunate enough to get bunks did not necessarily live in comfort. Some slept on palliases stuffed with wool that was left unchanged for month upon month, others had to use paper sacks. At a camp in a forested area the prisoners slept on palliases stuffed with pine branches and one particularly unfortunate work detachment of 250 men were all forced to sleep on bare boards since the previous inhabitants of the camp had burned the palliases to kill the bugs living in them. When members of one working party complained they were without bedding the Germans simply suggested they put cardboard on their bunks.

In some detachments there were too few beds leaving men sleeping on cold hard stone or wooden floors. Others found themselves sleeping not in bunks but on wooden shelves than ran around the walls. The winter of 1940 saw prisoners at a labour camp in Bromberg sleeping on the floor of an unheated stone house. At a work camp dependent on Stalag XIa 79 South African prisoners found themselves sharing just 54 blankets. Others found their blankets too small to sleep comfortably beneath and men on mining detachments found their blankets soiled with coal dust, meaning that after a hard day's work they returned still to be surrounded by the sooty reminders of their labours.

This was not the only darkness that impinged on the lives of the prisoners. In the dingy barrack rooms light was at a premium. With small windows, often shuttered even during daylight, the light failed to penetrate the gloom. At E734 a barrack room for 24 men was illuminated by just three 25-watt bulbs. Even in huts with lighting it was often found insufficient to allow reading at night. In one camp the prisoners reported being without light bulbs for two full years, leaving their activities confined to the hours of daylight – hours when they were usually at work. At another camp the punishment for escape attempts was the confiscation of all light bulbs, something that contravened the Geneva Convention in making collective reprisals for the actions of an individual. The shortage of light was not the only problem, the insistence of the guards about turning out lights at night also affected the prisoners. Some found themselves returning from work at 9.30 p.m. only to be told that lights out was at 10.30 p.m. With just an hour to eat and wash there was little time to spare before being plunged into darkness. There was no time for writing letters and repairing clothes, instead all they could do was lie in the darkness, smoke and make idle chatter until they fell asleep.

Other factors also came into play to spoil their enjoyment of the evenings. In many work detachments the prisoners were locked in their huts and had their trousers and boots taken away each night to prevent escape attempts. This left them confined to their dull, damp rooms for even longer hours each day, and without their trousers the men were forced into their bug-infested beds in an attempt to keep warm. Yet even if allowed to keep their trousers few would have anywhere to hang them at night. Wardrobes were unknown and many were even without cupboards, instead hanging the few clothes they had from nails hammered into the bare walls of their hut.

For some work parties the situation was even worse, all their work clothes and boots had to be handed in overnight. At some work detachments the guards allowed clothing to be dried overnight in their kitchens. Not all were so lucky. Instead their work clothes were bundled together into large sacks that were carried out and handed over to the guards. The unfortunate men detailed for this task had to make the journey in their underwear with bare feet. The next morning the process was reversed and the clothes were collected ready for them to start work again. In winter they found their work clothes wet or frozen. Pulling them on over their exhausted limbs they started the day feeling as cold and damp as they had finished the previous day and knowing that the next morning the process would begin all over again. For one group of Australians, used to the clement weather of their homeland, the winter weather endured at the Polish flax factory they worked in was more than they could bear. Via the Red Cross they requested that they be moved to camps further south in order to benefit from the warmer weather. Unsurprisingly their request was refused.

It was not only in winter that the living conditions troubled the prisoners. They spent many long summer's evenings locked within their accommodation. To miss out on fresh air and sunlight was frustrating for them. Often poorly ventilated with open drains nearby, foul smells filled the huts. Damp laundry, stinking socks and boots, the nightly stench of men breaking wind, all made the air heavy and difficult to breathe. Sometimes they were forced to keep their windows bolted shut and forbidden to open shutters. At one work camp the stated reason for sealing the windows was to prevent trading with locals and to stop contact between POWs and the 'village belles' with whom the prisoners had become friendly. In one work camp the situation was aggravated by a blocked chimney that poured smoke into their barrack room, in winter this offered a stark choice – keep warm and suffocate or freeze. Prisoners at a cigarette paper mill found themselves working in rooms filled by pulp steam all day. At night they retired to rooms on the floor above their workplace. As a result the air was heavy and damp. In an attempt to get fresh air the prisoners were forced to request regular walks outside the compound for fear they would all develop respiratory infections. At one farm the prisoners considered their situation a fire risk. Ten men were locked into a 5 by 6 metre room with just a single window and insufficient ventilation. With no escape route they feared the effects of fire, this was remedied by constructing a fire alarm made from a ploughshare and a heavy nail to act as a gong. When one commandant was challenged with regard to the poor ventilation endured by prisoners he offered the simple explanation that the problem of air quality was entirely the fault of the POWs who smoked all night long.

The unfortunate prisoners at Arbeitskommando E414 experienced conditions few would have wished on their worst enemies. Billeted on the ground floor of the leather factory in which they were employed, the prisoners found no escape from their day job, and the fact they had no drinking water on the premises was the least of their worries: 'New skins with meat still on them are placed outside the kitchen window, frightful smell and a breeding place for flies etc. Factory dump within 50 metres of billet.'[4] With their washroom still incomplete the POWs, often bloodstained from their work, were forced to wash in the same kitchens where they prepared their meals.

Whilst some prisoners were complaining about stuffy conditions within their barracks others had the opposite problem. Some huts had been erected quickly, were shoddily constructed and even in summer a cold wind whistled through them. Prisoners found water ran straight off the hillsides and through the walls of their barracks, leaving their possessions soaked and their beds permanently damp. The unfortunate prisoners soon reported suffering from chilblains courtesy of their permanently damp boots. In winter many huts were so cold prisoners awoke to find frost on their beds, others found ice had formed on the interior walls. In extreme cases prisoners awoke to find vegetables had frozen solid during the night, whilst the rains of both winter and summer poured through poorly covered roofs to soak the bunks of the men beneath. Prisoners at one farm were even billeted in a hut that didn't have a door.

Although wooden huts tended to let in more wind than the more solidly constructed stone buildings, conditions in the latter were seldom more comfortable. The more established buildings were often extremely damp. Even in summer the heat failed to penetrate the heavy walls. One 'thoroughly bad camp' housed work detachment AK175, from Stalag XXb. Based at a Danzig factory where the manager liked to threaten POWs with his revolver, the prisoners slept in three or four level bunks with little space between them. They had no tables or benches and were forced to buy their own buckets for washing. Added to these deprivations the building was infested with rats. The vermin were constantly seen scuttling from an open drain, covered only by wooden planks, which came from the kitchen and ran through their sleeping quarters. To add insult to injury the enterprise was laughingly named 'Neue Heimat' – new homeland.

The problem of rats was common to many of the labour camps. Farms were often full of them, nesting in the outbuildings and scuttling into huts to raid the prisoners' food supplies. At one quarry Australian prisoners were housed in a disused school building where a tiny rat-infested outhouse was used as a punishment cell, with offenders being forced to spend their sentence in the dark with the vermin. On many farms a solution was found by allowing the men to keep pet cats to keep the rats at bay. This worked most of the time, however at the AK62 work detachment from Stalag XXa the rats were so large they frightened the cat off and it ran away leaving the prisoners to fend for themselves.

In many cases the living conditions experienced by the prisoners depended on the generosity of the employers. On a farm at Alt Blumenau the prisoners reported all having two sets of clothing, local women washed their clothes for them and they were even paid in reichsmarks rather than the useless *Lagergeld*. Men on an agricultural detachment from Stalag XXb also reported sleeping in a pleasant room heated by an earthenware stove. They had three blankets each, plenty of good food and extra clothing given to them by the man they worked for. On top of this he had also loaned them a gramophone to listen to after work. Yet another detachment from the same Stalag found themselves lodged in peasant huts where their only water came from the drainage ditches in the surrounding fields, and in another farm the prisoners were housed a metre underground in a potato cellar beneath the farmhouse.

Despite the hardships endured by many of the working prisoners, for many there was an acceptance that good conditions could not be expected in wartime – whatever the circumstances: 'The conditions at the work camps were as good as those I'd known when I was first called up. I'd been in private billets in Guildford. The ladies who let the rooms out to us got sixpence a night but often we just had to sleep on the floor. So when you compare that, it wasn't too bad.'[5] The situation was much the same for one group of South Africans sent directly to a work camp from a POW camp in Italy. After long days of transit within the stifling confines of a train it was a joy for them to see bunks, even if they were triple-tiered. After sleeping on the bare boards of a railway wagon they considered a straw mattress 'heavenly'.[6]

The varying conditions found in work camps led to a certain amount of mixed emotion. Whilst mining became unpopular with the increasingly exhausted prisoners, it offered one advantage. At least most of the men employed underground had access to hot baths or showers at the pithead – although that wasn't always the case and at one mine the prisoners constructed their own showers since their employer offered no washing facilities, whilst others bathed in a clear pool found deep within a copper mine. Unlike the miners most prisoners working in German industry faced the daily grind of heavy labour without the benefits of a wash at the end of it. Instead they returned to their barracks still thick with sweat and stinking from their exertions. Few work camps had showers or baths and those that had access to hot water found it was often available just once a week, in one case prisoners working in a factory were allowed just one bath every month – and that was cold. Those camps with the luxury of showers seldom offered any great comforts, often with a single showerhead shared by hundreds. In one case 62 men shared a single cold tap. For the less fortunate there was no running water and it had to be drawn from wells or streams then heated in boilers, alternatively they had barrels of cold water in a courtyard in which to wash. At one farm the prisoners' only water came from a nearby lake and in winter the prisoners found themselves first breaking the ice to get washed. Others had to collect water from pumps or wells, dragging it back to their quarters between them. One man remembered the facilities on his East Prussian farm: 'The churn was put on the stove and heated over a wood fire. Then it was poured into the tin bath and two of you would share it. We did that once a week. We kept ourselves fairly clean.'7

Even those with running water were not guaranteed a good supply, between July and September 1944 the prisoners at work detachment E7111 reported water pipes remaining dry. Others reported having taps within their huts but that these were not actually fitted with drainage pipes. For some even drinking water was not available in their huts, instead they were forced to walk 400 yards just to slake their thirst. One detachment of 36 Palestinian Jews lived in facilities where they were denied access to any washing facilities.

Those with piped water were often unimpressed by its poor quality. They found water pipes to be rusty, leaving the water stained a reddish brown even after it had been boiled. When challenged by the Red Cross over the shortage of baths or showers the Germans had an excuse. They simply claimed that the men could only expect the same conditions as the local people, and since they seldom took baths why should the prisoners behave differently? Their captors may have found this argument convincing, and outsiders may have found the notion of an unwashed rural German population humorous, but to the 52 POWs forced to share a single baby bath as their only washing facility, it was not a laughing matter.

A further question vexed many of the men on work detachments. If they could get water, what would they use to heat it? Not all were offered sufficient fuel for heating both their rooms, their food and their water. Many huts were heated by briquettes of compressed coal dust rather than genuine lumps of coal. In one camp a group of ten men were offered just one cubic metre of wood for the entire winter. Harsh choices had to be made, balancing the fuel for various needs. Was it better to have a warm body, hot food or be clean but cold? For many the solution was simple, with no fuel they simply broke up their furniture. Starting with tables and chairs, some POWs eventually broke up their beds and the most desperate inmates even tore off doors and window frames to ensure a source of fuel.

Even if they could wash not all prisoners had a towel to dry themselves. Those who did often found the towels were small and thin and grew increasingly filthy as time passed. At one work detachment the prisoners were promised towels by their guards in August 1943. By March the next year the towels had still not arrived, leaving the prisoners to dry their bodies as best they could with old rags or discarded clothing. A further problem became the lack of soap. Issues of cleaning materials by the Germans were few and far between, with soap becoming a precious commodity even for civilians. The prisoners were forced to use whatever came in their Red Cross parcels and when the supply of parcels ran out so did the supply of soap. Once again the prisoners were forced to improvise. Some of the more inventive men collected small remnants of soap they found on the floor in shower rooms. They gathered up all they could find and put them into tins. The tins were then heated up causing the soap to melt. Once the tin cooled down they would have a complete and usable bar of soap.

Adding to their misery was the condition of camp latrines. Few work camps had porcelain toilets, and flushes were virtually unknown, instead most of the workforce had to make do with wooden latrines. These were often wooden planks with a hole in the middle that stood perched over open pits. In most places the men sat side by side with nothing to separate them from the next man. With no place for modesty they sat next to each other as the hideous aroma arose from the pits beneath. Others found themselves queuing to use the facilities, with often as many as 40 men sharing a single latrine. 'Bill' Sykes was among those who soon grew used to sharing: 'All in all it was a difficult time, but it had its lighter moments, have you ever sat on a tall oil drum acting as a lavatory, facing a large audience during the performance of your daily bodily functions? You can imagine the initial embarrassment. But when you've got to go, you've got to go, especially after standing in line for some length of time.'[8] At his work camp attached to a copper mine Alec Reynolds had a particularly nasty encounter with the latrines: 'We were told the manager of the mine had lost his gold watch in the latrine. So we had to clean it out. I had to climb down into the pit, it came up to my chest. It was all wet and sloshy. I had to fill buckets, someone would pass it up and then the others carried it off to be used on the fields as fertiliser. There was no gold watch, of course, they just used it as an excuse to get us to clean the pit out.'[9]

Prisoners in one camp reported their latrines being cleaned out just once every three weeks and in one particularly bad case the latrines were left unemptied between June and December. Foul smells rose from the pits beneath the latrines – smells that penetrated the senses, hanging over the camps and creating an atmosphere of decay. Even in one of the few camps with flushing toilets the location of the cesspit ensured the prisoners remained unhappy with their toilet arrangements. The raw sewage drained not into a sewer but into a pit directly beneath their sleeping quarters, causing its disgusting smell to torment them during their hours of rest. Even when latrines were finally emptied their contents were usually dumped on fields near to the work camps, the waste matter being used to fertilize the land. Unfortunately the raw human sewage acted as the breeding ground for thousands of flies that tormented prisoners during the summer.

A further problem, experienced by all prisoners, was the shortage of toilet paper. Men on working parties collected litter from the streets with which to wipe their backsides. Others were forced to use the labels from food tins that arrived in their Red Cross parcels. This changed when paper shortages meant the food arrived in labelless tins embossed with the name of the contents. When they became really desperate the prisoners resorted to using leaves, grass, or pages torn from books.

If their skin was becoming dirty it was nothing compared to the state of their uniforms, as one prisoner told the Red Cross: 'As the prisoners have only one outfit they have no time to wash or dry it. Consequently the clothing is sweaty, dirty and filthy.'[10] Some men went for months and years without washing their clothes. Where hot water was available some were able to at least rinse the worst of the dirt from their uniforms, though few could spare much of their precious soap to get them really clean. In some camps, in particular on farms, the men arranged for the women of the village to wash their uniforms – for a price. The problem was that few men had much spare clothing. If a man had a uniform for 'best' he would not want to wear it for work. But if he sent his work clothes to be cleaned would they be ready for him to wear in time? Prisoners at one mine discovered the answer when it took clothes over two weeks to return from a laundry.

Their uniforms were often marked to make the prisoners visible to the local population. No one could fail to notice the black triangles or red circles painted onto their backs or on their legs to show their status as prisoners. Some camp commandants insisted the letters 'KG' – for *Kriegsgefangene* – be painted on the backs of their jackets. In turn one leg of their trousers was marked with a 'k' the other with a 'g'. Their kit bags were also marked with yellow stripes to make them instantly recognizable if they embarked on escape attempts.

Yet such displays of their servitude were of little concern to the prisoners compared to their worries about the condition of their uniforms. The question of clothing constantly vexed the prisoners. The trials of battle meant that many had seen their clothing damaged even before they began the journey into captivity. Most lost all spare clothing and entered the Stalags with no more than what they stood up in. For the men of the BEF the weeks and months of constant marching soon took its toll on their uniforms. Socks and underwear, unchanged for weeks, became ragged and encrusted with sweat. The soles of their boots became worn and the heavy serge of their battledress wore thin as it rubbed at their crotches, making every step a living hell. With most having lost their 'housewife' sewing kits upon capture, few had any way of repairing their clothes. Rips and tears hung open and untouched, buttons fell off to be lost forever. Within months the POWs were dressed in rags, their tattered uniforms hanging from their malnourished frames. Desperate men took to wearing whatever they could find, even if that meant making shirts from cement sacks. In the first year of captivity their worn out clothing would only be replaced with the remnants of uniforms captured from the defeated armies of Europe. Soon the British POWs found themselves clad in Polish overcoats, French trousers, Dutch tunics – or any combination of any nationality. One man, who spent his war years working in gravel pits, factories and farms recalled the conditions in 1940: 'I was lucky, my battledress was quite good. But there was an issue of French and Belgian uniforms, which other people had to wear. I remember some were bloodstained so they must have come from corpses or wounded men.'[11]

Before long the prisoners were unable to distinguish between the various nationalities within the Stalags. It did not take long for their boots to start to wear out, one work detachment of 250 men found over 150 of them were in need of new boots. Thousands were reduced to wearing clogs issued by the Germans in place of their worn out boots, in which they shuffled around the camps. Worse still, many found the rough wood of the clogs could wear out a pair of socks in just one day. It was demoralizing for the prisoners to make their way to work each day, unable to lift their feet from the ground.

For some unfortunate men there was no replacement footwear and when clogs were not forthcoming from the Germans the prisoners found their own simple solution. They removed the battered leather uppers from the worn out soles and nailed them onto pieces of wood, constructing their own simple clogs. Some miners even used large rubber bands from machinery within the mines to repair their boots. Others had to send their boots out to be repaired, a process that could take weeks. In the meantime the prisoners had to beg, steal or borrow to make sure they were adequately shod for work. Some found that even after repairs the boots simply fell apart again within days. By 1942 one work detachment of over 700 POWs was all reported to be wearing clogs. When one working party was promised alpine boots by their guards they expected sturdy climbing boots. Instead they received clogs. They joked that whoever put the order in had filled in 'All pine' on the form. Even when military footwear was available in camp stores it was often found to be unsuitable. Much seemed to be surplus stock – shoes or boots in sizes few of the prisoners seemed to need. In particular the problem was felt by Indian prisoners whose feet tended to be smaller than their British counterparts. To ensure that their precious boots were kept in the best possible condition for work most prisoners chose to wear the German issued clogs whenever they were in their huts or within the compound – although they made sure they marked their names on their boots to prevent them from being stolen.

Socks also began to disintegrate. Many prisoners found their socks were darned so many times as to be unrecognizable from their original state. Once stocks of wool were exhausted and their socks were beyond repair the men were forced to improvise. In place of socks they were given *fusslappen*, strips of cloth which they wrapped around their feet, 'Russian Style'. If these were not available they simply bound their feet in rags or newspapers. To remedy this situation some men on working parties searched for any abandoned woollen articles which they took back to camp, unravelled and used for darning. Knitting needles and crochet hooks were improvised from the handles of worn out toothbrushes and those with a knowledge of crafts were able to make themselves clothes and blankets. This spirit of improvisation followed the prisoners throughout the work camps. Men with a talent for sewing sat down and used the remnants of worn out uniforms to make gloves to protect workers' hands during the winter. They also took two pairs of worn out trousers and took them apart, combining the pieces and patching where necessary to make one pair of wearable, if non-regulation, battledress trousers. In many cases the repairs had to be made with different coloured threads, giving the soldiers the appearance of tramps with their tattered and patched uniforms hanging from their malnourished frames.

Using such skills the ever-inventive prisoners were also able to make their own unit badges which they wore with pride in the place of those lost when their original uniforms had fallen to pieces. Particularly for the regular soldiers, such displays were a source of pride showing that despite their defeat on the battlefield they were still professional soldiers who were determined to return to their rightful place in the ranks of their own regiments. For the prisoners such embellishments became a small but important sign of their resistance to what was happening around them. It reassured them that despite their servitude they were still able to defy the enemy and display a sense of individuality.

In time the situation began to resolve itself. Complete sets of battledress arrived via the Red Cross, sent out by families of pre-war regulars many of whom had left their service dress at home when they went to war. Tailors and cobblers shops were even available at some of the larger work camps, where pre-war craftsmen from among the prisoners were able to ply their trade. Some of the working prisoners were even lucky enough to keep one spare uniform for 'best', that could be worn on days off or when they were allowed out of the camp. Gordon Barber was among them: 'Most of us sent home for spare uniforms. We asked the Red Cross to help since we had no clothes. My mum sent me mine. Mine was more ornate than most. We still had a bit of pride.'[12]

Underlying their complaints about clothing shortages was the awareness that there were vast stocks of captured uniforms in the Stalags, both British and those belonging to other nationalities, but the problem was distribution. The major shortages were of greatcoats and underwear. Most of the men had been captured in the summer of 1940 and had not been carrying winter clothing at the time, and with just one set of underwear this of course soon perished. When the British Red Cross dispatched 4,000 sets of underwear to Germany for British POWs the Germans intervened and sent the garments to a camp for Croatians. Such actions left thousands of prisoners with just one set of underwear. The iniquities regarding clothing enraged some of the prisoners. Whilst many of those heading out of the Stalags on work details were clothed in all manner of foreign uniforms and ragged battledress, those who remained in the camps often had adequate clothing, including sets for 'best' which they kept clean and well pressed. Some prisoners felt their own senior NCOs were responsible for keeping the best clothing within the Stalags, although in reality it was often the decision of the Germans to prevent clothing being fairly distributed.

The authorities frequently refused to issue new clothing unless worn out items were handed over. This was unfair on some of the POWs. Those captured in Greece often arrived in Germany clad in lightweight cotton uniforms that were unsuited to the harsh northern Europe winter. Some had even swum to safety when their ships were sunk and arrived with little more than shorts and shirts. When one detachment of 200 POWs arrived from Crete they were refused new uniforms. As they made their way to their first work detail many were still clad in sandals and shorts. The journey took its toll and one prisoner succumbed to the cold, dying before he reached the work camp. The irony was that in summer the prisoners on many work details were forbidden to wear khaki shorts and told they should continue to work in thick woollen battledress trousers despite the heat.

As prisoners were transferred between Stalags and work camps they soon realized how standards of clothing varied from place to place. Even after stocks of replacement battledress had arrived those prisoners who received new clothing continued to find some of it to be from the armies of other nations. In 1942 in one camp it was estimated that 30 per cent of British and Commonwealth inmates were dressed in foreign uniforms, 10 per cent were wearing clogs and they all had foreign greatcoats. Even as late as 1944 some were still clothed in foreign uniforms. By March that year one detachment of men working at a quarry were all seen to be wearing either Russian or French uniforms. Miners at Gleiwitz Oehringen described their clothing as being in 'unbearable' condition, since it had gone unchanged and unwashed for an entire year. Another group of 25 men employed in a tile and brick factory reported each having a solitary outfit to wear all day, every day. In early 1945 one mine was found to be staffed almost entirely by French Canadian soldiers who had been captured in Normandy. More than six months later they were still clothed in the same uniforms they had been wearing when they were captured and had not been issued with a single item of clothing. It was no surprise a Red Cross visitor to one camp reported: 'a large percentage of the men are dressed like tramps'.[13]

Those fortunate enough to have spare clothing were not always able to take advantage of it. Rules over clothing varied from place to place and were dependent on the attitudes of the employers or guards. On two Arbeitskommandos from Stalag XXa the prisoners were subjected to harsh rulings over their uniforms. Each man was allowed just one shirt or undershirt, one pair of pants, one pair of trousers, one jacket, one pair of socks and one pair of boots. All day they worked in the same clothes that they had to wear at night, sleeping in their vests and pants before re-dressing to start work again. Long hours were passed as prisoners squatted on their bunks in dimly lit barracks darning and sewing, making basic repairs to keep their clothing from falling to pieces. One of the few concessions made by the Germans was to allow prisoners to purchase some clothing. Vests and gloves were made available in some camps but the prisoners were forced to pay for them from their own money. As much as three complete days' wages were needed just to purchase a pair of gloves.

The stocks of clothing held at many camps ready to replace worn out uniforms did not always survive intact. At Stalag IVc the arrival of 400 prisoners evacuated from camps in Italy in late 1943 meant camps' stocks were soon exhausted. All needed to be fully re-clothed and once the remaining stores were issued there was nothing left for the rest of the camp's population. Soon it was reported that only 35 per cent had a spare outfit. At Stalag VIIIb the situation was even worse with the Red Cross reporting none of the 12,000 prisoners owning more than one outfit. Another group evacuated from Italy arrived in Germany to be stripped of all their possessions, such as blankets, spare clothing and boots. In another punitive move by the guards, at the end of winter prisoners were forced to hand back pullovers supplied by the Red Cross. Supposedly this was for safekeeping but, as many knew, they would not be returned in winter. When prisoners asked what had happened their guards admitted the pullovers had been issued to other nationalities.

In face of such appalling conditions it was the friendships shared among the prisoners that helped keep them sane. The sharing of adversity helped establish friendships that were to last a lifetime. Gordon Barber recalled life at a state farm in East Prussia:

> My mate Ken Wilats, he was lucky 'cause his mum and dad both had good jobs. They had a big house in Tooting and used to take in students. We used to get 50 or 100 fags from our parents. He used to get 500. But when he got them he'd go round and give us all at least five or ten each. I used to muck in with a bloke called Lofty Griggs and he was the cleverest man I ever knew. He could sew, he could iron, he could do all the

things I couldn't do. But in return he'd always say 'Nobby, when you go out tonight, bring me something back.' 'Cause I knew all the places to pinch food.'[14]

Sixty years on Barber has never forgotten the generosity shown by Wilats and they remain close friends.

The problems of cigarette shortages, in particular during the early and latter stages of the war, made life difficult for the smokers among the prisoners. Tobacco was vital to stave off the pangs of hunger that assaulted their bellies, yet the shortages of tobacco seemed to go hand in hand with food shortages. Often they were issued with Polish cigarettes, some of which were so foul that the prisoners would tie the tobacco inside rags, boil it, squeeze out the water and dry it before attempting to smoke it. At other times they were issued with cigarettes called 'Unacs' which were a small plug of tobacco at the end of a cardboard tube. Not only did they taste foul but they offered a very unsatisfactory smoke, as one man remembered: 'Two puffs and the end would fall off in your bed.'[15] In their desperation the POWs smoked anything they could get their hands on. They dried rose leaves and stuffed them into pipes. They waited till the tea leaves from their Red Cross parcels had been exhausted, then dried them and rolled them in scraps of paper. Men on work details desperately scavenged cigarette butts from the gutters and stuffed them into their pockets, before taking them to pieces and rolling the remaining tobacco.

For all the discomfort and desperate longing for the niceties of life endured by the working prisoners few even contemplated escape. It was little wonder anti-aircraft gunner John Tonkin, captured in Crete, entitled his unpublished memoirs *No Tunnels, No Wooden Horses*. With little time on their hands to plan escapes and with insufficient energy left to dig tunnels, they recognized they would have a slim chance of making a 'home run'. It was not that they did not yearn for freedom as much as any of their officer comrades or the airmen in their Stalag Lufts but quite simply any hopes of freedom were destroyed by the reality of their daily lives. Unlike officers who could devote long hours to plotting and scheming, the other ranks had their hours too fully occupied by work to have time for forging papers or converting uniforms into civilian outfits. Few had any real grasp of whereabouts they were, let alone how they might make their way to freedom, as one explained: 'We were what you'd call the illiterate mob. We didn't know anything. Officers could read a compass, I didn't have a clue.'[16]

Prisoners at a mine in Silesia. The letter 'K' on the back of their jackets identified them as 'Kreigsge-fangene' or Prisoners of War. These men were fortunate, few among the miners were issued with protective clothing. (Red Cross)

A group of prisoners posing for a photograph at the entrance to a salt mine. By the later stages of the war many POWS at salt mines were left with skin as white as the salt they mined, a legacy of the long hours they spent underground. They often worked 12 hours a day, 7 days a week. (Red Cross)

Prisoners loading wagons with earth. 'You worked for 8 hours a day without stopping. It was good for the muscles, but not good for the soul. You just stared at a gravel wall for most of the day. It was boring.' Ken Wilats, POW (Imperial War Museum HU 9210)

Prisoners in front of a vast wall of rock at a German quarry. (Red Cross)

Prisoners clearing a 20 foot snowdrift at Krima in March 1944. (Imperial War Museum)

Prisoners working to unload railway wagons in a German goods yard. (Red Cross)

POWs cooking their midday meal at a working party. (Red Cross)

Many prisoners were employed to level ground for German building or transport projects. These men are loading earth and rocks into wagons. (Red Cross)

Lack of mechanised transport meant prisoners were forced to carry out many tasks by hand. These men are pushing heavily laden wagons at a German building site. (Red Cross)

This lack of practical ability when it came to 'making a break for it' hampered Les Allan when he and a mate escaped from a working party. He had little thought of being successful. There was little heroic about his escape, he was simply 'fed up' and decided to 'shove off'. After three days and nights on the run, eating potatoes they stole from the fields, they eventually found themselves in some woods where they spent the night. The next morning they awoke to find themselves surrounded by German soldiers. They were soon put on a truck and sent back to the camp. There was a final ironic twist to their story: 'We'd been on the run for three days and nights but it only took about ten minutes to drive back to the camp!'[17] For their efforts they were both given 28 days in solitary confinement.

For the men on working parties the whole notion of tunnelling to freedom was absurd, as Ken Wilats recalled:

> I had no need to dig a tunnel. I could have walked out of the camp at any time but where would I have gone? I heard a story of some fellows who broke out. Their objective was to get to Danzig and to stow away on a boat and get to Sweden. After a bit of hardship they eventually reached Danzig and went to the docks. And what did they see? Prisoners of war, loading and unloading boats. So that rather crushed their morale. So it was tail between their legs and walk back to the working party.[18]

The ease with which it was possible to escape from many working parties was illustrated by Australian, Edward Sicklen. Whilst walking through an ill-lit Munich subway on his way to work he simply switched his uniform cap for a civilian hat. With that simple change he was able to mingle in with the crowds. Despite the ease of escape he failed to get far and like most escapers he was picked up within days. He was recaptured attempting to reach Belgrade by train, from where he hoped to change trains to reach neutral Turkey.

There was another important factor in preventing most POWs from making serious attempts to escape. Many realized they would have in-sufficient energy to be successful. The prisoners survived on pitifully small rations. Though some were able to hoard a little food to use in escape attempts most preferred simply to eat everything they received in a desperate struggle to maintain their health. It soon became clear to most that the notion of 'making a break for it' was a luxury they could ill afford. At Moosburg Bryan Willoughby contemplated his options:

At the back of my mind was the idea that I could get enough strength to take off and get down to the Swiss border. I would have had a go. But I realized I hadn't got the strength. One time coming back from working in Munich the train broke down and we had to walk the last seven miles. I only just made it. So that scotched that idea. Then a Yank pal of mine tried to persuade me to go, Sergeant Cox. He went but I stayed behind. I saw him back in the Stalag minus a foot. He'd taken off but was caught on the railway, he'd got frostbite and it had to be amputated. But if I'd been fit enough, I would have been silly enough to try it.[19]

One of those who did 'make a break for it' from an Arbeitskommando was D-Day paratrooper 'Bill' Sykes, an 18-year-old with an admittedly free spirit, who escaped during what he described as his 'contrarian period': 'As a very young man, I of course felt invincible and if anyone was going to die it certainly wasn't going to be me. I had of course anxious moments and was at times a little nervous but certainly never felt in need of the services of a psychiatrist. Remember – I was a street savvy youth and a survivor.' With little thought as to where he would go, or what he planned to do, he decided to make his move. There was not much need for planning or intrigue:

Escape from our particular work groups was relatively easy, you could just walk away when the armed civilian guards were otherwise occupied. A couple of times during my incarceration, I took off for a few days using the 'Sykes' confidence approach. I was very much a loner when it came to 'escaping', no cloak and dagger stuff. It was pretty obvious that I was a POW from my uniform with a large red circular patch on my back, but it's surprising how much you can get away with by using the 'I have a right to be here approach'. Travelling by local trains was not very difficult. Get into conversation with someone, preferably an older couple who spoke a little English, and hope that the ticket collector didn't call your bluff when you explained to him that the guard you were travelling with was in the toilet. I was eventually caught and apprehended by local police for obtaining food without having any local currency. It's called stealing – or in my book appropriation by reason of necessity. I was heading north for Berlin, why, who knows, just a whim that perhaps I could get lost in the big city. The first escape cost me seven days on a punishment diet of bread and water and a transfer to another camp. The second pathetic attempt, was more like a weekend affair, modesty forbids me to elaborate upon the precise circumstances. This cost me another week in the 'cooler'. After that, I resigned myself to waiting for the Allies to come to me, instead of vice-versa. I'm afraid that these two disappearing acts of a few days duration cannot be classified amongst the great escapes of World War Two.[20]

Although some prisoners, frustrated by the exertions and boredom of slave labour, did make a successful break to freedom most were unsuccessful. Many of those able to get away were men working in areas with strong partisan movements, such as Poland or Yugoslavia. Using contacts with local workers they were able to slip away into the relative safety of the partisan gangs. For those teaming up with Tito's men in Yugoslavia the route home would see them trekking across the mountains to either be flown homes on supply flights organized by British liaison officers or by meeting with the Royal Navy on the Dalmatian coast. But for most escape was a hopeless dream, a way of gaining a few days' freedom that more often than not ended in capture and 28 days solitary confinement. One band of men managed to hide in the covered railway wagons that left the mine where they worked. When the train came to a halt the next day they climbed out, hoping to make their way to freedom. To their dismay they were in the middle of a vast Wehrmacht base.

Such comical 'escapes' were not uncommon. Some prisoners were reported as escapers despite their lack of intention. Whilst one POW was working beside a railway line he asked his guard for permission to go to the toilet. Walking into the privacy of the thick forest he dropped his trousers, did his business, then attempted to return to the railway. Lost in the forest, he wandered until he found a village. Whilst he was asking for directions back to his work detail the police and guards were mobilized to look for him. Certain he had escaped they began to comb the local area, desperate to catch him before he got too far. When he was finally apprehended he was found sitting in a village inn enjoying a beer with the locals.

Added to the likelihood of failure was the very real knowledge of how their guards might react. Those men left behind in the aftermath of an escape often faced a clampdown by their guards. Rules forbidding the collective punishment of prisoners were ignored with the guards ordering frequent intrusive searches of the POWs' kit, the stopping of food parcels and interminable roll calls. Those who had enjoyed the opportunity to go swimming in lakes or wander around found themselves confined to their huts – all so someone else could enjoy a few hours or days of freedom. Thus any recaptured escapees, and few ever successfully got away for long, had to return to camps where their mates had faced increased harassment from the guards. Rather than being treated as heroes the recaptured prisoners were often treated with hostility for having indirectly inflicted punitive reprisals on the remaining men. As one persistent escaper later wrote, he and his like were: 'very unpopular people, nuisance and trouble makers who caused very considerable inconvenience to others'.[21]

Furthermore, those who had experienced brutality from their guards had no illusions about the fate that awaited them if they were spotted trying to get away at night. In the aftermath of an assault by a brutal guard Gordon Barber had to be talked out of making a break for freedom:

> I went to bed that night very tired. I said to Jock 'I'm going to piss off tonight. I can't stand any more of this. I'm going to take a chance. You coming?' He said no and I asked my mate Paddy. He said 'I wouldn't even think of it, Nobby. Look out there.' And I could see a cigarette burning outside. They'd put a guard outside. They weren't daft. They knew what we'd be thinking of doing. I'd said to the guard 'You wait till I get away'. So he probably thought I meant it.[22]

Some of those caught escaping faced the reality of what Barber had sensibly gathered awaited him if he tried to get away. When Alexander Dawson made a break from a work camp he was taken to the woods and shot through the back of the neck. At another Arbeitskommando a guard was summoned when local police caught two escaping prisoners. When the guard returned empty handed he revealed that he had collected the two men and executed them.

With the exertions of labour weighing heavy on the prisoners it was little wonder their attentions were focused on matters more immediate than escape. For vast periods the POWs found themselves hungry. Their bellies ached and began to crave for far more than the Germans were ever prepared to offer. Rations were minimal. They may have varied on every work detail but few locations ever offered enough food to stay healthy. In the early days of captivity rations had been poor. Most men newly captured in 1940 marched into Germany on rations that did little more than keep them alive. Yet even on this minimal fare plenty of men were sent immediately out to work. As a result they rapidly lost weight, their faces became lined, they walked with a stoop, their hair lost its youthful lustre – they looked around and noticed how the young men had grown middle aged in a matter of weeks. Ken Wilats remembered the arrival of the first Red Cross parcels whilst working in Poland: 'The first parcels arrived and they were divided up, one item per person. I was lucky I got the soap. At the start it seemed pretty disastrous, when you watched someone sitting down to eat a tin of corned beef and all you could do was wash. I took a dim view of that. But their corned beef only lasted a day, my soap lasted for two weeks. So we were all hungry again, but I was clean.'[23]

As the situation settled down they slowly began to regain their strength. Rations became more regular and the delivery of Red Cross parcels brought relief to men who had been on the brink of starvation. Yet despite these changes few among the prisoners would ever feel satisfied with food and most would spend their incarceration desperate to increase their meals any way possible. Beg, steal or borrow, they would do their utmost to quell their hunger.

It was little wonder they felt such hunger. Throughout the war the Germans did little to provide them with substantial food. The working prisoners' meals were supposed to be provided by their employers at the same rate of rations as given to civilians working in industry. Arrangements varied from location to location. A few employers simply ignored the plight of the prisoners, in one case they were simply sent to line up at a charity soup kitchen. In some camps civilian cooks were employed to prepare their food, a situation that often gave the prisoners a view of women that might otherwise have been denied to them. One South African prisoner reported how his work camp had two constantly bubbling cauldrons. In one was a seemingly never-ending supply of potatoes boiled in their jackets. In the other was a stew of swede, barley and turnips, that was heated and reheated day after day, constantly topped up with more vegetables and the occasional lumps of meat.

In many locations a prisoner was detailed to cook for his mates, with the man in question remaining in camp through the day to ensure a hot meal was ready on the soldiers' return from their factory shifts. Although the cooks avoided the heavy labour endured by their fellow prisoners it was not the 'cushy number' it might have appeared. Many among the cooks found their movements severely limited. One was confined to a barrack hut for eight long months, denied any chance to exercise outdoors. With a prisoner cooking for the men at night some civilian employers completely ignored their commitment to feed their labourers during the day. At AK404, a work detail from Stalag IIId, the prisoners were given a cup of 'coffee' for their breakfast at 6.15 a.m. They then remained unfed until their return from work at 6.30 p.m. Similar conditions were found at other camps. At one cement works a single hot meal was provided for the prisoners each day at midday. Thus those employed on the nightshift were forced to go through their shift unfed. Nor were lunch breaks necessarily a rest. Many among the prisoners found themselves allowed just half an hour's break. In that time they had to walk from the factory to their huts, eat their meal and walk back to the camp. There was no time for them to relax, they could merely devour their food and hurry back to take their place in the factory.

Although those employed at farms or in food processing plants often found they were well catered for – often with the foods they were able to 'appropriate' – many of the other working men found their rations no more than just enough to keep them alive. For men working in industry rations could be a little as a cup of bitter-tasting ersatz coffee made from acorns and a slice of bread for breakfast. That would be followed by a lunchtime bowl of soup or thin stew, then bread and margarine with fishpaste, meat or jam for their evening meal. On this they were expected to labour for up to 12 hours a day. Only occasionally would solid meals arrive for the workers, such as jacket potatoes served with dried swede. Sometimes tea would be served in place of coffee, but it was little comfort to the men for whom tea was their national drink. Just as German coffee had never been near Brazil, neither was the tea from the lush mountainsides of India. Instead it seemed to be made from any number of unidentifiable dried leaves, as one man later commented: 'it tasted like weeds soaked in hot water'.[24]

At lunchtimes prisoners queued clutching their battered mess tins, bowls or mugs. They watched as stews, often distributed from oil drums, were constantly stirred to prevent the little solid matter from settling to the bottom. In a world where a potato was a luxury, they joked that meat was like the Holy Grail – widely searched for, sometimes claimed, but never found. When a meat stew was claimed most found it was little more than bones, any flesh having already gone into someone else's pot. Promised sausage, they discovered instead inedible gristle, more fat than meat. If any flesh was found they would soon identify it as horsemeat. Instead most stews appeared to consist of barley or millet floating in a grey, watery mess of unidentifiable vegetable. Boiled swede, minced carrots, pumpkin, turnip or beet tops became the staple of their diets. Often what was dished up were mangel-wurzels or other root vegetables usually reserved solely for cattle feed. Copper miners in Silesia collected their 'meals' each day from a horse trough outside their barracks – it was usually a watery stew of either spinach or carrots. One man recalled how his evening meal, after a full day breaking rocks in a quarry, was no more than a cup of ersatz coffee and a slice of sponge cake. But to the eager prisoners it was food and food meant life.

Working at an open cast mine in eastern Germany, Bill Sykes became acquainted with the paucity of rations supplied by his employers:

> We worked from six o'clock in the morning until late afternoon, doing menial hard labour such as filling 20 ton railway hoppers with sand, carrying lengths of iron rail, and wooden rail ties. The winter months of 1944/5 were particularly rough, as food was not in plentiful supply and the bitter cold took its toll. It takes a lot of shovelling for a bunch of undernourished, starving men to shift 20 tons of sand. Our daily rations consisted mainly of a bowl of vegetable soup, 250 grammes of black bread, four or five potatoes and ersatz coffee. The rationing of the food was a lengthy and precise process, which took the wisdom of a saint and the accuracy of a surgeon to ensure fair distribution. You wouldn't believe the delays that hungry men will endure to ensure that they get their fair share. Potatoes were counted and sized on numerous occasions during the chain of distribution. The cutting of a loaf of bread, five men to a loaf, was an object lesson in concentration worthy of a master chess player. The pieces were measured for accuracy and handled by each party for weight assessment, before cutting the cards for priority of choice. Remember, the loaves of black bread had rounded ends, so an allowance had to be made for this small discrepancy. The one meal of the day took untold hours of deliberation and patience, but then, when it may be your 'last supper' why not savour the fruits of your labour! I was always more than anxious to get my hands on the small amount of food that would see me through the next 24 hours. Our constant thoughts, and discussions, were centred around food.[25]

Although Sykes and his comrades suffered much that winter they were fortunate to be able to avoid as much work as possible, as he later wrote: 'I must admit the long handled shovels made admirable leaning posts.'[26]

The rations issued to the working POWs were no more than just enough to keep them alive. As a result the contents of their Red Cross parcels were vital, something the prisoners were never able to forget: 'Every time I see a Red Cross box I put a pound in it. If it hadn't been for the Red Cross I'd have been dead.'[27] As another man put it: 'I never thought a cardboard box of food, about the same size as a shoe box, could make such a difference.'[28] Their regard for these life-saving parcels was not misplaced. It was simple, the food within meant survival. Although each parcel might vary all were designed to provide suitable sustenance for the prisoners, making sure they had enough energy to stay alive.

However, the distribution of these parcels remained at the whim of their guards. Depending on stocks of parcels the men might be issued one parcel per man per week or one to share between any number of men. Nor did they necessarily arrive each week. In some cases prisoners seldom or never received the hallowed parcels and instead were forced to survive solely on their rations or what they could steal. The system of distribution of the parcels from the main Stalags to the work camps depended on local conditions. Often this meant that when there were transportation problems parcels would not be forthcoming for weeks on end, even though the stores were full. As a result the working prisoners would go hungry until the stores could be replenished. When they did arrive at work detachments this meant a large batch would arrive at once. Despite the stores then being full the Germans still preferred to issue the parcels at one per week, rather than let the men enjoy the food they had previously missed out on. Often parcels were kept in a central store where the men could line up and collect certain items under the watchful eyes of their guards. If they took tinned foods the tins were opened to prevent hoarding food for escapes, and there was seldom any concern over allowing the men supplies that complemented each other. To receive a tin of condensed milk and a tin of corned beef was not unusual. Nor was the practice of refusing men the right to take the tins away, often they would have to bring mess tins into which their food would be deposited. This led to many of the prisoners gorging themselves when the parcels first arrived, meaning they would soon become hungry again until the next parcels arrived. The haphazard distribution of the contents of parcels meant many among the prisoners were to find themselves eating sardines with jam, all mixed together in a bowl, or other such unappetizing combinations. Not all guards allowed the men to have individual issues of food, instead allowing a daily allotment of food to be shared out among them. One 38-man detachment found itself sharing three tins of corned beef, two tins of meat, three tins of sardines, some milk and biscuits between them. Such rations could not supply a balanced or filling meal.

Despite all this some men were able to hoard food. Though escape was not on their minds they were careful not to eat too much for fear that the next day they might be without food. This process, known as 'mossing', allowed the men to eat a little each day rather than have one big blow-out as soon as the food was issued. The problem was that the 'mossers' ended up being able to eat whilst their fellow prisoners went hungry. Men whose bellies were crying out for food had to watch as more careful men ate what was left of their food, eking it out in the hope that it would last until the issue of the next parcel.

Others were able to improvise with the contents. Biscuits were crumbled then covered in melted chocolate to make them more inviting. Flour and raisins were mixed with condensed milk to bake puddings, anything to make a change from the uninviting fare they were usually faced with. One group of copper miners even attempted to liven up their meals with parsley sauce. They bought fresh parsley from their guards and mixed it with porridge oats then poured it over the tinned meat in the Red Cross parcels. The German guards who sold the fresh food to them were part of a racket that helped the prisoners subsist on official rations. At night the guards allowed some Russian prisoners to sneak out of the camp and steal from local vegetable gardens. The Germans then took a share of the loot that they sold on to British prisoners.

Even with food from the Red Cross parcels cooking was not a simple matter of standing at a stove waiting for a pot to boil. With just one stove in each hut there were almost constant queues of hungry men waiting to heat their food. Rotas were established with each 'combine' or 'team' allotted a time to prepare the food they shared. Using whatever implements they had been able to steal, scrounge or make, the prisoners heated their foods. Tinned meats were fried in margarine or small lumps of lard. Tinned stews were emptied into battered pots and heated through. In some more established camps the prisoners were able to build their own stoves, making them from scrap metal and old tins, hammering the tins together to prepare makeshift chimneys that fed out through windows. The most popular design even included a fan that pumped air into the stove causing the flames to intensify and heat the food more quickly. Despite such innovations prisoners at many camps had no facilities to keep their utensils clean and post-war investigations by both the British and American armies discovered most of the POWs had been cooking in unsanitary conditions.

Some however had no facilities and were forced to cook the contents of their Red Cross parcels outside. Squatting around small fires dug into holes in the compound, the prisoners heated up whatever food was available. The flames were seldom strong enough to cook complete meals, but food could be heated up just enough to ensure they had something warm to fill their aching bellies. It was not only the shortages of fuel or facilities that kept prisoners from heating up their food. At some work detachments the kitchen facilities were only available at certain times of the day. For men at E538 this meant they could only access the kitchen between 5 p.m. and 9 p.m. As a result all the men on the late shift were forced to eat their food uncooked, or to swap anything that needed heating with those on the early shift. Another detachment reported having tea but being without any container they could use to boil water.

When the parcels arrived they allowed the prisoners to share their good fortune. With enough food, if only for a few days, many among them were able to be generous towards the Russian prisoners they worked alongside. Knowing the hunger of their Russian allies they often allowed them to have the British share of midday stews and soups. It was a gesture the starving Russians could understand, most days they all shared hunger, and the spectre of disease and death haunted them all.

Food was not the only necessity in short supply. At some Arbeitskommandos fresh water was simply not available. With neither a tap nor a pump they were forced to collect water in churns and drag them up to camps for washing and cleaning. However in some cases what they collected was not fit for drinking. For men of one work detachment the only drinking water was what they could buy from canteens, yet they went for six weeks without any pay. With no money they were forced to beg, borrow, steal and scrounge to keep themselves hydrated.

Yet water was not the only drink on their minds. Despite the paucity of rations some prisoners still chose to donate their food for other, less nourishing, uses. Throughout the system of work camps there were men whose knowledge of chemistry allowed them to establish illicit stills in which they concocted evil tasting 'brews' of 'hooch' that were used to liven up Christmas and New Year celebrations. Most often they used tinned fruit and sugar from Red Cross parcels, a use the ever charitable Swiss organization could hardly have imagined. Others used potatoes 'appropriated' from farms or sugar taken from refineries where they worked. Whatever they used the end result was much the same, incredibly strong and often dangerous spirits. Maurice Newey remembered the effect of the 'jungle juice' distilled by his comrades: 'I was offered a drink and took a taste. It shot down my gullet, burnt a hole in my stomach, fired its way down my legs and burnt a hole in my socks and boots. At least that was the sensation. Cor, it was potent stuff. I stuck to the sweet tasting beer after that.'[29] However, not all of the fellow prisoners were so careful. After hearing nothing but silence from his mate's hut Newey went to investigate: 'Mystified we went outside to investigate. The lads were draped all over the place, heaving their hearts up. They had stored their jungle juice in galvanised buckets. The stuff was so potent it had taken the galvanising off the buckets. Fortunately they were so sick that they got rid of the poison before it did any real damage. They had to pour the tainted stuff away. All the wasted food and effort had gone down the drain.'[30]

Others on work details were able to acquire much safer spirits by trading the contents of Red Cross parcels with local workers to obtain bottles of vodka or schnapps. Those with sufficient funds opted for labelled bottles that had been bottled for human consumption. Those less well off bought dangerous homebrewed spirits, usually prepared in backyard stills. These came in unmarked bottles and ranged from the overstrong to the downright dangerous. Many watered down such drinks, mixing them with water or the lemonade they could sometimes buy in camp canteens. Others simply drank them neat, ignoring the risk to their health and trying to obliterate the misery of captivity.

Not all among them had to rely on trade. Men working in distilleries, even those producing industrial strength spirits, were able to steal alcohol. At one plant the prisoners made small incisions in the rubber pipes used for collecting the spirits. They drained off the strong liquid then diluted it with tea, adding sugar to produce a drink resembling whisky. When one prisoner overindulged in 'hooch' and woke up beneath his bunk with a raging headache and having been violently sick, his mates convinced the guards he was unfit for work due to a recurring bout of malaria.

Of course, drinking was not their only indulgence. Leisure was a precious commodity for men who often worked through most hours of daylight. Under official German rules they should all have one complete day off work each week, usually on a Sunday. This, in theory, became the day where their time was their own, when no one could order them to work. Making the most of their free time, they listened to gramophone records or had musical instruments sent by the Red Cross so they could form bands. A few of the more commercially minded prisoners even requested instruments to be sent from home despite being unable to play anything. Instead they used them for trade on the black market or swapped them for cigarettes. Saturday night dances were organized, with men taking regular dancing partners, during which they used up what little surplus energy they had making their way around the floor in their heavy boots or clogs. Somehow prisoners managed to find time to establish theatres, often converting disused buildings within the camps. Packing cases that had carried Red Cross parcels were dismantled and hammered together to build stages. The contents of Red Cross parcels were used to trade for costumes and materials to construct scenery. Their endeavours were a triumph of ingenuity and improvisation and even men exhausted by long hours of mining summoned up sufficient energy to put on plays and revues, or to organize pantomimes for Christmas. At one work camp the men called their concert party by a highly appropriate name 'Nena'. It was an anagram for the initials of 'Nicht Arbeit Nicht Essen' – or 'no work, no food' – the perpetual threat made to recalcitrant prisoners.

The entertainments often went beyond just stage shows. Some even organized beauty contests among the inmates, whilst some with artistic talent turned their hand to tattooing their fellow prisoners, often with unit badges. They played card games – usually gambling with their worthless *lagergeld* – darts, chess, draughts and monopoly. They read books sent out from the libraries of the Stalags, sketched, painted and produced handwritten camp newsletters. At one camp for men engaged in road building they even formed a troop of Boy Scouts. Many turned to new pursuits to fill the long hours after they were locked up for the night. Les Allan learnt to play chess in the most unusual circumstances – the aftermath of an unsuccessful escape:

> My mucker was in the next cell in the cooler. He asked me if I knew how to play chess. Then he started shouting out the instructions to me. I used a piece of soap to mark a chessboard on the blanket. He told me how many squares I needed and I used bits of paper as the pieces. He shouted out all the moves. By the time I got out after 28 days the first thing I wanted to do was get a Red Cross chess set. So when I played my first game I was in seventh heaven. Chess helped me get through a lot of boring hours, I was able to forget about life. The chess set was the only thing I took with me when we evacuated the camp, I prized it. I still have it to this day.[31]

Whilst some among the prisoners were involved in such cerebral pursuits much of the entertainment was trivial. In their boredom some resorted to the sort of behaviour expected of schoolboys. They organized raids on each other's huts, with gangs of men taking on their fellow prisoners in playful fights. The intention was to turf all the men out of a hut and claim a victory. Sometimes mobs would descend on huts with bootpolish and 'black' their victims. Others organized group fights, dividing up the combatants between those under 30 and those over. Such incidents were an ideal way for the men to let off steam and express a spontaneity and lust for life impossible during the rigid working days.

Yet above all else they played sport. Footballs were high on the list of items requested via the Red Cross. Boxing rings were constructed and fights were held between prisoners. If enough space was available in their compounds they played cricket or rugby, or held running races and athletic competitions. If they were allowed to visit rivers and lakes in the summer they held swimming races in the refreshing water that helped to soothe away the aches and pains of work. Others gave their word they would not attempt to escape and were simply let out of barracks to enjoy peaceful strolls around the countryside. It was a case of anything to keep themselves active.

Yet not all were able to indulge themselves in this manner. Throughout German industry access to sport and leisure was a lottery, some men were allowed, others were not. Some were housed in barbed wire enclosures with little space between the huts and the perimeter fence. They simply had no space to play sports. For others sport was forbidden by their employers, who felt they should save their energy for work, not fritter it away in meaningless games. For men at one Arbeitskommando there was no restriction on playing football, as the local team said their pitch could be used. There was just one catch, they could only play in football boots, something none of them had. Others found their activities restricted when recreation rooms were closed down to house incoming prisoners, meaning the only room left available was the space between the bunks of their overcrowded huts.

Some unlucky prisoners found their one day off per week was not the relaxing time it should have been. At one work camp it was not just the prisoners who were given Sunday off, their guard also had a day off. As a result the POWs were locked inside their huts, unable to enjoy their leisure time in the open air.

Yet despite the very real hardships endured by so many of the toiling POWs some among them were thrust into the confusing position of being sent to 'holiday camps'. Although many were mistrustful of these special camps, where prisoners with good disciplinary records were chosen for periods of rest, the reality was the camps really did provide a well-deserved break. Opened in 1943 the two camps, Special

Detachments 399 and 517, situated outside Berlin were expected to be propaganda camps where they would be paraded before the media from neutral countries and bombarded with Nazi rhetoric. Most prisoners were wary of the Germans' motives from the moment they heard about the camps. Their fears were confirmed when they were issued with the unheard of luxury of three Red Cross parcels in just one week. Indeed, when some prisoners arrived they insisted they be returned to their Stalags or work camps immediately. Although the Germans had initially hoped to use these camps as a method of enticing prisoners to join the British Free Corps to fight against the Red Army they made little headway with the 'holidaymakers'. Most of the prisoners were suspicious of their fellow Britons on the permanent staff of the camp, believing Sergeant Brown and Corporal Blewitt to be pre-war fascists.

As a result of the open hostility shown by many prisoners, they faced little in the way of propaganda and actually enjoyed a measure of comfort. For soldiers who had worked 12 hours a day, 6 days a week, the four-to-six-week break was the ideal opportunity to recuperate. Entertainment was provided by both the Dresden Philharmonic and the Berlin State Opera, with the British-born opera singer Miss Margery Booth paying a number of visits to the camp at Genshagen. They were also able to make trips to the cinema once a week and interpreters took them out on guided tours of the palaces at nearby Potsdam. When one prisoner, Clifford Allen, needed to visit the dentist he was sent into Berlin. His guard walked at a distance behind him and made no effort to interfere during the trip. Others found it was possible for them to make unofficial visits to the capital wearing borrowed civilian clothes. For all their fears about indoctrination the prisoners were able to relax and forget their troubles, knowing they would soon be back in their work camps.

Despite such facilities being on offer for a few, in the latter period of the war the trend was for decreasing living standards. Leisure became a thing of the past and all thoughts of plays or sport were cast from their minds as they became too weak to consider exercise. It was an ominous sign. By late 1944 the men who had endured real hardship upon capture and in the early days of their captivity knew how precarious their situation was. As the autumn turned to winter, and the German economy and infrastructure felt the effects of the relentless bombing, the situation changed for the prisoners. Red Cross parcels started to appear less and less frequently and all the certainties of their existence began to be washed away on a tide of hunger and fear. Words of warning came in 'Snips', the camp newsletter at a mine. The Christmas pantomime was cancelled since the leading actors all found they could summon up neither the energy not the enthusiasm for the proposed performance. In November 1944 the editor wrote: 'In this POW life to talk at all of relaxing is almost farcial, for now more than ever, we are living on our nerves, clutching at news and rumour, yet always with a half doubt in our minds. We wish and wish while we know that we can never hurry affairs with all the wishing in the world.'[32]

As a shadow of fear was cast over their lives many wondered if they would ever live to fulfil the dreams they had made during the long years of captivity. As the inevitable end of the war approached the prisoners were to face hardships and horrors few could ever have dreamt of. The final months of the war in Europe would be a period few would ever be able to forget, and that all who lived through it would be eternally grateful to have survived.

SIX

Friends, Enemies and Lovers

'Work together with German women should be restricted to the indispensable minimum.'[1]

'It was a well known fact that many German girls would drop their slacks for a bar of chocolate.'[2]

The prisoners leaving the Stalags to enter industry or take their place on farms soon realised that wartime Europe – even in the hands of the supposedly super-efficient Germans – was not the smooth-running machine of peacetime. In the wake of the German successes on the battlefield had come chaos. It was not always evident on the surface, but war had changed the world. All the certainties of life – for the conquering forces, German civilians, subject populations and, not least, the new captive workforce – had changed. Pre-war hopes and expectations had been swept away by the wave of violence unleashed on Europe and a new realism crept into the lives of those washed up by the tide.

For the first prisoners to enter the Reich the reaction from civilians was one of blatant hostility. As they were marched through the streets to the Stalags or work camps they were laughed at by local women, who found it comical to see the once proud soldiers reduced to wearing secondhand uniforms and rough wooden clogs. Men dropped cigarettes in the gutter and looked on in scorn as desperate prisoners scrabbled in the dirt to retrieve the butts. For the POWs their humiliation was complete, they had been defeated in battle, marched halfway across Europe, starved and then finally been paraded like slaves through the streets of the victorious nation. Yet as the people of Germany gloated and revelled in the fruits of their triumph the POWs had, deep within their minds, the feeling that the roles might one day be reversed.

In the years that followed many prisoners were to find themselves

increasingly confident about their position within German society. As
the war progressed German industry and agriculture were gradually
stripped of their loyal local workforce, sent off to the front to pursue
the vainglorious dreams of their leaders. In their place came a ragged
army of slaves – forced labourers from Poland and Russia, and POWs
from the armies of both the defeated nations and those who still fought
on. Alongside them worked people from across Europe, tempted into
Germany by the lure of high wages. When the German men were swallowed up by the armed forces the British and Commonwealth prisoners
slipped into their jobs and eventually, if they were lucky, into their beds.
It may have been a life of slavery, bound to work as ordered by those
who purchased their toil and sweat from the commandants of the Stalags, but it was a life most POWs would do their best to exploit. Eventually the chaos of the collapsing Reich would see many POWS able to
enjoy a life few could have envisaged when they first shuffled out of the
Stalags and into their work camps.

　　None knew what the attitude would be from the people they would
work alongside. Those POWs on farms across eastern Europe imagined
the conquered populations would be their friends and confidants, able
to succour them in their time of need, but few expected such assistance
from the natives of the newly enlarged Reich. The Germans and Aus-
trians of the pre-war state, and Volksdeutsch of the lands swallowed
during the advances eastwards, remained the enemy – and the prisoners expected to be treated as such by them. In this world of chaos and
confusion many expectations and preconceptions would be challenged
and friendships would grow in the vacuum caused by the dislocation of
war.

　　There was a measure of tension between the prisoners working in
some German industrial enterprises and the civilian labourers. Not all
were hostile to the prisoners, indeed for many it was little more than the
language barrier and the rules regarding fraternisation that kept the two
factions from developing friendships. In some mines the German workers were communists who had been sent to the mines as political prisoners and whose labour was forced as much as that of the prisoners. But in
every large factory or mine there seemed to be a few among the fellow
workers, foremen or managers who liked to make life difficult for the
prisoners. Some among the offenders were men whose foul nature made
them unpopular with their countrymen, something that was of little
consolation to the working prisoners. At one mine a Private Gray was
attacked by a fellow worker who swung a heavy pit lamp at his head.

Gray was left needing five stitches. Similarly, at Schlegel pit in Silesia the civilian overseers were a constant source of trouble for the prisoners, using rubber truncheons to beat the men into working harder.

Unsurprisingly it was with the Poles and Czechs who were living under German rule in the newly annexed lands of the Reich where the POWs made the first steps towards settling into life in the community. In particular, in the farms and small villages where they worked, the new labour force were viewed as allies by local labourers whose animosity towards their German neighbours long predated any conflict the British had known. These were lands that had been fought over enough times in recent history for the conquerors to know they were not among friends.

Trading for food began almost as soon as the POWS arrived in the Stalags and work camps that would become their new homes. In the harsh months following the defeat of the BEF in France, the men taken into captivity turned to barter to ensure they had enough food to survive. Imprisoned in Fort 17 at Stalag XXa, Ken Wilats witnessed the nascent trade that would over the years grow into a complete black market industry:

> The entrepreneurial side of people came to the fore. Working parties were going out and they had access to Poles. So if they had a gold watch they could swap it for bread which they could smuggle back into camp down their trousers. So consequently a black market arose, as men brought back bread and offered so many loaves for someone else's watch. Next time they went out they'd trade it at a higher value. So you got this commercial aspect to life in a very primitive state. I was lucky, I got onto a working party after about three weeks.[3]

Once the men had settled into their new homes – though few would ever consider them that – they began to look out for opportunities to enhance their existence and buy the few small luxuries that would help preserve their dignity. The local populations were the ideal source of supplies for the POWs. The contents of their Red Cross parcels were perfect for trading onto the black market – and trade they did, as one recalled: 'Give them a few fags, they'll get you anything.'[4] Although few prisoners could afford to sell their precious tinned foods, all across Europe POWs leaked other supplies into the local economy, providing goods many civilians had long given up hope of seeing again. Cigarettes, coffee, soap – all commanded high prices for the men behind the wire. The trade began at many of the smaller work camps where canteen facilities were unavailable. Instead the NCOs in charge of the work details were sent under escort to shop for what the men needed with whatever money they had available. In these quiet rural towns the shopkeepers often accepted the *lagergeld* offered by the prisoners and were able to exchange it for real money from the commandants of the Stalags. With prisoners making contact within the communities the local shopkeepers were able to begin a clandestine trade that would soon make many goods available to the local population. Chocolate bars handed over by the POWs meant extra loaves of bread appearing with the shopping, with the chocolate being sold on to eager local customers. It was not only foodstuffs that were used for trading. Whatever goods were short for civilians could be exchanged. When Polish workers were unable to buy woollen goods in the shops it was the POWs they turned to for help. The prisoners who had been lucky enough to receive clothing parcels from home were able to fill the gap. One prisoner was able to trade a pullover for 50 eggs, a chicken and several pounds of tomatoes and onions. Soon the black market trade became widespread, but some found such activities came at a price. For one prisoner the cost was 21 days hard labour, a sentence he received after committing an almost meaningless crime – the sale of a pair of underpants to a Polish worker.

It was not just the populations of the defeated nations who involved themselves in this trade. As soon as the Red Cross parcels began to arrive prisoners began to use them to curry favour with the guards. Working at a copper mine Alec Reynolds used what few Red Cross provisions he received to trade. He swapped his cigarettes for chocolate then used the chocolate to bribe guards to take him out of camp. In this way he was able to visit the local dentist for treatment, his offer of chocolate for the dentist to take home to his children ensuring he received a good standard of treatment. Such attempts at bribery were most successful at the work camps where the prisoners and their guards lived almost side by side. Collections were made among the working prisoners to ensure that their guards treated them fairly. At some factories guards began to look so favourably upon the prisoners that little work was done. The guards simply looked the other way as the POWs skived their way through the week and although such arrangements suited the immediate desires of the working prisoners they were of little benefit in the long run. As soon as levels of output fell to an obvious extent the employers had to take action. Since the employers were paying for the labour they expected to get the requisite hours of work. Soon the offending guards were replaced by men thought to be less corruptible. Such bribery could have other effects. At some camps attempts to corrupt the guards led to a clampdown in which prisoners were forbidden to have uncontrolled access to their food parcels. Instead commandants insisted on them being given just enough for each day – making sure the allowance of foodstuffs was removed from the packaging to prevent them using the contents in illegal trade.

For men on work details the illegal trade in goods meant they could buy overalls with which to cover their increasingly threadbare uniforms, or buy items they could never purchase with their comical *lagergeld*. A vast black market grew to replace the legal trade of the pre-war years, until by 1945 money had no value and all that mattered were the goods available for barter. High on the shopping lists of the prisoners were fresh fruit, vegetables and meat. They wanted 'real' food rather than tinned and yearned for a taste of home. They also wanted foods that could be easily smuggled back into their camps and which could be cooked simply and quickly. Long loaves of bread were slipped down inside trouser legs, thus hidden from the view of guards. One ingenious man even broke eggs into condoms then tied them around his waist, beneath his clothing. When the guard frisked him the soft contents of the condoms were not noticed and his eggs passed safely into the compound. Others used even simpler methods. When searches were made the prisoners raised their arms high above their heads so the guard could frisk them. As the guards patted them down they were blissfully unaware the prisoners were sometimes clutching eggs in their raised hands. Such was the level of exchange at one work camp that the commandant was shocked when he opened a cupboard only for a live goose to walk out into the room. Some didn't wait for the return to camp to have their fill of black market food. Those working in factories found there were plenty of places where food could be cooked. Blacksmith's forges could be used for cooking potatoes, meat could be cooked on the hot metal of factory machinery and pots of water could be boiled wherever heat was available.

Gordon Barber recalled the trade situation in the small East Prussian village that was his home for over three years:

> We had a bit of trouble with the Poles. It was a nice little village. The blacksmith's wife fancied me I think, but she wouldn't give anything. She was frightened. 'Cause if they got caught they had 'the camps' – we hadn't heard of Auschwitz or that – but they talked about these camps

you could get sent to. There was a lot of rivalry between us and the Poles, because we had things and we could barter for them. There was a bloke in the village he was like Fagin. If you had anything to swap or wanted anything you went to him. But I used to cut out the middle man and go directly to people. I wasn't going to give up two fags to him on each deal.

However, although such deals were welcomed by both sides they could lead to conflict between the two erstwhile allies, as Barber soon found out:

I said to the smith, 'I've got some fags, I want some eggs'. He said he'd get me some. That night the lads were playing football and I went to get my eggs. I went upstairs to his house which was above our billet, I think it used to be a Hitler Youth Summer Camp. I said 'Where are my eggs?' and this fucking Pole said 'I haven't got them'. I said 'Give us my bleedin' fags back'. No, he said he'll get the eggs next week. So we started having a go. He was a pretty strong lad and we finished up on the floor fighting. Then this other Pole – a horseman – he came in and he was wearing these clogs. He kicked me in the fucking head – bang! With that I was half out and they threw me down the stairs. Our cook was there, he said 'Hang on Nobby, I'll get the lads'. I said 'I'll wait till the morning, I'll get him'. So next day I got up nice and early 'cause the horseman has to go out early to feed and clean the horses. But I hadn't worked out a plan. I didn't think about what he might have in his hand. I hit him but not hard enough. He went out of the door and I went out after him. But he had a 'curry comb' – a horse brush - in his hand. I had my hands up to protect my face, it cut my hands open – I've still got the scars. He was ripping me with it. That wasn't pleasant, there was blood everywhere. Then three of our blokes came out. One threw me a billet of wood, from the foreman's woodpile. I grabbed it and I fucking really laid into this Pole. I whacked him all over the bleedin' show. But he was clever he kept taking it, all the time his whip was cracking but I was only worried about the curry comb. Then the guard came and sorted it out but they didn't do anything to me. After that the Poles were against me for a little while.[5]

Though Barber escaped punishment others were not so lucky, with some conflicts between prisoners and their guards or civilian overseers resulting in serious repercussions. At some work camps punishments were not just meted out to the prisoner responsible. When one of 80 POWs from Stalag XXa on detachment to a stove factory punched a civilian all of his comrades were punished. All had their midday soup ration halved to show them the price of defiance. One working party was forced to stand naked on a snow-covered parade ground as their clothes and possessions were searched for a stolen spanner. Another group of men caught slacking whilst clearing snow were forced to stand for an hour holding shovels in their outstretched arms. Tensions between the captors and the captive sometimes spilled over into open disobedience and even violence. Two men working at an iron ore mine playfully attacked a guard and stuffed snow down his shirt. For their crimes they were both given prison sentences, one receiving 18 months the other two years. Others found guilty of offences faced all manner of punishments. Bernard Smith, at a working party attached to a farm, received a 15-year sentence for 'laying out' a guard. Serious offenders, such as Smith, were sentenced by military courts and sent to military prisons where they served their sentences alongside offenders from the Wehrmacht. For some among them their sentences were spent in solitary confinement, with prisoners often found to be suffering from the ill effects of the poor diet and gruelling conditions. One man serving a four-year sentence was described by Red Cross inspectors as 'Weak and destitute'.[6]

For less serious offenders their punishments took place on site – either in the 'coolers' of the Stalags or in punishment cells at work camps. Punishments for POWs varied from camp to camp. In one camp the offenders were simply given odd jobs to do around the camp and then made to do one hour's gruelling pack-drill four times a day. In the words of the German authorities this was 're-education' rather than punishment. For the prisoners in question they must have wondered what value a 25lb pack could possibly have for their military education. At Arbeitskommando 7008, supplied by Stalag XIIIc, the Australian prisoners who offended were punished by being locked into a pitch-black cellar. For the duration of their sentence they were forced to stand in water four inches deep. The cold, damp liquid seeped into their boots, soaking the leather then softening their feet and exposing them to trench foot and other infections. Similarly, at a punishment camp in Chelms 150 POWs were housed in earth roofed wooden huts sunk one-and-a-half metres beneath the ground. Their punishment also included receiving no Red Cross parcels for 11 weeks.

Not all of the punishments were officially sanctioned. In some cases guards showed vindictiveness towards individual prisoners, carrying out personal vendettas against men who showed any defiance towards their captors. Powerless to react the prisoners could do little but watch help- lessly as guards dished out discriminating and humiliating treatment to their mates. They could complain to the Red Cross, a process that did occasionally see guards transferred, but few dared risk the wrath of an accused guard. Most were left to accept their punishment. At one agricultural work detail prisoners were forced to pull their guard behind them in a handcart, as they made the 5-mile round trip to deliver hot coffee to various groups of men on the farm. Gordon Barber, who came into conflict with both civilians and guards, fell foul of one particular guard. On the morning following a brutal beating by the guard he and a friend were singled out for punishment:

> We used to have to get our water from down in the village, from a farm. It was carried back in churns. Normally they got horses to drag it up. That day they made us do it. I got half way up the hill and I put it down. I said 'Fuck you mate, I'm not going any further. I'm worn out, I'm not carrying it.' And he kicked me right in the bottom of the spine. It was the only time I've ever been knocked out in my life. They dragged me back. You know what they made me do then? Our toilets were a plank over a wooden trough. They used to get the horses to pull it out and dump it on the fields. That morning they made me and Jock pull it out. That wasn't a pleasant sight.[7]

Barber, who eventually lost three teeth after a guard hit him in the face with a pistol, didn't forget his treatment and vowed to get his revenge. He waited for months before the opportunity arose whilst working in the farm store:

> In the corner I saw all these red cabbages. I put them in a basket and I was going to take them out and put them in a sack. I heard him coming down the stairs and I thought 'Sod it'. I kicked the basket into the corner hoping they'd fall out, but they didn't. He saw the cabbages and he laid into me with this little cane – like Charlie Chaplin's one – that he car- ried. He was trying to hit me in the face. I thought 'Enough is enough'. I grabbed him and held him against the wall, showed him my fist and said 'You hit me once more, you're gonna cop this!' He tried again so I whacked him and he cried out. Then the village smith and another bloke came and got me. I was sent back to Marienburg. I got 28 days in the cooler, just sitting on my own. Bread and water. There's not much you

can think about except 'I hope I get out of here quick'.[8]

He was not alone in facing the violent attentions of the Germans. Many working prisoners reported how local Nazi Party officials interfered at work camps to deliberately make their lives miserable. Prisoners at numerous work details used the visits by Red Cross representatives to report the abuse they faced. In a single monthly report on Arbeitskommandos dependent on Stalag VIIIb three camps came in for criticism. At E198 men complained they had been beaten by their guards and at E159 it was reported that one prisoner, John Gee, had been killed by a guard for no apparent reason. The worst of all was E51 which was closed down by the commandant of Stalag VIIIb after it was discovered that both guards and civilian workers had been beating the prisoners with knotted clubs. At AK7023, attached to Stalag III, the local Burgomeister paid visits to the camp to hit the working prisoners, whilst in Hanover overseers from the Todt organization used rubber truncheons on prisoners as well as slave labourers. The intervention of civilians did not only affect the POWs. Working at a benzene factory, prisoner Stuart Silcock noted how the Geneva Convention was 'flagrantly ignored' by the foremen and gangleaders, who were: 'entirely responsible for bad treatment, threatening German guards if they did not maintain forced work on the minimum food provided'.[9]

As a nation the Germans may have had a reputation for sticking to the rules but for many prisoners rules were constantly breached. Officially the commandants of the Stalags only loaned the POWs to civilian contractors, yet in some cases the civilians seemed to hold the real power. POW miners at Klausberg found that Herr Müller, the director of Abwehr Grube Klausberg, seemed to be able to override the military authorities and make life difficult for the prisoners. When prisoners complained to their guards they refused to help, telling them they had no power to act since the civilians were in charge. Some among the prisoners deliberately took note of the names of the offenders, hoping they might one day find a chance to ensure the man was punished. In a postwar report one prisoner noted the activities of Stabsfeldwebel Brandt, a middle-aged soldier from Magdeburg, who was: 'the cause of all the suffering which went on at Camp 340 where 50 per cent had malnutrition and quarter of the camp went to work half naked'.[10]

Of course not all relationships between prisoners and the guards and civilians were hostile. In many cases the prisoners were treated fairly by the men keeping them captive. At one work camp only the intervention of civilian workers saved the POWs from a particularly hostile guard. On three separate occasions the civilian workers intervened to take away the guard's rifle after he threatened to shoot the working prisoners. At other camps it was the guards who saved the men from violent civilians. At a quarry in Mittelangenau the owner ordered the guards to strike the prisoners and stab them with bayonets. When Gunner Clarence Scott was injured in a rockfall he laughed at him and said he should have been killed. Few realized how serious he was until he then ordered a guard to shoot the injured Scott. Fortunately for the prisoner the guard refused. Once recovered and transferred to a farm Scott again found himself with a violent boss. The farm owner, Richard Kuhne, ordered guards to beat Scott to death. Once more he was only saved by the refusal of the guards to carry out the order.

Yet some of the factory owners and farmers were generous towards their prisoners. One factory owner even secretly provided a truck to ensure that supplies of Red Cross parcels could continue to reach 'his' prisoners after the military transport network had begun to collapse. For many among the prisoners it was a confusing situation finding guards friendly at one moment and then violently antagonistic the next, as one prisoner later wrote: 'Merry Christmas today and a bayonet up the arse tomorrow.'[11] Many of the guards were soldiers who had been wounded in battle and for some of them POW work camps were merely a place they were sent to recuperate. Often they retained a respect for their fellow fighting men and had no wish to mistreat them. On smaller work detachments both guards and prisoners lived in the same huts, although the guards were not locked in at night. Ken Wilats, working on a farm in East Prussia recalled the relationship between the guards and the prisoners:

> The guards were very relaxed. It depended on the individual and there were vast differences between the ones you could get. Remember – without having particular sympathy for them – they weren't on a good job. We had people we could talk to but they were on their own. They must have been bored out of their minds. But remember, the alternative was the Russian front. So which is better, being lonely or being at the front getting killed? So they thanked their lucky stars. Some were ordinary chaps. Some were men who'd been wounded on the Russian front. Some had medical problems. By and large they weren't too bad.[12]

Spending all day every day side by side it was easy to see why a hesitant camaraderie was established between the two factions. Cigarettes from Red Cross parcels were able to help bridge the gap between the factions, with many guards amenable to bribery. They happily turned their heads away and ignored the misdemeanours and black market dealings of the POWs. The bribery and corruption resulted in many work camps being full of contraband goods, something the guards could not fail to be aware of. The problem was that there existed an ever present threat of spot checks by the Gestapo. Where the guards were complicit in the misdeeds of the prisoners this was a great worry but they simply alerted the prisoners that a search was imminent and took the contraband into safe keeping until the search was complete.

In such circumstances it was not surprising that both guards and prisoners established good relations. A few built up close friendships, going out together at night to visit local bars. At one work camp there was a great commotion after a guard and his prisoner were seen returning to the camp late at night drunkenly singing whilst walking with their arms around each other's shoulders. Some of the most amenable guards allowed men to sneak out of the work camps in exchange for cigarettes, with a few using this method to attend Christmas parties in the compounds reserved for the foreign labourers they worked alongside. It was simple, the guards would make openings in the wire and agree to turn their backs, just so long as the men made sure they returned before the morning roll call.

At one East Prussian farm the guard was invited to a Christmas party. The party was livened up by a brew concocted by the prisoners. Gordon Barber recalled his role in the makeshift distillery:

> We got the guard pissed at Christmas. We made our own still. To this day they're probably still wondering what happened to the copper piping on the reserve tractor. I know because I took it off. The others asked me to find some piping so one night, just before we were locked in, I got them to tell the guard I'd just gone down to do some work for someone – they would never check – and so I went and stripped the pipes off. That put the tractor out of action. So I got the bits and pieces and this bloke made a still. The brew was really lethal and it was really good. And we got the guard pissed. I wish we could've had photographs of that.[13]

His fellow prisoner Ken Wilats recalled what happened:

> We had some fun with our guard. We had dried and sliced sugar beet,

they called it schnitzel. This was the remnants of the stuff we grew
which was sent back by the factories as cattle feed. Each day we'd put
it into the inside pockets of our battledress, bring it back home, mix
it with sugar and prunes from the Red Cross parcels, put it in a milk
churn, keep it for a few weeks then distil it. We then made ourselves a
highly volatile drink. It was so strong you could set light to it. We'd save
it for the Christmas party. The farmer's wife gave us a firkin of nettle
beer – about 0.5 per cent alcohol – and we mixed this with our firewater.
Our guard was a nice sort of chap – middle-aged – and he was obviously
lonely because he hung around with us. So we offered him a glass of
beer but we couldn't let him know we'd got this brew going. So we went
into a separate room to fetch our drinks. But he latched onto this and
so we had no option but to let him in on our secret. He got as drunk as
could be. So we got his rifle and we were marching up and down with it
whilst he's laying on the bed, spark out.[14]

Not all drunken guards were so friendly. At one mining camp a drunken
guard threatened to shoot prisoners who refused to clean their room
at Christmas. He was only placated when the frightened prisoners re-
trieved their own stock of precious alcohol and offered him a drink.

Other relationships appeared to go beyond such good-natured fun.
In a rather suspicious case a group of prisoners arrived at a remote Silesian forestry camp where there was a curious relationship between
some of the prisoners and their guards. At night they spotted how some
among the prisoners went to great lengths to prepare themselves for
an evening's entertainment. They dressed in civilian clothes, including
shirts and ties, and combed their hair meticulously. Then they made
their way to the guards' quarters. When the newcomers enquired what
the men were doing they were told they were going to work. The homo-
sexual overtones of the curious behaviour of the POWs was obvious and
the newcomers contrived to get themselves transferred away as soon as
possible.

There was a darker side to relationships between captors and captive. Many disagreements broke out between factions who believed the
POWs should do their work quickly and efficiently, in order to ensure a
quiet life, and those who believed they should make all efforts to undermine the Nazi industry. Those who believed they should endeavour to
sabotage German industry were playing a dangerous game for the Germans openly proclaimed they would execute men for any acts of sabotage. Yet in the minds of the prisoners it was the only way they could

play an active part in the war, doing whatever would hinder the efforts of the enemy to run an efficient military machine. All knew they had to be careful, meaning there were few attempts at serious sabotage, but any small personal act of defiance helped to liven up an otherwise dull day. 'Pinpricks' they may have been when compared to the bombs dropped on German cities or the bullets fired by their comrades, but these acts of sabotage provided a psychological support for the prisoners – a way of saying 'I'm still fighting for my country'. For some it was as simple as mixing cement weakly so that in time the building would show defects, or putting sand or gravel into the workings of machinery. Others cut wires and cables before laying them, making sure their guards would not be able to trace the perpetrators. Some simply let the brakes off on mine wagons when going round corners, ensuring the wagon would derail.

The sabotage of tools was among the most common of all the efforts made by the prisoners to slow down their work. They simply waited until no one was watching, broke their tools and wandered over to the foreman to report what had happened. Some even used the excuse that the accident had happened because of how hard they were working. At one road-building site one man managed to break two picks within 15 minutes. When the guards became irritated by the incessant breakages they ordered all the men to parade at bayonet point. They were then informed that they had to own up to the sabotage. With little choice but to comply the perpetrators admitted their crimes and were joined in their confessions by numerous other prisoners. Eventually the number of prisoners admitting to breaking tools was greater than the number of tools broken, leaving the guards powerless to punish the offenders.

Such 'accidents' slowed down production without harming anyone or damaging any machinery. The overseers merely shouted and urged the men to get working again quickly. At one factory prisoners urinated over sacks of coffee, whilst others put salt into sacks of flour or switched the contents of seed packets – all silent, if ineffectual, protests against their enforced labour.

But some prisoners had a desire to make a real impact upon the enemy. Men at one work camp in eastern Germany destroyed a grain conveyor across the River Oder, whilst others put a mine out of action for two days simply by cutting through the main power cable. Australian Sergeant Royce Simmons struck a blow for the prisoners' cause when he destroyed 300 gallons of milk destined for the German army. A further act of defiance brought even more comfort to Simmons and his fellow working prisoners when he stole 144,000 German army cigarettes.

For men prepared to take such risks by sabotaging German industry there was little understanding of the dedicated work of some of
their comrades. They could understand why a prisoner would do his
job properly but why would anyone show enthusiasm whilst working
for the enemy? Some of the enthusiasts were accused of treachery, with
rumours circulating about the reasons behind their conscientious industrial efforts. Maurice Newey was among their critics: 'the BAU battalion were a brainwashed lot, the way they used to work. I was under
the impression that it was our duty to hinder the enemy, not help him.
These chaps worked like the clappers and it was rumoured one man had
been presented with a Workers medal for the amount of work that he
had achieved.'[15] The keenness shown by some men for their work led to
uncomfortable situations and conflicts. In April 1945 prisoners at Wargl
refused to work on a bomb-damaged railway for fear of future air raids.
With the men on strike a Sergeant Patterson, captured at Arnhem, de-
fied his comrades and volunteered to keep working. His actions only
further inflamed the situation when he was reported to have apologised
to the Germans for the behaviour of his fellow Britons.

In some industrial enterprises the over-enthusiastic workers were
considered to be attempting to curry favour with the guards, wanting
to be singled out for special treatment at the expense of others. In June
1944 'Snips', the secret handwritten camp newspaper at a copper mine,
dared to be critical of the behaviour of a number of prisoners:

> On Friday 2nd June the 'Big Bad Wolf' inspected the mine, he warmly
> complimented two of our 'comrades' on their efficient drilling and bor-
> ing, another as being an 'excellent' worker in district sixteen. He quoted
> two other examples, one a shoveller on the face who, when kept waiting
> for an 'empty' does his own trekking, another on a tipping machine,
> who goes as far as to tell his gang to 'hurry up'! Names of these men will
> be supplied on application.[16]

For all the accusations of treachery against fellow prisoners, in most
cases the men who were deemed over-enthusiastic at work were simply
trying to make their lives as easy as possible, caring little about what
this meant for their fellow prisoners. Often it was simply that they had
made arrangements with the foreman that once a job was finished they
would be allowed to rest, hiding in the factory smoking and playing
cards. Others were allowed by their guards to fulfil their daily tasks then
return to their barracks, whiling away the hours of daylight they would

otherwise seldom have seen.

Some among the prisoners had a simple solution to the behaviour of such men thought to be too close to the enemy. On a work detail in Poznan one POW posed for photographs with a group of German soldiers, in return for cigarettes he was persuaded to give a Nazi salute. His actions did not impress his fellow prisoners and that night he was forced to run the gauntlet of men who each punched him. After his beating his humiliation was compounded when the offending cigarettes were stamped into the ground. Gordon Barber was one of those POWs who happily responded to such collaboration with violence: 'They sent me to a lumber camp. I didn't last three weeks there. I saw too many blokes with broken arms and legs. I smacked the bloke in charge – one of our blokes – in the mouth. He was too far up the Germans' arses. He had a nice billet and we had the shit. One day he started giving me a lot of mouth so I hit him.'[17]

Whilst some of the camp leaders used their position to curry favour with the Germans most worked tirelessly for the welfare of their men. They put aside their fears of what might happen to them and used their official position to act as a mouthpiece for those whose rights were quite often being abused by their captors. They knew they would not be able to win many concessions from the enemy but also knew every little bit would help. It also gave the prisoners great faith to know someone was trying to help. The difficulty for camp leaders was that they always knew that if they complained too much they would be transferred away and replaced by a more pliable character. One of those who managed to perform this delicate balancing act was Bombardier Norton, the camp leader for a detachment of prisoners working in a copper mine. Norton, a solicitor's clerk, law student and Communist Party member who had been captured in North Africa, was revered by the copper miners for his efforts: 'In this camp he worked consistently for our welfare, always maintaining an even temper and a cool attitude towards our captors. His reward? Our gratitude and appreciation and the knowledge, we trust, that he has performed a difficult task in fine style and spirit.'[18]

The divisions between prisoners also fell along national lines. Right from the collapse of the 1940 campaign British and French troops had clashed angrily, often with violent results. This hostility often continued once behind the wire, with little co-operation between the erstwhile allies. Many among the French considered Dunkirk a betrayal whilst the British thought the French had too often surrendered without a fight. Worse still were the frequent differences between British and Commonwealth troops, most notably the South Africans. Whether fair or not, stories spread through the camps about how the Boers among the South Africans were over-friendly towards the Germans. Many were considered sympathetic to the Nazi cause, and rumours spread that they had deliberately capitulated at Tobruk, allowing the Germans to capture the town. The same rumours suggested many among them yearned for a Nazi victory, after which they would be free from the British Empire.

There was an altogether different situation between the British and American prisoners. Those prisoners who could remember the Americans back in Britain could only visualise men swaggering about confidently, spending their money on having a good time with British women. They were so casual nothing seemed to worry them. However, once within the POW camps many found the Americans a shadow of their former selves, something to be pitied rather than envied. One man later wrote that the Americans were: 'a sorry, scruffy lot who couldn't take captivity'. He went on to explain how distant this was from their public image: 'The scene bore out our theory that there was a lot of difference between victorious advancing Yanks, sitting on tanks blowing kisses to the girls, and Yanks in adversity.'[19]

Whilst the GIs in Britain were attracting the attentions of British women it was a different group of uniformed men who were befriending the women of Hitler's expanding Reich. For the thousands of men working in the farms and factories of the Reich employment outside the Stalags was more than just a change of scenery. The relative freedom of life on an Arbeitskommando also gave them access to a most important commodity – sex. Right from the start of imprisonment sex had been an important issue for many of the newly captive men. Many of those men of the BEF captured in June 1940 had been regular visitors to the French brothels that had thrived in the towns around their camps. Much the same situation had existed in North Africa where the whores of Cairo and Alexandria had done a roaring trade among the troops passing through their towns. Married men missed the regular attentions of their wives, but once 'behind the wire' all the prisoners had to find a substitute. The obvious solution was to indulge themselves, but conditions within the Stalags meant there were few solitary moments when masturbation could be enjoyed. With cramped huts and overcrowded washrooms the men had little choice but to wait until after lights out when they could furtively relieve their frustration under the threadbare blankets of their bunks. Despite the restrictive situation, pornography became a widely traded source of visual stimulation for the men known as 'mutton floggers', 'bishop bashers', 'wire pullers' or, more simply, 'wankers' – men whose hands were known as 'the five fingered widow'. One prisoner was so famed for his regular self relief he became known as 'Wanker Bill' and his room mates joked how he even 'wanked between wanks'.[20] and was famed for still being interested in sex even after most of his fellow prisoners had physically lost the ability to get erections. One of his mates, initially held in Italy and then in Germany, later wrote:

> Onanism was widely practised and there would have been hardly a man who hadn't indulged at one time or the other. It seemed the married men were the worst because when their stomachs were full they would spend hours reliving their courting days, the wedding night, the honeymoon and sundry Sunday afternoons on the carpet. Not that the single men hadn't any memories to look back on. They had, but our sex lives had tended to be more spasmodic, so that we were used to going without it.[21]

Many of the prisoners noted how their sexual urges were suppressed whenever food supplies were bad but recovered with the arrival of Red Cross parcels. The same situation was found in winter when the cold dampened their ardour, only for the awakenings of spring to restore their urges and once more the 'one-eyed milkman' was brought fully back into action.

Among those confined to the Stalags there was another outlet for their urges – homosexuality. Although commonly laughed about by the prisoners – who would joke about dropping their soap in the showers and what would happen when they bent over – open homosexuality was uncommon. Some men developed close bonds, not always sexual, with their fellow prisoners. The men were not always obviously suited as one POW recalled: 'Liaisons sprang up between all kinds of people, tall and short, fat and thin, and the good, the bad and the ugly. Relationships took many forms from parcel sharing, holding hands, heavy petting and actual indulging.'[22] Some formed inseparable couples, embroidering matching monograms on their jumpers, as if to seal their relationship in lieu of marriage. Men developed crushes on other prisoners, some unrequited, some reciprocated. One camp medic noticed what he called 'abnormal acquaintances' between inmates. They would go on parade together dressed alike and holding hands like a normal courting couple. He also noticed how anyone who played the female role in the camp theatre was considered a heart throb, whose every movement was followed by the admiring gaze of fellow prisoners. In some Stalags desperate men waited outside camp theatres for the chance to meet 'leading ladies' and even fought each other for their attentions.

With those confined to the Stalags having to find their own entertainment the men sent out on working parties discovered opportunities for encounters with someone other than their own hands or their fellow prisoners. A few desperate working prisoners were able to find an outlet for their sexual urges among the local workforce. In one Polish mine a few local teenage boys prostituted themselves to the prisoners for a few cigarettes. It was desperate behaviour on the behalf of both parties and their acts were carried out in the privacy of dark corners of the mine. Unable to converse and unable to see the boys the prisoners simply did their best to clear their minds and concentrate on the sexual relief rather than who was providing it. Such acts were rare and there was little criticism from others for those who indulged.

Yet not many of the working prisoners had any interest in homosexuality, what they really wanted was contact with local women. At first many had been wary of the women they met, uncertain as to what might happen if they were caught having sex with them. Rumours went round that the prisoners found having sex with women whose husbands were in the German army would be tried in German military courts and their sentences served in civilian prisons. Notices put up within work camps soon confirmed their fears: 'Prisoners of War are strictly forbidden to approach German women or girls in any way or have intercourse with them. This order is issued with the command that any contravention of same will result in a court martial and besides imprisonment, for serious cases – sexual intercourse for instance – the death penalty will be imposed.'[23] In reality such extreme options were not used by their captors and punishments varied from place to place – in Munich both the male and female offenders were stripped and paraded naked through the streets of the city carrying placards proclaiming their misdeeds.

It was not just the reaction of their guards that worried them, they also feared the reactions of local people – both German and Polish – knowing that hostility could make their lives uncomfortable. As a result the prisoners remained wary of those they met in the course of their work, but with time it was difficult to suppress the urges brought on by mutual attraction. It was on work detachments to farms where relationships first flourished.

Initially many of the working prisoners had faced hostility whenever they appeared in public. One man working as a dustman in Munich had been clearing bins from a girls' boarding school when one of the pupils threw a used sanitary towel at him. Indian prisoners reported how German civilians spat at them in the street and even stopped to slap the faces of the humiliated POWs. Yet such attitudes did not endure throughout the war years. Initially the changes were noticed in Poland where local women seemed to hang around in areas where they could be seen by the prisoners. Each time the prisoners had to march through towns they noticed how women watched their every movement with interest, with flirtatious glances being shared between them. With an air of sexual tension simmering between the two factions it was not long before men on many working parties were able to exploit the situation to their benefit. The common trick was to bribe guards to allow them to go out on walks in the evening or on Sunday afternoons. Whilst out of the camp the guard would escort them to a meeting place where they could spend time alone with their chosen woman. The danger was that outsiders might discover what was happening – something which could bring these privileges to a swift end. For the guards the threat was even more real, they faced a transfer away from the safety of a POW camp to the hell of the Russian front. To counter the threat of being seen whilst walking through the local town one prisoner borrowed women's clothing and made his way in safety to his girlfriend's house.

In one work camp the guards decided such nights out were too dangerous and chose a simpler course of action. Rather than taking the men out they simply invited in a local prostitute who was hidden in the prisoners' washhouse. The men then paid a fee to the guard to be escorted to meet her. The same men were also able to sate their desires when taking the commandant's laundry to be washed. The men established a rota for the weekly visits since the washerwoman was known to have a voracious sexual appetite, always being willing to entertain whoever visited her.

As the war progressed it was not just the Polish women who became enamoured with the prisoners, with so many of the German men away at the front their wives sought comfort in the arms of other men in uniform – the prisoners. On a working party from Stalag XXb Gordon Barber, who had already come into conflict with both the German farm managers and the Polish workers soon formed a more harmonious relationship, with a local woman known to the POWs as 'Frau Stinkabit':

Some of us used to get our ends away. The Poles were against me but

I didn't bother because by that time I'd got in with a married woman, Frieda, she was about 35 or 40. In that village a lot of our blokes did, there was a bit of the other going on. You've got to remember we'd been out there for over three years. We were working and we were fit. We were all about 23 or 24 and the young women – in their thirties and forties – liked us. The governor of this big state farm used to make us go and help with their smallholdings. One Sunday I had to take the boar down to her sow. That was a bit funny. I remember watching the boar have a little bit. I could speak quite a lot of German by that time. I said 'Good job we're not like that!' She said 'What are you like?' That was the opening. She wasn't a bad looking woman. But nothing happened that day. But then on my birthday, 26 February 1943, she promised me some cake. I was doing the painting in her bedroom, then she came in and put her arms around my neck. And that was the start of a beautiful friendship. My mates'll tell you I was the only bloke walking out on a Sunday afternoon all spit and polish, going down to see his ladylove. When I put me best uniform on they all knew I was going to see Frieda.[24]

For all the pleasure taken with the local girls the POWs faced immense risks for consorting with German women. Some of Barber's fellow prisoners made a conscious effort to avoid their attentions. They did not fear for themselves but for what might happen to the women: 'I never had a relationship with any of the women. The maximum sentence I would get would be 28 days, but that did not apply to the women. She would probably have gone to prison for years or been shot. So it wasn't a very fair risk. I just lay on my bed and kept myself to myself. I kept my head down.'[25]

He was wise to do so. Despite the 20-day sentences some men expected to get for such liaisons there were plenty of offenders who faced more severe punishments. One inmate of Stalag XXb was given a four-year prison sentence for his liaisons whilst others were threatened with execution – a policy that was used to force some unwillingly to join the British Freikorps. Gordon Barber was lucky not to be caught: 'Frieda had two kids and I used to take them chocolate and the kids used to run out to see me. But we had a new guard and as we were walking by the kids ran up shouting "Uncle Nobby! Uncle Nobby! Chocolade". So you had to be very careful. But in the end she started going with the governor of the farm.'[26]

Some of the men working on farms picked up strange stories about the war from the women they met. On one East Prussian farm the workers heard about secret weapons being developed by the enemy:

> There was an evacuee woman who had been bombed out of her home
> by the British. Her husband was in the Luftwaffe and she came to live
> with a family in the village. One of our chaps, Sparks, got friendly with
> her. He would spend his spare hours, between coming back from work
> and being locked up for the night, with her. He told us that he couldn't
> meet her because her husband was going on a secret mission and he was
> coming to see her. Sparks said the husband was working on a pilotless
> plane – the V1. We took it all with a pinch of salt. We later saw leaflets
> dropped by the airforce showing a V1, and saying that the British knew
> all about the flying bombs. This confirmed what Sparks' girlfriend had
> told us. So we knew all about it before the people back home.[27]

Whilst the men working on farms were enjoying liaisons with the local
women, those in industry initially had less good fortune. There were
few women within factories or working in urban locations and prisoners had less freedom to mix with the local populace than did those in
rural areas. Some of the more adventurous men were able to slip away
from work camps to brothels, where they paid for the prostitute's services with bars of Red Cross chocolate. They simply turned their overalls
inside out and slipped away to visit the brothels designated for the use
of foreign workers. These were staffed entirely by foreign prostitutes,
which meant the prisoners were safe in the knowledge they were not
infringing the Germans' draconian racial purity laws. The girls had a
secondary function in that they were often amenable to hiding any prisoners who went on the run. Paradoxically though many among the prisoners were desperate for sex some soon realised it didn't actually cost
them anything except their time. In Munich during the middle years of
the war the soldiers were able to buy sex for a tin of coffee or a bar of
soap, and would get three reichsmarks change. Such was the exchange
rate for commodities such as coffee, chocolate or soap that it seemed
to the prisoners that the girls were paying them. They received the soap
and coffee for free in their parcels and in exchange could get sex and the
equivalent of four days' wages. For some it was a risk worth taking.

For others the thought of sneaking away to have sex was too risky,
they simply bided their time until circumstances changed. Then as time
passed and the manpower situation in Germany became more serious,
changes took place within the factories. The POWs found themselves
working alongside women from throughout occupied Europe. Many

were slave labourers brought in to bolster the workforce but others were attracted to the Reich by the offer of high wages. These women, whatever their circumstances, would become a source of much comfort to the men who worked alongside them.

In one case John Elwyn, a Welsh Guardsman captured during the fall of France in 1940, began a relationship with a Polish girl at a factory. By night he would sneak from the camp to meet her at her lodgings. Their relationship blossomed until he eventually proposed to her. Their wedding was carried out in secret and so began a brief but intense relationship, tempered only by the impossible circumstances surrounding their love. Eventually the new groom and one of his mates were apprehended whilst on a visit to the bride and the camp was subject to a new strict regime of extra guards and increased security. Despite the increasing restrictions in the work camp, the prisoner was able to continue to make occasional trips to visit his bride. Their love was only curtailed when she fell sick and eventually died. For Elwyn this was the spur for him to continue with his escape attempts until he was eventually able to flee across the Baltic to Sweden.

However, it was not only the Germans who disapproved of such contacts between POWs and women, the Red Cross also complained about the situation. In 1942 they reported to London about the behaviour of four men from Stalag XXb working at Arbeitskommando 9 who had been caught sneaking through the wire into an enclosure for female workers. Though they had acted with the consent of the girls their actions were considered irresponsible and the Red Cross, though blaming the women for 'provocation', felt measures should be taken by the Germans to prevent such contact. They didn't bother to report the opinion of the POWs.

During the latter stages of the war the prisoners discovered new sexual horizons opening up before them. When escapes were discovered by the guards they more often than not apprehended the prisoners not desperately heading towards the Swiss border but tucked up in the beds of their girlfriends. Just like their more celebrated comrades in the camps for officers some among the working men scrounged tools to dig tunnels. Yet they had no intention of escaping. Instead these were 'Tunnels of Love', dug to connect their compounds with those of the female labourers. After work each night the POWs crawled along the dark tunnels to emerge in the foreign labourers' enclosures and spend the night alongside their girlfriends, retracing their steps at dawn in time for roll call. Prisoners also swapped clothes with civilian labourers so that they could enter the civilian compound to visit their girlfriends. In return the civilians would be able to stay overnight in the POW compound where they could share the luxuries of the prisoners' Red Cross parcels. In some cases tunnels were unnecessary. Fifty cigarettes were enough to make guards avert their gaze and allow prisoners out of their huts to attend parties with the foreign workers. Those amenable guards were in turn given chits confirming their compliance and good will that could be showed to liberating troops once the final defeat of Germany came.

As more and more German men left the factories for the front German women soon began to flood into the factories. One artilleryman, James Witte, was offered the chance to meet a female crane operator. In the knowledge that sex was on offer he agreed, arranging to meet her in the cab of her crane: 'She promptly undid the braces of her overalls revealing that she was stark naked underneath. She then lay on the floor and opened her legs. To my horror I realised that I wasn't going to be able to do anything. Dolly began to get impatient, eyeing my limp organ with disfavour.'[28] Ironically, for the rest of the day, realising the opportunity he had missed, he kept getting erections. This made Witte realise that he had to conquer his fears and find a woman in circumstances where he would be able to perform. In the aftermath of his failure he began sneaking into the enclosure for foreign labourers and there built up a relationship with a foreign worker.

On one work detail a Belgian labourer came up with an interesting offer for a group of POWs. For a price he could arrange for one of his countrywomen to meet with the prisoners. On the allotted day the prisoners drew lots to decide the order in which they would take their turn with the woman. When the time came, one by one the prisoners approached the guard and requested they be allowed to go to the toilet where the girl was hidden. For the price of a packet of cigarettes each man had his way with her. The 19-year-old girl seemed nervous, visibly trembling and obviously not enjoying her task, as one of the prisoners remembered: 'She was in a dreadful state of fear, trembling and her eyes were rolling. She whispered "Be quick" but there was no pleasure in it at all. I left, feeling that I had been cheated. After all my expectations it had been a complete let down. I gave the nod to the next man and off he went.'[29] For the men it was intense, passionless and, in the most part, very quick. The men couldn't help but realise her plight, but like her they were desperate. They longed for the intimacy of a woman's touch and she for the purchasing power she acquired from the western cigarettes. So they took their place in line, relieving the sexual tension of years of imprisonment. It is hard to blame the prisoners for playing their role in this degrading scenario, in the closing months of the war there was little room for the niceties of pre-war civilian morality. With death an almost constant companion, and starvation a very real prospect, life was cheap. Who could afford to be afraid for someone's moral welfare when tomorrow they might all be dead?

In the final, chaotic months of war it was the prisoners working in German towns and cities who were able to benefit most from contact with civilians. Throughout the war years, prisoners based in large cities had maintained regular contact with the locals. In Munich prisoners employed to sweep the streets took shelter from the winter weather by bribing the attendants of public toilets to allow them to shelter beside their stoves. Similarly, on their one day's rest, the prisoners could bribe their guards to allow them out into the city. The bribes would ensure only the most amenable guards were sent to accompany them, something that would allow them an afternoon's peace drinking in the bars. One guard found his party of prisoners seated at a table alongside a group of soldiers from the Afrika Korps, happily getting drunk together. In Munich an Australian POW entered into a clever arrangement with the foreman of his working party. Although a non-smoker the Australian ordered cigarettes in bulk from his friends and family back home. These, along with his ration from Red Cross parcels, were then passed to the German who traded them on the black market. The astonishing profits from these deals were then used for the Australian to purchase a house, paying off his mortgage instalments as each parcel arrived.

As Germany was plunged deeper into economic and social turmoil more and more prisoners were able to exploit the contacts they made whilst working. Despite not yet having fully recovered from the wounds he sustained at Arnhem, Bryan Willoughby, in Stalag VIIb, made sure he got onto working details sent out from the camp each day into Munich. Wearing what he described as 'the remains of a uniform', including an overcoat with deep 'loot pockets' that he had acquired he joined the queues of working prisoners that assembled each morning within the compound:

> The working parties used to go out to the station at 4 o'clock in the morning, and go 30 kms down to Munich. Munich was in an awful state, big piles of rubble everywhere. Then first time I went out I found it was tough, boring work. Most of the guards were all right. Occasionally some of our chaps would get a bit obstreperous and they'd get hit

with rifle butts. But mostly it was all very peaceful. You'd see German troops marching along, singing their Waffen SS songs, but no one took any notice of them. The whole place was in such a state nobody cared about anything. There was no hard feeling anywhere. We didn't have many feelings at all. I soon realised, as I got into the way of things, that some of the blokes were so advanced they had an entrepreneurial spirit – with the rackets. They built up a stock of stuff. Some of them used to go down to Munich on a working party, stay with a Russian woman for a couple of weeks and then come back. They didn't bother escaping. You don't read about this in the books. The way they did it was that the cattle wagons would start from Moosburg station and they'd do the count. We'd do all sorts of things to make them miscount. They would count 40 yet maybe 43 actually went. They'd just stay down in Munich, staying with their Russian women. How they had the strength to do it I don't know! Munich was a hell of a place. Maybe you'd work on the railways or on the roads – pick and shovel work, but nobody did very much. We just played at it. On one particular occasion I was emptying dustbins in the Café Leopold, a high class café. When I was down in the kitchen a woman emptied a big ladle of stew into a bowl and said '*Essen Schnell!*' So I '*essened*' schnell. I had to get the hang of this trading business. I'd bring 25 cigarettes from the camp and hang around looking out for a likely civilian – whether they were German or not I wouldn't know, they could've been any nationality. You'd get a two kilo loaf for the price of five cigarettes. You took it back to the camp and you could flog the loaf for 20 or 25 fags. So it was a clear profit of maybe 15 or 20 cigarettes.[30]

The obvious economic sense of such transactions meant few of the working prisoners failed to exploit the opportunity for trade. The only problem was that they still had to get their day's haul back into the camp, as Willoughby recalled:

You took a chance of being searched. On the way back there'd be maybe a quarter of a mile column of prisoners all shuffling along being shouted at. They'd pick out a certain group and everyone in it was searched. If you were in there you were unlucky, if you had bread you lost it. But you took that chance. But on the average you would gain.[31]

However, he soon discovered it was not just the attentions of the guards he had to worry about. Willoughby found himself in Munich carrying three 2-kilo loaves, the fruits of a trading deal with local civilians:

As luck would have it an air raid happened and we went into these catacombs. Before the raid stopped in came the Gestapo. They started searching everybody. Some people got bashed with the butt of a rifle. I was waiting and waiting, getting nearer the end. They were knocking hell out of a bloke and I got down on my hands and knees and crawled behind them. I got clean away with three loaves of bread.[32]

The trade between civilians and prisoners was not an entirely two-way process and not all of the hungry POWs had to trade cigarettes for food. There were plenty of German civilians who witnessed the suffering of the prisoners and decided to help. With Red Cross parcels failing to reach some prisoners, and employers giving them just starvation rations, some became desperate. One prisoner, housed in the cellar of the railway station where he worked, reported kindly civilians passing food to him through the barred windows. Elsewhere a Frau Gramgg helped prisoners to escape from a disciplinary camp, giving them information on patrols and passing them a compass and map. At Graz a Fraulein Kaplan risked her life to help a prisoner employed to build air raid shelters. For 16 months she gave food and cigarettes to Sidney Banner, despite being arrested and questioned three times by the Gestapo. The threat to such brave civilians was real, in Czechoslovakia Freda Wybreck was given a three-year prison sentence for helping prisoners. Such acts of selfless kindness offered by such courageous women were something few among the prisoners had ever expected, but all appreciated.

As the end of the war approached the prisoners began to look forward to more than just food as they craved the chance to meet the women in the towns and villages around their camps. They knew, or rather hoped, that if the liberating troops arrived they would be set free to enjoy themselves. At one copper mine the prisoners discussed the matter and were told by a French prisoner working alongside them that the: 'Eisleben girls are awaiting "Der tag" with pleasant anticipation. When warned that the Tommies had been separated from the fair sex for some years they replied "We are not at all anxious. Only English and Frenchmen know how to make love!"'[33] Such news helped the prisoners sustain their morale in the desperate last months of the war. Indeed, the mine was liberated without serious incident and the American troops simply passed them by and left the prisoners to explore the delights of the town. It was a peaceful end to a dangerous period in their lives – an end which would not be enjoyed by most among the workforce of POWs.

SEVEN

Danger, Disease, Decay and Death

Scenes of wanton and unnecessarily brutal treatment, sheer neglect and dying.[1]

They are now positively suffering from hunger. They are also in such a weakened condition that they cannot throw off any illness and cannot finish their work thoroughly or undertake short marches.[2]

In the aftermath of the initial period of deprivation endured by the prisoners most saw a recovery in health and living conditions that buoyed their spirits. As the Red Cross food and clothing parcels gradually helped them be restored to health and pride, life for the prisoners underwent a phenomenal change. No longer starving and dressed like tramps they could once more walk past their guards with their heads held high. Feeling more like soldiers than slaves they prepared themselves for a life of industry.

Yet as time passed, this life became increasingly uncomfortable. When a senior surgeon from the US Public Health Service visited 22 camps in 1941 he found them satisfactory with regard to food, sanitation, health and clothing. Working prisoners were receiving up to 60 per cent more food than the camp rations and there was no malnutrition. Barracks had adequate heat, light, sanitation, ventilation and drainage. It was a situation that would not last and by 1945 many of the prisoners were desperately struggling to survive. As one Red Cross inspector predicted in 1943, if the situation did not improve the prisoners would soon be completely and utterly exhausted. As food shortages and worsening living conditions reduced the prisoners to mere shadows of their former selves, they had every reason to fear an ominous future, as one prisoner later explained: 'Freud reckoned everything we do is motivated by sex. Not true – when women and food are not available there is still fear!'[3]

Although in the early war years such fears were far from the minds of most working prisoners the situation was not the same everywhere. In some work camps conditions had remained below standard right from the start of the war, with the Red Cross reporting: 'very unsatisfactory conditions in Stalag XVIIIa and in practically all its labour detachments'.[4] Many stayed clad in rags and shuffling along in clogs throughout the war and false teeth remained in short supply, as did razor blades, glasses, toothbrushes and toothpaste.

As the war continued even those who had known tolerable conditions in the early years found their situation worsening. In 1941 the men of Bau und Arbeitsbattaillon (BUA) No 20 had found themselves living in a German fort. Each member of the three work companies was given a weekly beer ration of one and a half bottles, and each man had a new battledress and boots. Ironically, in light of what would follow, their main complaints were about the poor quality of the carrots in their rations. In another camp the prisoners were even able to keep pets, with turkeys, ducks and goats all being smuggled into the camp. One prisoner even bought a horse from a local civilian but found himself unable to smuggle it past the camp guards.

Gradually conditions for BUA20 began to deteriorate. In May 1942 they moved to south-east Germany and their shifts were increased to 10 hours a day. By the end of the year they reported that medical supplies were running short and they were forced to rely on what could be supplied via the Red Cross. These shortages were exacerbated by the knowledge that some Stalags had an excess of doctors whilst few work camps had trained medical personnel and were instead left to rely on whatever assistance they were offered by the Germans. In some cases men on work detachments even had to purchase their medicines from their guards. If sick prisoners were refused a chance to return to the camps for treatment they had to keep working. For some this meant continuing to work even with open sores on their faces – something the guards could not have missed.

Soon the shortages began to bite. Boils began appearing on the bodies of men whose diets lacked many of the vitamins fresh fruit and vegetables would have given them. By early 1943 the clothing situation was starting to deteriorate. Although most still had one uniform for work and one for 'best' many pairs of trousers were beginning to wear out. In March that year they were merged with another work unit to form a camp of 1,200 men. With the drug shortages deepening the prisoners were hit by a serious outbreak of diarrhoea. The long hours of work and the lack of fresh food meant the numbers of men unfit for work also increased.

It was the lack of food that took the greatest toll on health. When potatoes were issued they were found to be poor quality. All tinned foods from Red Cross parcels were opened by the guards ensuring they had to be used immediately and could not be stored for later use. Meat in meals was often found to be as much as 40 per cent bone and the tea substitute issued by their guards was so bad most men simply discarded it. The shortages were only aggravated by the empty shelves of the camp canteen, where the prisoners had once been able to spend their weekly wages. By June 1944 they found even potatoes were off the menu, having been replaced by inedible millet and dried vegetables, usually turnip or cabbage, with little or no taste.

This gradual decline in living conditions was replicated throughout the system of Arbeitskommandos, until by 1945 many were facing the twin threats of disease and starvation. At one work detachment from Stalag XXa prisoners reported receiving meat in their meals just once every three weeks. As the food supplies got worse and the labour got heavier more men suffered. It was little wonder some work detachments had as many as 10 per cent of prisoners in hospitals at any time.

The prisoners grew to rely upon food from outside sources since the supply of Red Cross parcels was often erratic. Whilst some prisoners found parcels arrived on a regular basis others rarely saw them. At one work detachment no parcels arrived between November 1941 and March 1942, and men arriving at Fallingbostel after the capitulation of Italy had to wait for three months before parcels were issued. Others found parcels were often missing soap and chocolate, two commodities that were highly prized on the black market – something both guards and prisoners were keenly aware of. Some guards were even spotted wearing Red Cross issue shirts. At one camp the guards made searches of prisoners and allowed them to keep up to 50 cigarettes, two bars of soap and half a pound of chocolate – anything else was confiscated.

Yet despite the shortages of food some prisoners used their meagre supplies for other purposes. At Rennes in France, a group of Indian prisoners pooled their supplies of butter and cooking oil in order to cremate a fellow prisoner. As a Sikh he was obliged, under the rules of his religion, to be cremated and have his ashes scattered, but the guards refused to supply the fuel. Unable to convince the Germans of the man's religious obligations they improvised and collected enough oil to ensure the success of the cremation. They were then forced to request replacement supplies via the Red Cross. It was ironic, since the Germans were cremating millions against their will in camps throughout the Reich.

Though the harsh and deteriorating conditions of labour made life uncomfortable for the prisoners, little struck fear into their hearts more than the knowledge that they were at the mercy of their guards. The actions of many, both military and civilian, left them in little doubt their lives were constantly under threat. Many of the prisoners took chances, mocked their guards, laughed at them and refused their orders – up to a point. Until the moment was reached when continued defiance could mean but one thing – death.

They had every right to be frightened. One group of prisoners had watched as their guard killed a fellow worker – a Russian POW – with an axe. Others even saw Russian prisoners being buried alive. In the face of such violence most prisoners believed their guards could easily turn on them, despite these real fears many continued to defy their guards, attempting to get away with as little work as possible. Some were successful, their defiance meaning they were transferred away from a working party back to the Stalag. In turn some were labelled troublemakers and forbidden to go out on working parties, a sentence that saved them the physical burden of work but which condemned them to the stupefying tedium of Stalag life. The punishment for others was imprisonment. Some sentences were light – seldom more than 28 days in solitary confinement – but others were a physical and mental burden for the men. Such was the level of disobedience in some camps that offenders were keep waiting before being sent to serve sentences in the 'Bunker'. With all punishment facilities full they simply had to wait their turn.

For others the situation was more serious. One POW received a sentence of 19 months for talking to civilians, another was sentenced to two years for refusing to work, and a third was sentenced to 30 months for disobedience. For sabotage in the workplace sentences of up to eight years were passed. Conditions for men sent to prison were far worse than those endured in the Stalags. Few had access to outdoor exercise and most were held in solitary confinement. One prisoner recorded losing 2 stone in five months, having existed on a diet of bread and water for three days and with normal rations handed out just every fourth day.

They could, however, consider themselves lucky. Between January 1941 and July 1943 the Germans admitted to shooting 68 British prisoners, many of them on labour detachments. Their crimes were many and varied – some serious such as attacking guards or organising strikes, others less serious such as failing to salute German NCOs. Not all the shootings were the responsibility of Wehrmacht guards. In some work camps, in particular in the mines, the guards kept away once their charges were at work. In their place came armed overseers among the civilian staff. Although technically a breach of the Geneva Convention, which stated only soldiers could guard prisoners, many armed civilians were placed in charge of working gangs. Many among these were accused of overstepping the mark with regard to discipline. Some among the prisoners took risks with both their guards and overseers. When they considered a task too dangerous – such as working in gas-filled areas of mines – they simply refused. Sometimes they were lucky, and were able to appeal to the better nature of their guards – sometimes they were not.

The entire war was marked by the killing of working prisoners. In 1942 William Evans and John Flynn were shot at Stalag XVIIIa for refusing to work. The following year saw three men shot and killed for refusing to work on railway detachment, Bauhof II. A Private Miller on detachment from Stalag XXb was shot and killed for smoking at work and a Private Russel was shot for arguing. In early 1943 two Palestinian prisoners, on detachment from Stalag VIIIb, were even shot and killed whilst working below ground in a coal mine and a Private Kallender was killed whilst waiting for the pit cage. The same fate befell an Australian, Private Devlin, who was murdered at the Gruba Gotha mine. Another POW miner, George Strachan, was killed for arguing with a guard after arriving late for roll call. When he arrived smoking a cigarette the guard knocked it from his mouth. Strachan reacted by hitting the German, who then retaliated by lunging at him with his bayonet. The guard then called for Feldwebel Rolle who executed Strachan in cold blood.

At Auschwitz Lance Corporal Reynolds was shot and killed for refusing to climb an icy steel pylon without rubber boots and gloves, the guard who fired the shot later claimed Reynolds had been 'running away'. Gunner Thomas Crook, from Stalag XXa, was shot for trying to organise a strike. Another working prisoner, Trooper Jack Brown, was shot by a guard for walking outside the factory whilst on an official break from his nightshift, his 'crime' was that prisoners were not allowed out at night. Such was the vicious nature of some of the guards that men were shot for the most ridiculous of reasons. One of the victims was a Fusilier Rigby. His crime? Whistling on the way to work. Another unfortunate victim, Private Harry Hudson, working at a farm, was shot in his own bed after he refused to get up for early morning milking. He was taken to hospital but died there, being refused treatment since the guards were convinced he was a Russian. Another man died in the arms of his brother after having been shot by a guard, described by prisoners as a 'rabid aryan', for returning to the barrack hut rather than continue working in torrential rain, whilst at a copper mine two men were shot and killed for standing outside applauding an Allied air raid. In one particularly sad case Private Archibald Alexander was killed by a guard in May 1942. By September his unfortunate parents had still not received the news and continued to write to him enquiring why he no longer answered their letters.

A constant stream of names were sent back to London of those killed at work. Month by month the list grew – Driver Brown from New Zealand, Sergeant H. Robertson, John Marshall, Roy Jagger, Joe Gee, John Jack, Frank Curtis, Peterson, Lovett, Gould, Kerr, Young, Troy, May, Francis, Coulson, Halsell, Zassler, Bull, Slade, Weeks, Kavanagh and Cullity – all young men killed far from home whilst slaving for the enemy. From one of the worst camps, Stalag VIIIb, reports came that 28 men had been shot whilst attempting to escape. Included among them were Joseph Reid and Samuel Green at Arbeitskommando E22. After they were shot and killed their bodies were left out in the open for two days as a warning. It was a warning few could fail to heed. Not all of those shot whilst escaping were killed in cold blood. When two Palestinian Jews, Krause and Eisenberg, escaped from a working party near Katowicz in the summer of 1944 they were recaptured and brought back to the camp to show how they had escaped. They were then shot by the guards, their bodies falling at the point where they had escaped. Krause was killed immediately but Eisenberg survived the shooting, only to later die of pneumonia.

In October 1942 a group of men returning to camp from a work detail witnessed the arbitrary violence of guards. The incident arose from arguments over a guard's suitcase:

The guard was asking those in the shed to take the case back to the camp and I, amongst others, refused, walked out of the shed and made my way to the road where the others were fell in. I saw the guard carrying the case himself to the road. He placed the case down still asking the men who were near to take it and they refused. The guard was 30-35 yards from where the majority of the party was standing. [Another man continued]: Suddenly without warning a shot was fired. This took us completely by surprise and Wynne fell down saying he had been hit and Potts did not fall but said the same. I had seen nothing that in my opinion would have provoked the guard to shoot at us. Certainly nobody who had fallen in was laughing at the guard and many did not even know about the case.[5]

Christmas 1943 saw another senselessly brutal incident. At work camp E563 two soldiers, Englishman Sid Smith and Australian Douglas Burling, were shot whilst in the bathhouse of the camp. The two men were defenceless at the time of the attack and fellow POWs reported that Burling had been naked when he was shot. In another vicious attack a group of prisoners attempting to pass food through a latrine wall to a starving Russian were shot. As he reached for the food the Russian was bayoneted by the German guard who then opened fire on the prisoners when they remonstrated with him. They were lucky to all survive the attack, although a number were seriously injured.

It was not just the arbitrary nature of such violence that concerned the prisoners, some among the guards viewed POWs as expendable. In August 1944 John Hankinson, a private in the Durham Light Infantry, paid the ultimate price for defying the guards. After a fight between him and a guard Hankinson was left wounded by shots fired by another guard. Still breathing the 22-year-old was carried to a shed where his fellow prisoners expected he would be treated. To their horror another guard arrived and entered the hut. Moments later a shot was fired and the guard emerged carrying his revolver.

Such violence was extreme but it was not rare. Many prisoners experienced guards who made their lives unbearable. Some prisoners were beaten to the floor and kicked repeatedly by their guards. One man reported being struck with a rifle butt whilst in his sick bed, whilst others found bayonets and butts were frequently used to cajole them into working harder. Les Allan was working at a brewery when he was attacked by a guard:

The brewery master gave me a broom and told me to follow him. He went to open a small door, I heard someone shout to the guard. The brewery bloke had handed me a club hammer. I can only assume I must have looked at the hammer then looked at the guard longingly and he thought I was going to hit him. He got it in first. Hit me with the rifle butt. He beat me up something shocking. I got my jaw broken. It still haunts me now.[6]

The violence was something many of the prisoners grew to accept. Yet when Private Sherwood escaped from a working party few could have known the fate awaiting him. After recapture he was paraded in front of the entire camp. Then the beatings began. In front of his gathered comrades Sherwood was beaten to the ground, where the attacked continued: 'My neck hands and back were lacerated and bullet wounds which had not quite healed were broken open and bled for some time'.[7] Despite his wounds his ordeal was not over. The guards told a British sergeant to join in the beating and when he refused he too was hit with a rifle butt. The guards then dragged the private away, beating him all the time. Thrown into the coal shed he might have thought he would be left alone, once again he was wrong. Instead the assault ended in a sickening scene of humiliation: 'each German soldier of the party came in turn and either kicked me or hit me with something. These men also defecated on me'.[8]

Although his humiliation was complete it was at least over fairly quickly. He took his punishment and was then released into the comradeship of the work camp. Others suffered more enduring punishments and in some cases mental cruelty was favoured. When a Corporal Shortland attempted to refuse to work on the grounds of his rank he was immediately transferred away from his mates. His punishment, though no physical strain, was cruel. He was sent to a work camp for French prisoners where, as the only British inmate, he was alone and isolated.

Yet the threat to the safety of the working prisoners did not just come from the weapons of their enemies. The ever more frequent Allied bombing raids soon took their toll of prisoners labouring in the very enterprises the airforces were hellbent on destroying. By 1944 raids were a regular feature of life for thousands of working prisoners, in particular those at the synthetic fuel plants so vital to the war effort. Many work camps and the barracks for the labourers were built in the heart of industrial areas, leaving the prisoners exposed to attack from above. Railway yards, mines, factories, refineries – all were targets for the bomber fleets whose tactic of inaccurate saturation bombing meant both industrial enterprises and any buildings for miles around were likely victims. Between May and August that year 651 British and Commonwealth prisoners died in air raids, and a further 72 had been killed by Christmas. Ironically, included among the dead were men employed to build air raid shelters.

Such was the fear of bombing that some prisoners took direct action in an attempt to protect themselves. POW miner Alec Reynolds decided the bombing crews needed to be warned: 'I climbed out onto the top of the winding gear and hung up a white sheet with a red cross painted on it. When we were up there the Germans were shooting at us, but it was worth it. I'd seen the results of bombing. I saw the Yanks dive bombing trains, coming right down out of the sky. It was a shame, they hit a train full of schoolkids.'[9] His efforts were worthwhile and the mine was never bombed.

The worst single bombing incident was at Epinal in France where 400 Indians were killed during an air raid, whilst a raid on Aquilla in Italy killed a further 140 men. Other raids saw further larger death tolls: 36 men constructing a factory in the Sudentenland, 38 on a work detachment from Stalag VIIIb, and 56 killed and wounded at Stalag E798. A further 80 were reported missing after a raid on an I.G. Farben plant at Ludwigshafen and 24 were killed during a raid on Leipzig in February 1945. At Linz two prisoners were killed when Allied fighters strafed the site they were working at, whilst at Auschwitz it was not just the Jewish deportees and slaves who faced death and 38 British prisoners were killed during an Allied bombing raid on the factory complex. Ironically the Red Cross blamed the prisoners for having refused to enter air raid shelters, instead preferring to remain outside and watch the bombing.

Work camp E793, part of Stalag 344, was among those hit during these raids. At 12.20 on 2 December 1944 the sirens sounded, signalling the start of an hour-long raid. With the sound of heavy bombers in the skies above them the prisoners raced for the dubious cover of their shelters. As they cowered within the reinforced concrete buildings they could hear the explosions of bombs falling around them. Seven bombs fell within the camp with two hitting a single shelter in which 65 British POWs had taken cover. As their comrades rushed to their assistance they found a scene of almost indescribable horror. Twenty-eight of the occupants were dead with a further 28 seriously wounded. The 40-centimetre-thick concrete had been no match for the high explosive bomb. Most of the dead were badly mutilated. Among the wounded many had serious head injuries, limbs were smashed and two men had been badly crushed. Other bombs had flattened three barrack huts, the wash house, the clothing store and the Red Cross parcel store. Another hut had burned to the ground. Every building of the camp was either destroyed or damaged and both the water and electricity supplies were cut off. Fortunately for the prisoners only 500 of the usual 1,100 inmates were in camp at the time of the attack.

The experience of repeated bombing shattered the nerves of many prisoners, the crazed stampede for safety destroying all notion of the calm and order the Germans were so famed for. One POW died in such a stampede when he slipped and fell under the wheels of a lorry. At one camp the workers came to recognise the signal for the start of a raid – it was the sight of the factory managers fleeing the site at top speed in their cars. At one working party, loading and unloading at a sugar refinery, the prisoners were forbidden to leave their posts when the sirens sounded. Only when the planes were directly overhead were they allowed to seek sanctuary in the shelters. For prisoners at a factory in Trieben the situation was even worse, with the factory manager Herr Stillner forcing POWs to remain at work during air raids despite their guards having told them they were free to seek the sanctuary of the shelters.

Such raids were a difficult time for many. The sight and sound of Allied bombers gave them the feeling that they had not been forgotten and that the war was finally catching up with them. There was also comfort in the knowledge that the destruction caused by the raids might mean a day off work. However, there were other emotions at play. The prisoners cursed the irony of a situation where aircrew set out from Britain to destroy German industry – an industry staffed by their fellow countrymen. It was uncomfortable for them to be trapped within their camps in areas targeted by their supposed saviours. No one wanted to survive the rigours of battle only to lose their life to the attentions of their own airforce.

Men working in one factory encountered a downed pilot who gave them ominous news. Since their workplace had not yet been attacked he could guarantee it would soon become a target. He was not wrong, just days later James Witte witnessed the promised raid:

> As we ran we heard the menacing roar of hundreds of bombers. We looked up and saw the sky was black with them, so much so they almost blotted out the sun. What happened next was a blur. I ran for my life and flung myself into a ditch as the first load of bombs fell in the fields. I felt the blast travel across the ditch …. When the all clear went I struggled out of the ditch, dazed but unhurt, and still clutching my overcoat and haversack. We assembled for a roll call and found out that six lads were missing. They were blown to pieces. Somewhere nearby a woman was screaming hysterically. She had just found her husband's decapitated body. She started to rush around looking for his head.[10]

Though being out in the open during a bombing raid was a terrifying experience it could not compare to the fear felt by the men working underground. Although deep within the earth the miners could still feel the ominous rumbling of bombs that were landing a mile above them. All felt the dread of being buried alive in a pitch black tomb, unable to find a way out from the darkness, slowly dying as the air grew thin. At one Silesian mine the prisoners were trapped underground for an hour and a half after bombing had knocked out the power supply. With the electricity shut down the working prisoners relied on the dim light of their carbide lamps as they awaited their fate. When they finally climbed from the bowels of the earth most could not believe they were still alive.

They may have been shaken by the experience but there were plenty of prisoners growing desperate to seek shelter far beneath ground. The fears regarding bombing were exacerbated by the knowledge that many air raid shelters were inadequate. Frequently shelters were added as an afterthought. At one work detachment in Munich the shelters remained unfinished five months after the camp had opened. Elsewhere in the city prisoners were actually evicted from shelters during air raids by policemen and Nazi Party members. In some locations shelters were little more than trenches dug in soft, sandy soil with boards and soil laid over the top. Even the more substantial shelters were often unlit and poorly ventilated.

After the nightly fears endured during bombing raids their ordeal was not necessarily over. With so many German cities in ruins, the prisoners were a perfect source of labour to clear up the damage caused by the bombing. They were marched into towns, faced a hostile populace and began their work. Prisoners dug in the rubble in search of corpses or survivors. They collected bricks, knocking away the remains of mortar so they could be used again, and piled them high ready for the Germans to begin reconstruction. When the Allied armies arrived in the flattened towns they marvelled at how the enemy had already begun the work to raise their towns from the ashes of defeat – little did they know how much of the reconstruction work had been done by the bedraggled inmates of POW camps.

Back in London the War Office didn't object to the prisoners being employed on clearing bomb sites on the condition that the prisoners were not housed in the area at night. Yet for many the question of overnight accommodation was irrelevant. One of the greatest dangers for those clearing the rubble was the likelihood of planes returning to hit the same target in the daytime. In the latter stages of the war, with the Allied bombing fleets given almost free reign of the skies above Germany, repeat missions became frighteningly familiar. One group of prisoners, who had marched all the way from Poland, were employed to spend all day filling bomb craters only to have to repeat the task the very next day in the aftermath of a follow up raid. In spring 1945 Jim Sims was among a detachment sent to clear bomb damage at a railway station when the American bombers returned:

> We were attacked by USAF Thunderbolts straffing Uelzen station and then subjected to a raid by Flying Fortresses. We fled from the station area and it was a race between POWs, guards, women, kids and SS as to who got to the dubious shelter of some woods. We were not unduly upset by POWs killed in the raid but dead children upset us. We had some sympathy for German women and children, but it all seemed such a waste.[11]

Sims and his fellow prisoners were lucky, they escaped the attentions of both the fighters and the bombers. Others were not so fortunate. One hundred and seventeen POWs died when Allied aircraft attacked a column of prisoners evacuated from Stalag VIIIc. Among the dead were 13 Britons.

Worst of all, some prisoners were detailed to work on clearing un-exploded bombs. New Zealand prisoners held in Greece were sent on bomb disposal details and in the early war years Americans living in Berlin reported seeing British prisoners carrying bombs with delayed action fuses, taking them to explode away from built up areas. As the bombing grew increasingly heavy this type of labour increased. In the aftermath of a raid in January 1945, which had destroyed the accommodation for 300 POWs at Brux, killing nine men and severely wounding 12 more, a group of 50 POWs were sent to clear a bomb-damaged area. When they arrived they were turned back by civilians who told them there were unexploded bombs in the area, insisting it was unsafe to work. Despite the pleas the guards forced them into the area and when they refused to work they were threatened with machine guns. The message was clear, work or die. They worked. As the camp commandant later admitted, the guards were serious and would have carried out their threats.

It was not just the dangers from the guards, civilian workers and bombing that was putting a strain upon the prisoners. As early as October 1942 the Red Cross noted how prisoners' rations needed an additional 2-and-a-half kilograms of fats and milk a month to make up the required calories – and that was just for men within Stalags, those on work detachments would require even more. As the German economic resources were stretched to the limit so too were their supplies of food. With the infrastructure under constant air attack and the lands of the Reich continually shrinking, the supply of food to POWs was not a primary concern for the authorities – something the prisoners did not take long to notice. Increasingly, many prisoners found the Red Cross parcels, so vital for providing sustenance, were 'irregular and spasmodic',[12] and their arrival was never a foregone conclusion. Then as the Allies advanced through France the parcels, which had previously arrived via neutral Portugal, began to dry up. At a mine in Bourecit it was reported that no parcels were available for a period of three months over the winter of 1944-45 – instead the prisoners had to work 12 hours a day surviving solely on weak stews provided by their employers. Even as early as October 1944 the lack of Red Cross parcels at Stalag XIIa left many prisoners too weak to stand. Undernourished and starved of hope, all activity became a strain and the prisoners started fainting from hunger, with an ever-increasing number being carried off to hospital by their starving mates.

By September 1944 the Swiss government informed the British of the visit by its representatives to work detachments from Stalag IVa:

> The effects of long working hours over the past three or four years are becoming evident among British prisoners in this area. In many cases low grade fever persisting for several days with listlessness, lack of appetite and headache is seen. Boils are very prevalent. During the recent hot weather many men suffered from heat exhaustion. Gastric complaints, abdominal pains, diarrhoea and vomiting are common. It must be borne in mind that the men of this area were in A1 category when they were captured.[13]

Even colds and chills were a major feature of life in many camps since they had to keep windows open in all weathers to counteract the overcrowding within the barrack rooms. Ironically when some German doctors saw the boils suffered by working prisoners who reported sick they had a simple explanation. They blamed rich food contained within Red Cross parcels and as a result the sick men were denied the contents.

By Christmas 1944 prisoners were recording growing arguments among them over how food should be distributed. Some men simply swapped the contents of parcels for cigarettes without giving a choice to those they shared with. In these conditions the prisoners had to work hard to prevent relationships worsening between them. It was little wonder friendships were strained during this period. In March 1945 Eric Laker, working beneath the surface of a Silesian mine recorded how low the daily rations for the miners had fallen. Each day they received just 285 grammes of bread, with no margarine to spread upon it. There were few potatoes in their soup, which seemed to consist of just flour and water. Occasionally a sausage would appear in the soup. On these pitiful rations the prisoners continued to toil below ground for over 10 hours each day. At another mine it was recorded that the daily bread ration had fallen as low as one loaf between 17 men.

The treatment experienced by the growing numbers of sick varied. At work camps where a British doctor was available a simple system evolved to make life as comfortable as possible for the prisoners. The ever efficient Germans informed the doctors that only a certain percentage of men would ever be allowed to report sick. Ever ingenious the British ensured the quota was always full, regardless of whether men were really sick. Men with minor complaints were thus admitted to hospitals or confined to their beds with official backing. The only concern for the doctors was to make sure there were always beds available for the truly sick. Such systems, usually based around a rota, allowed vital periods of rest. However, as time went on prisoners were increasingly denied the luxury of avoiding work in such a manner – even if they were genuinely sick.

As the arduous work and decreasing rations took their toll, plenty of genuinely sick men were forced to keep working. Even those unfortunate men who had never fully recovered from their wounds were selected to go on work parties. One prisoner was forced down a coal mine despite having a bullet lodged in his back and another man with both shrapnel wounds and arthritis was unable to avoid labouring underground. In a work camp on the Austrian railways an Unteroffizer Lins held a revolver to the head of sick prisoners to force them out of bed and back to work. At Bad Lausick – ironically a spa town where German civilians went to recuperate – a prisoner with a badly swollen foot was punched by a guard for refusing to work. The general rule was that if a man didn't have a high temperature then he was fit enough to continue work. Such decisions were arbitrary since few had thermometers to record their temperatures and it was left to the whim of guards or foremen as to whether a man could report sick. When one prisoner with a heart condition was seen by a doctor he simply had his throat examined and was sent back to work. The commandant then put him under arrest for malingering. When the prisoner requested to see a heart specialist he was threatened with a month's imprisonment if he was found to be faking his condition. Another man who even the Germans admitted had heart disease, was put on 'light duties' only to find that meant carrying heavy machine parts around a factory.

Even with broken fingers POWs were expected to report for work, strapping their injured digits together with whatever was available. Some found their fingers becoming permanently disfigured after receiving no treatment. When one POW's hand was trapped beneath a railway sleeper he was refused treatment for hours. When finally excused from work the unfortunate soldier was taken to hospital. Even then he was unable to seek treatment since the doctors refused to see him. As a result of their obstruction the soldier lost two of his fingertips. South African prisoners at the E579 work camp reported that civilian workers interfered with the work of the medical staff. They claimed they had the right to decide who could go sick and who was fit for work. Some of those men who still attempted to report sick were punished with beatings by pistol-wielding civilians whilst others were forced to work shifts of up to 17 hours. In one case a prisoner died two days after the owner of a quarry, Herr Dumling, refused him permission to report sick.

The seriously wounded were expected to work, despite having clear evidence of their conditions. Even showing X-rays revealing lung infections and spinal damage was not enough to get one man excused, instead he was given 14 days' detention on a diet of bread and water for refusing to work. When Private Thomas Barclay fractured his spine in a fall in a coal mine he received full treatment but despite the severity of the damage he failed to pass a medical board for repatriation and remained at work until he was liberated in 1945. Even those whose wounds meant they were passed for repatriation were not always excused from labour. One group of 67 men who had been approved for repatriation to Britain were sent on a work detachment to a tobacco factory in Nordhausen, with the Germans claiming they had volunteered.

By forcing the sick to work it was little wonder the numbers of dead began to grow. Even those allowed to report sick were not always afforded suitable attention. When Sergeant Leslie Hudson reported sick with a stomach infection that made him unable to eat or relieve himself he was told the doctor would not come to him. Instead the prisoner, hardly able to walk, was forced to leave his bed and visit the doctor. When he was finally seen it was too late and he died in hospital. At many work camps medical orderlies had to carry bed-ridden prisoners for miles to visit doctors, whilst more mobile men were forced to make the journey unaided. One prisoner with a temperature of 40°C was made to walk 20 kilometres to visit a doctor and a man with pneumonia reported a march of 11 kilometres. A Private Tallis died after contracting pneumonia and pleurisy. In his weakened condition he was taken to hospital by horse and cart, a journey that lasted 5 hours. The freezing weather of January 1945 was too much for him and by the end of the journey he was dead. At an iron ore mine one prisoner showed his toes to the German doctor. He looked down at the prisoner's feet, the nails were loose and pus was seeping from beneath them, then without a word of warning he ripped the nail from the toe. When the prisoner passed out he continued his work and ripped off the remaining nail. Others reported being held down in dentists' chairs by their guards and given no anaesthetic except a spray of iced water, whilst dentists tore out their teeth. For New Zealander Stuart Cunningham the price of poor treatment was even higher. He died whilst being treated for peritonitis, the failure of the operation being blamed on the carelessness of the German doctor.

Such seemingly brutal treatment was not uncommon. The prisoners often faced doctors and dentists who had little concern for their welfare. That was not to say there were not plenty of German doctors who treated them with the utmost regard, it was just the memories of painful encounters made a lasting impression on those who suffered. When one South African showed a large, multi-headed boil to a doctor, he was forced to help with the lancing. The doctor produced a kidney dish for the unfortunate man to hold. He then proceeded to prod around with a blunt instrument until the boil finally burst, leaving the man to collect the stream of his own pus.

Rather than allow prisoners to report sick some commandants instructed prisoners to keep working and the local doctor would pay them a visit. However doctors were not always reliable with some taking up to two weeks to bother to attend sick prisoners. The delays caused by obstinate guards and doctors meant that many eventually found their health deteriorating in a manner that could have been prevented. Hospital staff noticed how patients arrived for treatment with wounds that would have easily cleared up with rapid treatment but which had instead become infected. The lack of attention soon caused a growing list of names of POWs who fell victim to disease. Among them was Robert Metcalf who died at Stalag VIIIb after contracting diphtheria and receiving no medical attention. Alongside Metcalf were men such as Private Young, an Australian who died of pneumonia whilst working as a coal miner and Privates Botfield and Mackintosh, both victims of medical neglect.

Despite the Germans forcing the POWs to keep working, the camp *lazaretts* – or hospitals – were constantly full. At the POW infirmary in Bad Lausick bedsheets were left unchanged for six weeks, whilst conditions at the 'Kopernikus Lager' of Stalag XXa were such that only surgical cases were allowed sheets on their beds. Most patients slept in bunks, had to use a pump to collect their water, and were forced to walk a hundred yards to reach the latrine, where they had to squat over an open pit. Another POW hospital was without a supply of fresh drinking water and the patients were instead forced to purchase bottles of mineral water to ensure they didn't contract illnesses from water-borne viruses. At one hospital even the operating theatre had no running water, and bandages remained in short supply despite the efforts of the Red Cross to provide them. In extreme cases conditions were so poor that rats were seen scurrying over the beds of the patients at night.

Paratrooper Bryan Willoughby was taken from the comfort of a hospital in the Netherlands to the *lazarett* at Stalag VIIa at Moosburg. He arrived in the winter of 1944 – for Willoughby and his fellow POWs it was not a season of goodwill:

> There were all sorts of nationalities in this hospital. We were in a hut next door to where they did the operations. There were a mixture of French, Yanks, Poles, Russians – you name it. The Ruskies didn't get Red Cross parcels. They used to make things like bellows and sell those for about twenty cigarettes – that was wealth! American cigarettes were currency. It was very boring but it wasn't uncomfortable. I used to make the point of going out of the hut every morning and trying to exercise because I wanted to get on my feet as quickly as possible. I didn't want to stay in there, I wanted to get in on the rackets. I used to walk about a hundred yards up and back, and talk to the Russians – all dressed in rags and trying to pick up cigarette butts. Mostly they were in there with open TB. It was very boring, we used to play cut throat games of Monopoly just for a sweet from a Red Cross parcel, but the parcels were few and far between. If they did come you'd probably get one between 12 for two weeks. You couldn't exist on German rations, they were very poor. You'd have a piece of bread and be very careful of how it was distributed. I remember one morning thirty Russians came in and they were doing amputations next door. I shouldn't say this but the only time we had meat in the pot was the day after they did all these amputations. It

made me think. I thought about it, I must admit, but we were always so hungry we just ate anything.[14]

Although camp hospitals should have been places for rest and recovery many of the sick prisoners found the behaviour of the Germans unlikely to aid the healing process. One group of men were raised from their sick beds and sent to bury the bodies of Allied airmen found at crash sites. At Fallingbostel those confined to hospital beds were forced to spend their days naked, with no pyjamas and no new clothing issued until they were discharged. New prisoners arriving at the camp hospital were ordered to hand over their own blankets and informed that whilst patients they could use just one camp issue blanket. By early 1945 the POW doctors were forced to abandon any hope of performing surgery since there was no power for the sterilising equipment. The medical staff were also forced to sign a declaration stating they had no right to state that a patient was ill. The message was clear, the German doctor could override all decisions. With this power he could condemn a sick man to return to the harsh regime of a mine or a quarry – which for some was tantamount to a death sentence. Indeed, by early 1945 some prisoners in Stalag XIb were reporting as many as seven deaths a day among the POWs. It was clear that if liberation did not come soon many of them would not live to see it.

As the war continued those engaged in heavy industrial work found the burden of their work increasing. Later enquiries by investigators from the Allied Supreme Headquarters found few, if any of the men engaged on heavy manual labour had ever received the correct rations. Where once men had put on shows and concerts they no longer had the energy: 'Christmas 1944 looked like being the blackest ever as prisoners of war. The proposed pantomime was washed out because those who were suited for leading parts just could not summon up the energy or interest.'[15]

There were plenty of prisoners who found sickness followed them throughout their captivity. For some their afflictions were no more serious than having to work without glasses – itself enough of a burden for those whose eyesight was failing – or being in need of false teeth, but for others the effects of constant deprivation pushed them to the very limit of their endurance. Canadian prisoners reported men with heart conditions brought on by being underfed, whilst hernias affected hundreds of POWs made to carry heavy weights at work. Some reported suffering from bronchitis on and off for years, whilst others complained of persistent pain from sciatica and lumbago from sleeping on cold stone floors. Ulcers became common, with one prisoner suffering from an ulcerated foot for six months, believing it to be caused by ill-fitting footwear. Even more unfortunate was the paratrooper who endured an abcess on his arm for eighteen months. Another long-suffering prisoner, Driver Stuart Silcock of the Royal Signals, found himself almost constantly suffering from cramp for a year and a half. It was a condition he attributed to the general conditions within the Stalags and work camps. Stomach ulcers and gastritis also became widespread, mostly as a result of the poor diet.

As early as 1941 medics were complaining that many of the POWs suffering from diphtheria were arriving at hospital already partially paralysed by the disease, their conditions having been aggravated by the failure of the authorities to release them for prompt treatment. By 1943 the miners of work detachment E22 were found to be suffering from various ailments. In particular many were suffering from chronic bronchitis and discharges from the ear. These ear infections, known as otitis media, were even found among men engaged in surface work since they were constantly exposed to coal dust. These infections were of such seriousness that many prisoners were expected to suffer permanent deafness, yet few ever received suitable treatment. Railway workers were also found to be prone to eye infections and inflammation caused by working conditions. Men working in some mines were found to suffer from extreme cases of athlete's foot. With their feet constantly soaked by the waters of the mine, and no way of drying either their boots or socks, they were unable to prevent the spread of infection. At one camp hospital it was calculated that a majority of men they treated had foot injuries deemed to be the result of the clogs they wore. However, the problem went much deeper and medics at one work detachment found an average of 20 men out of 400 were off sick each day with work-related complaints. Of the 136 South Africans of AK1225, 60 among them suffered from recurring bouts of malaria but found there was no quinine available for treatment. Instead they worked on as similar scenes were being played out across the Reich. The Red Cross visitors and the doctors working in the Stalags continually diagnosed ailments they blamed upon the conditions endured by the prisoners. When inspections were made of men working in a salt mine eight out of a group of 83 were found to have chronic surgical lesions. Others were found to be suffering from akylosis of the joints, osteomyelitis and lesions of the nerve plexus of the upper extremities. At other camps the inspectors found men suffering from furunculosis and other skin diseases caused by a lack of vitamins in the diet. The list of medical problems resulting from the conditions endured by the prisoners grew: weight loss, muscle atrophy, oedema, cheiloses, night blindness, muscle tenderness. With many of the POWs lying in their bunks scratching lice covered bodies night after night hyperkeratosis was also noticed. This was a chronic thickening of the outer layers of skin in which the normal skin markings became prominent. It most commonly results from scratching or rubbing – something many among them were familiar with. Other POWs, examined by doctors after liberation, were found to have loose, flabby skin, or rough skin, much of which was peeling. Pellagrous stomatitis was also noticed, where the tongue becomes raw and swollen, causing excessive salivation. In later stages of the condition the surface of the tongue became smooth and pink but could also be cracked. The men found their tongues becoming sensitive making them unable to eat hot foods, and even smoking caused pain. Others suffered from nocturnal polyuria, a complaint resulting in them passing large amounts of urine during the night, caused by the altered secretion of hormones controlling urine production. Yet for the men suffering from these ailments, it was not the unfamiliar names and detailed diagnosis that mattered – all they cared about was whether they would ever be free to recover.

With increasing levels of disease and deprivation recovery times for those taken sick began to increase. This was due to 'a general state of fatigue'[16] and the fact that few among the prisoners had previously been used to such heavy work. For some of those employed in excessively heavy labour the sickness noticed had the potential for causing serious long-term damage. An Indian doctor working at Reserve Lazarett Elsterhorst, and mainly treating prisoners employed in mining, noted as early as 1942 how he was encountering increasing levels of heart trouble among his patients. This he put down to 'overworking and nervous strain'[17] among the men, many of whom were unsuited to heavy manual labour.

Those suffering work-related injuries or sickness had plenty on their minds. Not only was their health of concern, they also found their wages being docked by their employers. For three days they were forced to pay their own board and lodging to compensate their employer for the loss of labour. Some workers even found they had to provide the food for their mates who had fallen sick. As soup or stew was dished out a portion was removed to represent the number of men taken sick. It was an extreme example of the 'no work, no pay' rule, under which all suffered. In the later stages of the war any such loss of food or wages to buy extra food put an incredible strain on the physical welfare of the prisoners. In the worsening conditions it was no wonder TB began to make an appearance, as did typhus. As early as 1942 one of the worst camps, Stalag VIIIb, had to be quarantined after an outbreak of typhus. Though the POWs came through the outbreak without serious infection the same would not be said two years later.

As their health failed there were obvious and widespread physical manifestations. Weight loss was noticeable to all but for many there was worse to come, as one recalled: 'Living conditions were not that pleasant. We all got ulcers on our legs. I've seen men with ulcers the size of a fist, and deep to the bone. And all they used to give us was charcoal and paper bandages – like toilet paper. Some of them were terrible. It came from the lice. I can remember looking under my arm and it was full of lice. Even now I'm still frightened of getting ulcers.'[18]

There was a staggering change in appearance of those at work details. With their ragged uniforms and increasingly thin bodies many looked less like soldiers than they had during the early years of captivity. With shortages of razor blades they went unshaven for long periods. Fortunately, many among them found that as they reduced how often they shaved their facial hair began to grow more slowly, but that was not the case on top of their heads. Since barber's tools were seldom available many took to wearing their hair long, as one NCO reported: 'all his men look like poets with their long hair'.[19]

By late 1944 the British government had recognised the changes endured by the working prisoners. It was clear the relatively comfortable conditions of the early war years had been swept away. Just as the war itself was becoming increasingly ferocious, so too was the treatment meted out to the men behind the wire. One group of 682 prisoners were found to be housed in a single room just 58 by 62 feet. As the Foreign Office informed the Swiss government in December:

In the opinion of His Majesty's government it is intolerable that prisoners of war should thus be worked as slaves without regard to their health, which in consequence of this treatment and the meagre rations and inadequate medical facilities supplied by the German authorities has in many cases deteriorated to a marked degree. Such treatment is entirely contrary to the spirit and terms of the Geneva Convention.[20]

It was not just their physical welfare that was threatened, some prisoners began to suffer mental deterioration as the long years of captivity continued with no hope of release in the foreseeable future. It was easy to see why the prisoners should be struck by despair. They were working long hours in boringly repetitive labour. Their bodies were exhausted yet they had little time to themselves to rest and recover. And hanging over them was a sense of dread that this might continue forever. With the fear that the Germans might win the war quickly many had been sustained by the knowledge they might be released soon. But as the months, then years, of war dragged on there seemed no prospect of freedom. There was a fear that a stalemate might be reached where the war stopped but no settlement was reached. In such circumstances might they be left to rot, eternal slaves to Hitler's dream of European domination?

Even when it became clear the once mighty German military and economic machine was crumbling it was not clear to the prisoners that their fate was secure. Their treatment had shown they were expendable and that the Germans might hold them as hostages, bartering their lives in exchange for freedom for the Nazi elite. Ken Wilats found some of the thoughts that entered his head were depressing:

When you are sitting on a farm in East Prussia and your home is in Elmfield Way, Balham, you cannot possibly see what events could take place to remove you from this little hamlet back to the hustle and bustle of London, SW12. You couldn't imagine how that could come about. It seemed impossible that you would one day be back in normal life. So that was daunting. One realised that if Germany did win the war you'd be there for many, many years. That was a very real thought. I suppose we were optimistic enough to realise that in the end England would win the war. But morale went up and down. One of the most dev-astating photographs I saw was in the propaganda newspaper. It showed a German officer talking to an English policeman in Jersey. We couldn't believe it. But once you'd determined the war was going to be over by Christmas – every Christmas – you were all right. There was no point thinking anything else. It could drive you mad, you'd torture yourself. Quite honestly it was good to work. We were doing physical work from dawn till dusk. So at night you didn't have time to think about anything except playing a game of cards, reading a book and going to sleep.[21]

The notion that life was passing them by was one that played on the minds of many prisoners. They read letters about children being born or people dying but had no real connection with that world. Yet some

POWs learned many new skills whilst employed on farms including learning Polish phrases to control horses ploughing, 'Ho-com' to move forward and 'Ha-com' to turn right. (Red Cross)

As the years passed, those men employed on farms established close relationships with local families. These men are harvesting crops alongside German women and children. (Red Cross)

Forestry work was heavy and tiring for the prisoners, but at least they worked in the fresh air. The outdoor life was popular with those who had previously worked in mines and factories. (Red Cross)

Harvest time saw many prisoners working from sunrise to sunset, in all conditions, to ensure the crops could be gathered. Most prisoners employed on farms soon realised their work changed with the seasons but seldom stopped except in the depth of winter. (Red Cross)

Above: In spring 1945 prisoners in Stalag XIb at Fallingbostel were forced to break up their huts for firewood. These South African prisoners were captured at Tobruk. (Imperial War Museum BU 3867)

Below: As prisoners were evacuated westwards many camps became overcrowded, forcing the men to be housed within hastily erected tents like these at Langwasser near Nuremberg. (National Archive)

Above: In the latter stages of the war conditions within the Stalags and work camps deteriorated as more and more prisoners were crammed 'behind the wire'. Many latrines likes these ones, were left overflowing for weeks on end. (National Archive)

Above: By the time the camps were liberated many prisoners were suffering from malnutrition. This man, Private Buchanan from Glasgow, was liberated at Stalag XIb in April 1945. (Imperial War Museum BU 3866)

Right: This emaciated torso belonged to Guardsman Thompson of Palmers Green in North London, also liberated at Stalag XIb. (Imperial War Museum BU 4086)

Below: Starvation and disease were not the only dangers faced by the prisoners. This mass POW funeral was for the victims of an Allied bombing raid on a factory at Brux in the Sudetenland where hundreds of prisoners were employed. (Red Cross)

were faced with additional burdens. The regular soldiers among them were tormented by the knowledge that whilst they languished behind the wire other people were taking their place. NCOs realised they were missing out on promotion to men who probably never wanted to be soldiers. It was vexing to know they would eventually be released into an army where reluctant 'civilian soldiers' would be the ones giving them orders. They felt cursed by POW status, as if it would forever be a black mark against them. Not only that but they were missing out on the war they had always trained to fight. Sergeant Liddell, a Canadian of the Essex-Scottish Rifles, wrote of how imprisonment had impacted on his career. He was particularly bitter that whilst in battle he had led his platoon after his officers were all killed, yet felt he would be viewed as a failure: 'I was hit and taken prisoner. My officers were killed. My career in the army is finished and nobody gives a damn.'[22]

As some prisoners fought to contain their disillusionment most adopted their own ways of coping with the pressures, both consciously and unconsciously. Most chose to settle into their work, much as they would as civilians, and concentrate on living as normally as possible. Adjusting to the conditions they simply got on with life, as one recalled: 'It was just all mates together, talking about what we'd done at work. No worries about anything else. Everyone seemed to be the same. The outside world didn't matter. Like being at home with more restrictions. We knew we'd be liberated one day, especially when we could see our planes coming over every day.'[23] In the minds of many was understanding that war was an awful business, but at least a work camp was safer than the front line, as one miner recalled: 'I was there, I knew nothing could change it. You do what you can to make the best of it. You've got to realise I'd done three and a half years in the desert. And that was worse than going down the pit. It was boiling during the day and freezing at night. So going into the working camp was more comfortable. The only problem was the lack of freedom.'[24]

Whilst most buckled down to a life of heavy labour, albeit reluctantly, others chose to move around as much as possible, contriving to make sure they were transferred as often as possible. Such men went from working party back to Stalag and then onto another working party, on a regular basis. They became known as 'Cook's Tourists' after the famous British travel agent, Thomas Cook. The frequent changes meant they were constantly faced with new challenges, never staying in one place long enough to stagnate, always looking for new experiences that would help keep their minds active.

In light of the emotional pressures of captivity the minds of some were thrown into turmoil. One of those who suffered a nervous breakdown traced the roots of his condition to having been forced to work as a weaver despite having poor eyesight and having had his glasses confiscated by the enemy. Madness seized the minds of some prisoners to the extent they were committed to asylums. One Polish hospital housed 11 British prisoners from Stalag XXa, mostly schizophrenics. Among the behaviour exhibited when Red Cross inspectors visited them was a man suffering hallucinations, open homosexuality, a man 'seized with frenzy' and another simply described as 'silly'. At one camp a prisoner took a cowboy costume from the camp theatre and wore it continuously, convinced he was a sheriff. A Canadian prisoner had to be committed to a psychiatric ward after his divorce papers came through from his wife. In his desperation he became an alcoholic, over-indulging himself with wickedly strong home-brewed alcohol. Such was his desperate condition he was repatriated to Canada. Fortunately he was able to make a full recovery after his return home. John Gambarill, a New Zealander, was not so fortunate. He had remained in the Stalag at Lamsdorf despite suffering from psychiatric problems. In his confusion the unfortunate prisoner crossed the warning wire around the perimeter fence and was shot dead by a guard.

Although only a handful of the POWs succumbed to the pressures of captivity in such a way, all among them experienced a degree of mental strain whilst working for the enemy – it was simply that most were able to cope with it. Their morale was constantly assailed by the rumours that surged through the camps. These rumours took all forms, some true some false, and seemed to cover every subject, from everyday concerns about the arrival of Red Cross parcels to news regarding Allied victories or defeats. In the middle years of the war one prisoner noted down the various stories doing the rounds within his workplace. They heard how the British and Americans had supposedly landed in France, long before the planning for D-Day had even started. Finland was rumoured to have swapped sides and the Swedes and Turks had supposedly joined the Allied cause. Other stories included peace talks between the warring factions to allow the Germans to fight Russia unhindered and that Churchill had resigned with Anthony Eden taking his place.

One of the most common causes of falling morale and emotional upset was the effect of the prisoners' separation from their loved ones. Men who missed their wives were particularly touched by their enforced captivity, second only to those men whose wives requested divorces or whose girlfriends broke off relationships. This was one of the greatest blows a prisoner could face. Some men tried to make light of it, posting their 'Dear John' letters on noticeboards or forming themselves into 'Broken Hearts Clubs'. Yet others were unable to face the situation and grew embittered, assailing their mates with promises of what they would do to their wife's lover when they finally got home.

The burden of lovesick prisoners was one that was sometimes shared by all within a working party. Gordon Barber, on an agricultural detachment from Stalag XXb, shared accommodation with a man who was unable to handle the rigours of captivity:

> One chap went stir crazy. This quiet young bloke Phipps, he said to me 'I've fallen in love'. Then one night when we were all asleep, all of a sudden we heard this voice singing. It sounded lovely. He was singing a song called 'Rosemarie', the name of this local girl. It was uncanny, it frightened us. What the fucking hell was going on? All night he stood by the window holding the bars, gazing into the darkness and singing about his lover. My mate Ken went up to him and said 'What's wrong?' He said 'I love her. I don't care what the guards say I'm going to see her tonight.' He'd gone. He'd flipped. All you could see were fag ends burning. None of us could handle it. Next morning he wouldn't go to work. We saw him with his hands through the barbed wire. The guards said they'd shoot him. We said 'You can't shoot him, he's gone crazy'. So 'Dixie' Dean walks over, says 'Phipper, you've got to go'. Then hits him and knocks him straight out. We carried him to the fields, but he was useless. When the sergeant in charge of us came round they took him away. He got sent home.[25]

Not all were so lucky as to have the help of mates to protect them. Some were transferred around the system of work camps and Stalags at random, staying in one camp for a few weeks before being moved on. Others spent years working alongside the same men, getting to know every small detail about their fellow prisoners. For some of those who were separated from their friends it was a burden not to have anyone to support them. In one camp a soldier was seen to go 'crazy' and was noticed constantly talking about his wife. To the surprise of his fellow prisoners he began to miss his meals, a sure sign something had to be seriously wrong. Eventually he tried to break out of camp. The next morning he was found hanging from the perimeter wire, unconscious but alive. He'd been shot by the guards who simply left him to die. Barely alive, he was taken to hospital where, although, he recovered from his wounds, his mind failed to recover. The sad man was returned to the Stalag where he was spotted wandering around the camp, eating soap and sand.

Some among the prisoners, though not losing their minds completely, took extreme measures to avoid work. A few were able to outwit the guards and doctors by giving themselves the appearance of being sick. Silver paper was chewed and swallowed in the hope that it would show as an ulcer on an X-ray. One prisoner feigned a heart condition by holding his breath for as long as possible just before doctors were due to examine him. This got his heart racing and earned him a certificate to say he was exempt from work. Others went even further, smoking a combination of tea leaves and crushed saccharine to ensure their hearts would race prior to any examination. Those unable to pull off such scams sometimes became so desperate that they inflicted wounds upon themselves, preferring the humdrum life of Stalags and hospitals to the never ending toil of the Arbeitskommandos. Some deliberately infected wounds by rubbing dirt into them, causing them to fester and swell. Others placed their fingers on railway lines allowing them to be crushed and forcing amputation. Deep within the mines prisoners deliberately placed their arms between pit wagons then got their mates to push the wagons together, ensuring fractured bones. For those too squeamish to self harm there were always individuals willing to help. At one camp an Australian prisoner was paid by his co-workers to inflict injuries. This he did by removing the leg from a stool and using it to crush the fingers of his willing victim. Possibly the most unusual ruse used to avoid work was perpetrated by a prisoner at a mine. He claimed his foreskin was causing him intense pain and was able to trick the doctors into returning him to the hospital at his Stalag to be circumcised.

Many who despaired became known as 'sackhounds', men who spent any spare time in their bunks. They could raise no enthusiasm for any aspects of life except to do the absolute minimum. They worked, collected food and attended roll calls, then for the rest of their time they kept themselves to themselves, sinking into the enforced apathy of captivity. Some among the 'sackhounds' eventually crossed into a state of madness. In one camp a South African was found lying on his bunk with his blankets pulled up to his chin. When his comrades pulled back the blankets they found he had slashed open his forearms in a suicide bid. He was fortunately saved by the camp doctors.

Yet such extreme acts were in a minority and the majority of prisoners were able to maintain a certain level of morale. When the Canadian army made assessments of wounded men captured at Dieppe and repatriated from POW camps in 1944 they saw few signs of 'Stalag mentality' and reported on how they felt their men had adapted well to life in the camps: 'They had organised themselves to resist the Nazis in the Stalags and had united together with the object of making the best of conditions as they found them. By these means they had maintained their sanity and balance.' As a result two years in captivity: 'did not seem to have affected their mental health to any noticeable degree, although it may have left marks which will only reveal themselves at a later date'.[26] When reporting on why the Canadians had not been shown signs of 'brooding introspection' Lieutenant Chas Counsell wrote: 'Canadians don't like to stick around reading books and arguing all the time; they like to get out and play a game of ball. That is what we used to do in the camps.'[27]

Yet despite this optimism the study of the returning Canadians also revealed some pertinent points about the men left behind in the Stalags. The Canadian troops, who were mostly young, noted how many of the older men in the camps were suffering: 'Most men report four years of imprisonment is seriously affecting the sanity of British prisoners.'[28] The Canadians also curiously reported how anti-semitism seemed to be on the rise among British, Australian and New Zealand POWs, and how there was an increasing tendency for the men to openly criticise both their allies and their own military leaders. Such was the strength of opinion that the prisoners were suffering from the effects of incarceration, that one Canadian colonel noted in the report that those who had been prisoners for four or five years were more deserving of repatriation than those wounded men who had been captured more recently. In his opinion their mental state meant they were more desperate. Les Allan, who arrived at Stalag XIb in Fallingbostel in the final weeks of the war, recalled the attitudes of many of his fellow prisoners in the camp: 'By this time – the 1940 ones had been prisoners for five years. They'd got used to it, they never knew any different. If a guard beat up somebody they immediately thought the prisoner must have done something wrong. They were what we called, "Stalag Happy". The hunger and the filth – they just accepted it.'[29]

As the Canadians had noted, some prisoners seemed inspired by adversity and made the most of appalling conditions. As one expressed it: 'I would say that thanks to the Red Cross, life as a POW in a working camp, although definitely not a pleasure is at least bearable.'[30] Those whose spirit was not broken examined the world they lived in. One POW focused on world economics and how it played its part in the turmoil of the 1930s in the lead up to war. Though his words concerned the lessons of the past he might have been talking of his own life when he wrote: 'Is this the ideal of life? Is this civilisation? This progess? Or is it rather the hastening of decay? The encroachment of the Dark Age against which we must all fight, the oozing of the slime that would engulf us all and drive us back into the dark and gloom from which we have emerged.'[31]

The 'slime' engulfing the prisoners was war itself, but on a day to day basis it translated to the complete uncertainty of their continued existence:

> This camp is our world: for the time being anyway, and events which would seem insignificant to an outsider are of paramount importance to us. We have no parallel case whatsoever; some comparison of this life might be made with a boarding school, a monastery, a civilian prison, but in these cases there is contact with outside society, time limits and so on.[32]

One particular group felt the pressures of POW life in a manner experienced by few others. The 'Irishmen' assembled into a segregated Arbeitskommando at Friesack had difficulty maintaining morale. Although their living and working conditions remained good it was the psychological rather than physical pressures that vexed them, due in no small part to the fact that the camp population remained static for three years. None had been able to leave and no new men had arrived causing a stagnation that became the breeding ground for tensions and conflicts among the inmates. In most camps the population was constantly shifting, yet at Friesack they were trapped. By spring 1944 most hated the sight of each other. They knew every irritating detail about everyone else and the same conversations were repeated on a daily basis. With no fresh news from outside and no real source of rumours their life had grown stale. In the words of their 'Man of Confidence', Private Morgan Ferries: 'We have all we want yet we are an unhappy crowd.'[33] It was little wonder many among them admitted they would prefer to be transferred to a coal mine rather than remain trapped within the stupefying confines of Arbeitskommando 961.

That most prisoners managed to keep their spirits up was based around certain aspects of their life. As long as they had regular mail, food and cigarettes they could endure almost anything. It was only when these things stopped that a growing sense of despair clutched their hearts. Such was the regard for mail that complaints about the lack of concern for their correspondence led to the dismissal of the 'Man of Confidence' at Stalag IXc. Mail deliveries, in both directions, were often fitful, with post being unknown for weeks or months on end and then sometimes suddenly arriving all at once. By the summer of 1944 men at an Arbeitskommando in Leipzig reported they had only been allowed to write home once in four months, whilst others found they had still not received parcels posted to them two years earlier. One group of Australians were forced to endure a lonely Christmas when parcels sent from home failed to arrive. By March the following year the parcels had still not reached them. For men who found that regular mail was their only contact with the outside world the lack of it was intolerable. Letters came referring to the contents of previous letters that had never arrived, leaving the recipients confused as to the mysterious news they had missed.

The situation was complicated by German rules. Few among the Australians realised their letters could be sent by airmail for a fee of 40 pfennigs. Instead they continued to send letters by sea. Men from across the Empire were frustrated by the German insistence that only letters written in English could be passed by their censors, thus POWs from families unable to write the language were tormented by never receiving news from home. For all prisoners there was one very real emotion at play. Without the chance to prove to their families that they were alive there grew very real doubts in the minds of all those not receiving mail. It seemed they were just existing, rather than actually living. Indeed, with no parcels coming from the Red Cross it seemed they had been forgotten, and with no facilities for recreation the prisoners felt they could do nothing worthwhile with their lives. As one man wrote in a poem composed whilst in captivity: 'The skies may be grey, but to me they seem blue, when there's a letter from you.'[34] Despite the uplifting of emotion enjoyed by most prisoners upon the arrival of mail, not all felt the same. For some there was the feeling that mail was simply a painful reminder of the outside world – something some felt they would never see again.

Another factor that helped maintain morale was the existence of illicit wireless sets. Usually swapped for Red Cross food and kept carefully hidden from the guards, the sets were used to tune into news reports about the progress of the war. This allowed the men to work out the truth behind the propaganda they heard from official German sources. Although few radios were available in the early years of the war – when

most of the news was bad and could be heard from the constant influx of new prisoners – from late 1942 onwards the prisoners heard all
the details of the Allied advances which convinced them that salvation
would eventually come.

Another concern for some POWs was the access, or lack of it, to religious facilities. Again facilities varied from place to place. For some regular church services were available, usually conducted by captive army
chaplains. Others found lay preachers among their fellow inmates, or
simply found someone prepared to read prayers and lead hymn singing.
For those in the smaller work detachments any such religious facilities
were haphazard. In areas with large populations of French workers the
Catholics among the prisoners were able to attend services.

Those of other faiths were often left to their own devices. The many
faiths embraced by those from the British Empire were all found within
the camps. Every conceivable Christian denomination from the British
Isles – from the mighty Anglican church down to the smallest Baptist
sect, from the pomp of Catholicism to the austerity of the Presbyterians
– were found. And that was before those of other faiths: the Moslems,
Sikhs and Hindus of India, the Jews of both Britain and Palestine, the
Orthodox Cypriots, Calvinists from South Africa – all formed their own
congregations and prayer groups. Despite Nazi claims of European su-
periority, the Germans were surprisingly tolerant towards the religious
groups. Muslim prisoners at work camps were even given Fridays off
work in order to practise their faith, instead working on Sundays whilst
the Christians were at rest. One camp commandant even admitted that
he would happily have allowed them their own imam except for one
small problem: 'we have not yet caught any Mohammedan priests'.[35]

Even when chaplains were available their efforts to attend to the
needs of 'their flocks' were often frustrated by restrictions on their
movements. At Stalag XIa the chaplain found he was unable to make
visits to many of the distant working camps since he was forbidden to
make overnight stays. Furthermore the few available chaplains were unable to perform services at working parties each Sunday since the camps
were often spread out across a wide area. Maybe a few could be fitted
in during the one day of rest but for plenty of the prisoners there was
simply no access to religious services.

For the average prisoner the notion of religion was no more or less
important than it had been in civilian life. Most among them displayed
a *laissez faire* attitude towards both God and the views of the strong
believers. One prisoner recalled the feelings shared by him and his fel-

low POWs:

> Remember we had padres who prayed for our success in battle and the
> Germans wore a belt buckle with the words '*Gott Mitt Uns*' – 'God
> With Us' – in the middle. So God was in a bit of a dilemma if he was on
> both sides. There wasn't much religion in the camps. There was one hut
> each Sunday given over to religion, I think it was one of the Salvationist
> groups. The Germans allowed the hut to be comfortably warm – so that
> guaranteed a good turn out. So we sat and sang the hymns, but it wasn't
> a very deep religious conviction. It was just a chance to keep warm and
> that there wasn't a lot else to do.[36]

Of course, the attitudes towards religion varied between the men, with
plenty finding religion as others abandoned it. Some were buoyed by
the thought of a divine force that would eventually offer them salvation
from their living hell. Others simply felt abandoned by God and rejected
any notion of divinity. One man later recalled that as he sat reading his
bible some among his fellow POWs would call out to him 'Where's your
God now?'[37] It was little wonder that as the men suffered the agonies of
the long march westwards many prisoners retained their bibles as their
only possession, whilst others simply abandoned them in the snow.

The psychological pressures of captivity were increased by the
knowledge that since they were being treated as slaves they could easily be disposed of. Nearly every prisoner had experienced ill treatment,
starvation and cruelty at some point since their capture. Most had seen
the cruel treatment of Russian prisoners, with many having witnessed
executions of those no longer fit enough to be of use. Some had witnessed the arbitrary murder of concentration camp inmates and slave
labourers. All knew stories of men who had been shot whilst escaping
or who had been beaten or killed for refusing to work. By the winter of
1945 hunger was the norm as disease, deprivation and death became
the men's constant companions. With their bodies growing weaker and
labour becoming an increasing burden, few did not consider the future
– and in minds of many the approaching end to the war might herald
the moment they were considered expendable.

These real fears were not unfounded and with increasing chaos in
the crumbling Reich some of the labourers fell victim to defiant Nazis.
In February 1945 600 British POWs from the E393 work camp in Upper
Silesia were reported killed at Ratibor in an attack by an SS unit. They
were being marched away from the advancing Red Army when the Ger-

man unit struck the multinational column. In total around 2,000 men were reported dead. Only those inhabitants who had been too sick to join the march survived the atrocity and they later saw the carnage left in the aftermath. The road was littered with the bloodstained corpses of Russian and British POWs – men who thought they were being safely evacuated but who were left to an anonymous death on a foreign roadside. The attack was an ominous portent for what might happen in those final months of war.

EIGHT

The Column of the Damned

'We walked … and we walked … and we walked…'[1]

Starving, clad in rags, frozen to the very bone – a vast wave of humanity shuffled along the roads of eastern Europe in early 1945. Sick with fear, thick with lice and ravaged by dysentery, these miserable hordes were herded along frozen roads, some in small groups others in seemingly never ending columns, all heading for an unknown destination somewhere in the heart of the Reich. Bodies lay by the roadside. Some, too tired to move another yard, had been shot by their guards. Others were dead from starvation. Disease and deprivation were the daily realities, liberation a distant dream and survival an almost unimaginable concept.

Among this tide of misery were concentration camp inmates, slave labourers and the POWs of all the Allied nations. They shared the roads with retreating German soldiers and civilians fleeing the revenge they knew would come from the advancing Red Army. For the prisoners, many of whom had spent years slaving in the fields and factories of the Reich, this would be their greatest hurdle on the road to liberation. It was a hurdle that hundreds, possibly thousands, failed to cross.

For those men who had spent as many as five years labouring for the enemy the news that they would be moved westwards was no surprise. Most were aware of the progress of the war and once they could hear the Russian artillery in the distance they knew their lives would soon be changing. What would happen to them none could tell. They had heard plenty of rumours which plagued the lives of the prisoners throughout those final desperate months of war. They heard of camps where the SS had departed only after throwing hand grenades into each hut, or the mine where working parties of POWs were deliberately trapped below ground. True or false, such stories weighed heavily on their minds. Would they be left behind to be liberated by the Red Army? Would they be marched back into Germany and held hostage by Nazi leaders desperate to do a deal to save their own necks? Or would they simply be executed as no longer being of any value to the Reich? It was a question that hung over many POWs that Christmas – would the New Year be a time of hope or of despair? It was also a question that many would never live to see answered.

When the news came that they would be evacuated westwards a sense of relief swept through the work detachments and Stalags. Few expected the journey to be easy, most had made the same trip in the opposite direction back in the summer of 1940 and knew a repeat performance in the depths of winter would be a terrible experience.

Before the massed marches could begin, the men on work detachments had to return to their parent Stalags. In early 1945 prisoners at farms and factories across eastern areas of the Reich began to leave the camps that had been their homes for years. Les Allan was working near Königsberg in East Prussia when the command came to depart. It was an unexpected order that would cause Allan much misery in the months that followed:

In those days you conserved your clothing as much as possible. In the barracks you walked around in your clogs, never your leather boots. You saved them, you never knew when you were really going to need them. The temperature was 25 degrees below zero for much of the time. To be in that temperature is hard enough even if you are well dressed. If you were called for work you put on your boots, but often they had these *Appells* – roll calls – in the middle of the night. It was just to check none of us had run off, mind you who's going to escape when it's 25 degrees below? So at night you just put on what you needed, you wouldn't put your leather boots on, so you left them at your bunk – they wouldn't be stolen because they had your name on them. But you took all your bits of food and anything you prized. I had a chess set, so I put that under my coat. We would never mess them about, we just wanted to get back inside. But on one night it was different. We went outside and we were surrounded by front line Wehrmacht troops. They just marched us out of the gates and away. So I just had a pair of wooden clogs, a British uniform the Red Cross had issued to me, and an army overcoat. I had no hat. We headed off along the Baltic coast and walked for 600 miles. No one has ever disclosed how many people died on those marches.[2]

The suddenness of their departure, that left Allan and many of his fellow prisoners wearing just clogs upon their feet, meant they faced an immediate difficulty. For Allan his situation worsened when he slipped on the ice and fractured his ankle. With no treatment available he was forced to keep walking. He and all the men in the columns knew they had no choice – it was march or die.

Gordon Barber was on a working party at Adlesbruck when he got the news:

All of a sudden the guard came along and said we'd all got to move. We could already hear the Russian guns, we worried about that because we didn't want them to get us. We'd heard so many atrocity stories about them. They didn't care if you were their friend or enemy – if you were in their way they'd shoot you. On 3 January we marched out. When we came out it was cold, really cold – I'll tell you what you couldn't dig a spade into the ground. You couldn't dig with a bulldozer, the frost was so deep. We didn't have much clothing, just what we were wearing. I still had the French overcoat I'd kept since 1940. I had a British army cap and a big balaclava my mother had sent me. It covered my face, I'd have done as a bank robber. And it was warm. We had blankets round our shoulders. I still had a pair of boots. That was the good thing about the Red Cross, you might have to wait six months but you got it in the end. As we left there were five of us – Ken Wilats, Frank Turton from Nottingham, Stevie from Devon, Lofty Griggs from London and myself. We said we'd stick together but if one of us went sick we'd share everything out. We'd been together three years so we knew who we could trust. When we knew we were going, and had a few days to get our gear together, we made a great big knapsack and put all our food in it. I said I'd carry it since I was the strongest. Lofty carried all the utensils, the rest was spread out. They'd made two bleedin' big straps and they lifted it up onto my shoulders.[3]

With the homemade knapsack on his bag Barber and his mates, along with the rest of their detachment, began the long march back towards the heart of Germany. At the same time all across eastern areas of the Reich small work detachments were converging on the Stalags where they would assemble ready to begin the final march. After an overnight march through the snow Barber and his mates made their first stop, at Stalag XXb in Marienburg – the camp from which they had been detailed to farm work three years earlier. Even in the early war years, whilst many of the inhabitants had been out at work, the inmates had complained of overcrowding. Barber and his mates soon realised they were not the only men returning to the vast camp:

> We walked about 15 miles to the Stalag. It was solid, you couldn't move for blokes. You went in these big huts and there were thousands of us. It was cold and damp, there was snow everywhere. I remember distinctly, there was a little jazz band in the corner playing the 'Okey Cokey'. They were dancing, it was ' the end of the war is nearly in sight', and all that bollocks. The Red Cross hut was being emptied so we all dived out to get parcels.[4]

His mate Ken Wilats remembered: 'It was frightful, bulging at the seams. Absolutely terrible. We found a space in the washroom and kipped down in there. There was no proper accommodation.'[5]

As thousands of prisoners tried to get parcels Barber and Wilats decided to try to get extra parcels from another source, the French Red Cross parcel store:

> I said to him 'I've got a French overcoat and you've got a French hat. And you speak French' – because he was a chef. I said 'Let's go down there, and when they're throwing them out we'll get one.' I was stupid, I told him to shout out in French. They're throwing them out and everyone was grabbing them, pulling them off each other. All of a sudden I got this big box and I shouted out 'Ken, I've got one!' I realised what I'd done and I had all these Frenchmen around me, but they were way too slow – I'd gone. I knocked them out of the way. I didn't get a kicking that time, they weren't expecting a Brit to be there. Ken said to me afterwards 'What a prat! Why didn't you keep your mouth shut?' Well, I wanted to let him know not to try to catch one. Well he was a nice bloke, he couldn't have caught a cold.[6]

Similar scenes were played out in POW camps throughout the region. Rumours flew that the moment for departure had come, only to become outdated as soon as a new one began to do the rounds. Announcements were made by the guards, only to be cancelled or superseded by new instructions. The camps were awash with conflicting reports of departure times. Responding to the confusion some men simply lay down and rested, conserving their energy for the moment it would finally be needed. Others worked frantically – mending clothes, repairing boots, swapping their possessions for food, cooking meat and preparing bundles of firewood. Others squatted on the floor hammering at empty food tins, shaping them into small stoves that could be carried in their haversacks. Some fashioned small sledges and trailers upon which to carry their meagre possessions. A few men took sacks of straw with them, in which to put their legs at night, hoping the straw would insulate them from the cold. Many among the prisoners began sorting through the things they'd acquired over years of captivity, deciding what to take and what had to be left behind. Books that had been read, loaned out, reread and carefully hoarded were burnt on fires. Spare clothes were swapped for food and cigarettes were exchanged for boots. Men without haversacks improvised by sewing up the bottoms of spare shirts, stuffing them full of food and tying the arms around their necks. Others bundled up tins of food inside blankets and swung them over their shoulders. Some were left in tears as they abandoned things that had meant so much to them, others packaged together every last item and attempted to carry them away to safety. For many their lives were changing just as drastically as they had on the day they had been captured. Once more they were heading out into the chaos of the unknown and, unlike during the long years of captivity, their futures were no longer mapped out for them.

Then after hours or days of waiting came the familiar shout of 'Raus' and they began their long march towards home. Gordon Barber was among the expectant prisoners at Marienburg, who started their journey by walking across an ominously frozen river:

> We just wanted to get home. We were fit – well we were when we started. We started on about 3 January and finished on 12 April. That's a long time walking. We stayed in barns, in stations – there were thousands of us. It was cold, it was snowing, and they had to give us stops at the side of the road every four or five hours. Food was non existent, 'cause the Germans were fleeing as well.[7]

Thousands of the men in the columns that snaked through the snow were the very same men who had walked out of France back in the summer of 1940. Then their enemy had been the scorching sun and their desperate thirst. Now it was cold and hunger that threatened them. Back in 1940 they had been relatively fit, now many of the marchers had been existing on watery stews for many months. However, the marchers of 1945 had one advantage. Five years earlier they were marching into the unknown – at least now they knew they were heading home. All knew well the extremes of the Polish weather, indeed for many this was their fifth winter of captivity. Most had shovelled the deep snow from blocked roads or chipped ice from frozen railway lines. Thousands among them had spent the early part of winter in the fields, pulling up sugar beet from the frosty ground, their fingers numb with cold, their backs aching from stooping for hours on end. Some had stood on the frozen rivers and sawed blocks of ice, others had walked the beaches along the Baltic building paths as the icy wind bit through their clothing. Yet this was something new. Now the cold was relentless. There were no barracks to return to at night. No stoves to huddle around and no blankets to wrap around their thin bodies as they settled into their bunks for the night. Now there was just cold – for day upon day, week after week. As the prisoners marched their whole world was reduced to a vision of whiteness. They trudged along roads that seemed to have no end, the horizon disappearing between the snowy ground and the white of the sky. Their vision was limited to the whiteness to either side of the column or the hunched brown figures shuffling along in front of them.

Often alongside columns of civilians also fleeing from the Russians, the POWs marched, and marched, and marched. Some among the prisoners witnessed chilling scenes that served to remind them just how fragile was their hold on life. Those who marched out of the work camps of Auschwitz walked through hundreds of frozen corpses of the inmates of the concentration camp. Most had died from starvation and exhaustion, but there were plenty who had clearly been executed. The dirty grey sky above them offered no comfort and a bitterly cold wind bit through their thin uniforms, burning their skin and bringing tears to their eyes. They hunched their shoulders, dug their hands deep into their pockets and lowered their heads to avoid the icy blasts. Such were the extremes of temperature that men found their eyelids freezing together, leaving them to rub their faces vigorously to restore their sight. Nothing in life could have prepared them for this – not the terror of the battlefield nor the unrelenting work camps. Even those wearing layer upon layer of clothing became numb with cold. It started with the extremities. Their feet were the first things to feel the strain. Thousands were shod in worn out boots or clogs, with laces made from the string that had once held together their Red Cross parcels. Some had slip-on clogs that meant they could hardly lift their feet from the icy roads. There were men without socks whose feet were wrapped in rags. Others were hit by the opposite problem. Upon evacuation stores of clothing had been opened and some men began the journey in brand new British army boots. The stiff leather was too much for their feet, blistering the skin and cutting into their ankles. Worse still, the metal studs on the soles were treacherous on the ice of the frozen roads, leaving the men slipping and sliding as they tried to march.

Then the icy cold struck their hands. Fingertips became numb as their gloves fought to preserve circulation. For many their gloves were threadbare, worn out during years of tilling the soil or wielding pick axes. Others had simply cut out pocket linings from inside their great-coats and fashioned basic mittens. To prevent frostbite they wrapped their faces in scarves and towels, using their hats to hold the thin coverings in place. Collars were turned up and hands forced deep into pockets. Thin blankets were wrapped around their shoulders and heads like stinking grey shawls, with only their eyes shining from the shadows. They were eyes that did not shine for long.

Yet for all their precautions, still they froze. Some men recorded icicles hanging from their bearded chins and one man later wrote:

> Agony is almost unbearable now. We marched until 2 a.m. They told us it was 20 below freezing, and made us wait for two hours on the road. We froze to the marrow, not used to this at all. When almost asleep on our feet, were taken into a large barn. Shivered all through the rest of the night, … no interest in anything at all.[8]

Thousands of men crowded into barns where they desperately attempted to seek shelter from the elements, snuggling down into the straw, ignoring the insects that bit them and the rats that scurried among them. Men raced to reach the upper levels of the barn, knowing that those on the ground floor might be soaked during the night since those upstairs, afraid of losing their sleeping place, would simply urinate down through the floor. When no more space was left others were left outside in the snow to spend the nights in agony. Such was the cold that some men elected to sleep in dung piles in order to keep warm. Even inside farm buildings men awoke to find frost on their clothing. Those who had removed their boots to rest their aching feet found the leather frozen stiff. Unable to put them on they simply bound their feet in rags and continued on their journey, hoping their boots would defrost before frostbite struck their feet and toes.

As the days passed even the fittest among them grew exhausted. Some nights were spent indoors, others were passed in the open with the prisoners remaining on their feet for fear of freezing to death on the ground. As frostbite hit the pain turned to agony and as they lost circulation in their extremities the real dangers set in. The unfortunate men began to lose all feeling in their toes, fingers and ears and then they turned black. Eventually they faced the inevitable conclusion. Joseph Healey, captured in Norway in 1940 was one of the victims. After 14 days marching without medical treatment his big toe was finally lost.

With the increasingly weak men struggling to move through the snow they abandoned all surplus weight from their packs in the knowledge that survival was all that mattered. Musical instruments and books were the first to go, along with treasured possessions and souvenirs constructed or collected during captivity. And so it continued until all they carried in their haversacks were the remains of their Red Cross parcels. Only a few were able to retain mementoes of their time in captivity. All thoughts of the past were obliterated from their memories – food, heat and rest were the only things that mattered now. When they asked the guards how much further they received no definite answer, maybe a shrug of the shoulders or an uncertain, unknown destination always a few more kilometres away.

Their stomachs tormented by hunger, the miserable prisoners ate whatever was available and cooked it by burning any fuel they could find. Books and bibles, diaries and letters from home, lovingly preserved for years, were consumed by the flames of fires lit in desperate attempts to banish the cold. Some days there were issues of food, sometimes a little bread, maybe a weak unidentifiable stew or soup, maybe just a scoop of sauerkraut. If they thought they had been hungry in the camps they realised they had never known real hunger until now. Some men received tinned meat that resembled dog food, which they ate with the fervour of the starving. Others considered themselves blessed to receive soup powder and dehydrated meat.

Such rations may have seemed a godsend but it was seldom enough to stave off starvation. Some cursed as they marched past SS columns moving towards the eastern front openly carrying cartloads of stolen Red Cross parcels. Others who had been forbidden to empty the parcel stores within their camps watched in desperate envy as their guards devoured their contents. In desperation many of those shuffling through the snow decided to risk the wrath of their guards and scour the towns and villages for food. Even when they were given hot drinks by sympathetic civilians their guards often knocked them out of their hands. Finding grain husks and molasses, one group of men bribed a farmer's wife to bake the concoction for them – anything to stave off the pangs of hunger. Other men jumped into pigsties and kicked the animals away in order to reach the food that had been left for them. Some searched farmhouses, regardless of who was at home:

> I sneaked off a couple of times and went into farmhouses. I went into a shop, but it didn't sell anything edible. In one house I found a big bowl of stuff that looked edible. I thought 'I'll have that'. When we started eating someone said 'This is chicken feed, you prat!' We threw it away, it was bloody horrible. Anything you could see that was edible, you'd eat. I remember going into a house and a kid was sitting there eating some food. That went – we had that. That was the worst thing I'd done.[9]

With just an average of little over six hundred calories a day being consumed it was little wonder many among them fell victim to exhaustion. Gordon Barber and his team of 'muckers' became aware of the problem early on in the march:

> I remember this night, the snow was really coming down and the five of us were sitting there. Then we got up to go on. We'd not got very far when we looked round and I said 'Where's Ken?' Stevie said 'He was getting ever so tired. But from what I remember he was leaning against a tree.' We were all getting tired. So I gave Lofty the haversack and told him to take it easy. Then me and Stevie went back to find him. He was by the tree. We got hold of him, he was fucking cold. His teeth were chattering. I said 'You'll die if you stop there. You won't be tired anymore.' So we put our arms round his shoulders and off we went and caught the others up. We were lucky that night we found a barn to sleep in. I said 'Put Ken between us, he's really cold. I think he's got something wrong with him.' The next morning it was sunny. I went out and found a horsedrawn wagon the Germans were carrying the sick on. Ken was just frozen so we got him on this wagon and they went. I never saw him again until we got home. That was one of the worst things that happened.[10]

Wilats had begun the journey wearing just his battledress, boots, a balaclava and a greatcoat. With only a pair of mittens made from pockets cut from his greatcoat, and without a blanket to sleep beneath, it was little wonder the cold soon took effect. He recalled those final hours before he was carried to the wagon that brought him salvation:

> The first night was horrendous. We walked all night and all day. Then we were marched into a field late at night. The temperature must have been 30 degrees below zero. There was no cover. I was carrying a tin of Red Cross corned beef. I got it out to eat and the meat was frozen stiff. I couldn't get it out of the tin, that's how cold it was. When we got up in the morning I was so exhausted I could hear music playing and see houses – I was hallucinating. I saw these houses that weren't there. It was then I decided I would sit down and have a sleep. Of course, if Gordon hadn't come back for me I would have been dead. My survival instinct was gone. It was as if I had been anaesthetised. I was at the limit of my endurance.[11]

It was not just the prisoners who were tormented by the journey westwards, many of the guards were also suffering. Although some had transport – bicycles, motorbikes or horses and carts – most walked alongside the prisoners. They too were freezing and short of food. And just like the prisoners they were uncertain of their destination. But unlike their captives the guards were staring defeat in the face. They had no hope of liberation, they realised their destiny was life behind the wire of an Allied POW camp – if they were lucky. Maybe it was this sense of hopelessness that inspired some guards to mistreat prisoners. For the East Prussians among them they knew their homes were being taken over by the Poles or destroyed by the rampaging Russian hordes. They had little idea where their families were, and most feared the worst. They knew that for the retreating women rape was the best they could hope for.

The fears and apprehensions of some guards led to a state of terror:

> We had reasonable guards at first, but we had one who looked like the actor, Alan Ladd. Blond and really good looking but he was the biggest bastard alive. He used to ride around on a little motorbike or in a squad car. He carried this machine gun. Nothing would stop him, he'd use it. We saw him use it. He shot blokes but you never knew who they were.[12]

There were plenty like him, guards who had no qualms about shooting a sick man who fell out of the column or someone who stepped out of line to accept food from a civilian. It was a lottery, with a very deadly and expensive prize. Some men who refused to walk any further were left behind to fend for themselves, the guards unconcerned by their actions. Others who offered the merest defiance were left in the snow, a patch of dark blood growing beneath their soon to be frozen bodies. As one man later wrote of the help given by the guards: 'assistance for the stragglers in the form of a blow from a rifle butt'.[13] Maurice Newey was among those who witnessed the killing of a prisoner by a guard:

> Not knowing how much longer we would be left standing an older chap wearily walked out of the column and sat down on a stone parapet. A young guard ran up to him and ordered him back to the column. The fellow was so tired that he limply raised an arm and said 'F – off'. The guard became hysterical screaming F- F- F- at him then pointed his rifle at him and shot him straight through the heart. ... We learned later that the dead soldier had been a POW for five years. He was a father of four children. What a tragic way to die after all those years in captivity.[14]

Some of the vindictive guards continued to terrorise the prisoners even in the final days before liberation. The Alan Ladd lookalike was among them:

> A bloke got shot, I think he was one who was a bit 'handy' – an Indian army boxing champion. He had a go at the guard and they shot him through the stomach. They wouldn't let us go and sort him out. He lay out there all night crying – calling out 'Help me, help me' until he died. I'll always remember that.[15]

No one was keeping a count of those who succumbed to the extremes of the weather, were executed, or who starved to death. One man who marched west from Stalag VIIIb estimated that between four and six hundred prisoners had died. Yet in truth no one could tell what had happened to those who had gone missing. Some among the sick had fallen out and died at the roadside, whilst others had been taken away for treatment, or crawled into the safety of civilian homes. Columns had been split up almost at random with friends losing each other in the chaos, often never to meet again.

However not all of the deaths on the marches went unrecorded. As the columns of men snaked their way across east and central Europe the Red Cross representatives tried to keep track of them. It was not an easy task and deliveries of food or medical relief were rare, yet still they kept trying. Some of the Red Cross staff located the marching columns and noted down offences committed by guards in those final desperate weeks. In April 1945, when the Red Cross men caught up with the evacuees from Stalag 344, they took notes of the names of the Germans' victims. Among them were two men who died from malnutrition, a Private Russell who was shot dead for stopping to rest during the march, and Mullins and MacLean who died for lack of medical attention. Other individuals made mental notes about those they saw die, hoping the news could eventually be passed on to desperate families – men such as Guardsman Sweetman who died in April 1945 after receiving no medical treatment for pneumonia and pleurisy. Just the simple act of recording their names meant they were not consigned to the lists of the forgotten.

It was not just the attentions of the guards that were a cause for concern – the advancing Allies also put the wretched POWs in danger, as Les Allan remembered:

> For the first month we kept being bombed by Russian planes, they must have thought we were retreating Germans, otherwise they wouldn't have wasted their bombs. But we didn't hold them in terror, our attitude was that they were foreigners and they couldn't hit a barn door at ten yards. So when they came over we just dived for cover and hoped for the best. Then there was a period when we were beyond the reach of their airforce, we were too far from the front. Then we came under attack by RAF Typhoons. We'd never seen these planes before, we'd never heard of rockets. They came down and smashed into us, and we were astonished to see red white and blue rings on the planes. From then on we were terrified, whenever we saw planes in the sky we knew they were our planes and the RAF could never miss. And we were the target![16]

At least the marching men had somewhere to run to. Some of those evacuated westwards were sent by ship from Danzig. It was a terrifying time for the prisoners, locked deep into the freezing hold as the ship slowly made its way along the Baltic coast. For two weeks they travelled, their only food being three pounds of bread per man but the lack of food, the miserable conditions, the cold and the rats were not their only concern. Their greatest fear was drowning. Locked into the hold they were trapped within a steel coffin. A single torpedo from a lurking Russian submarine, a magnetic mine, or an air raid by the increasingly dominant Allied airforces, would all have spelt doom for the POWs. Fortunately their fears were not realised and two weeks after their departure they finally disembarked at Lübeck in Germany.

Whether marching, sailing, or travelling by train, the friendships that had survived the rigours of years of imprisonment soon began to be put under strain. Unsurprisingly the men began to lose all thought of others and concentrate on their personal survival. Tempers frayed and friends fell out over tiny morsels of food. When the Germans provided rations no queues were formed, instead everyone rushed to claim their share of whatever was on offer. One among these mobs later wrote:

> Without any bias or prejudice, our boys, myself included, are a rotten crowd. Each one wishes to be at the head of the queue, and the result is a rush and a push ... brawling, cursing crowd jammed round the cook-house. Animals and starving at that. ..... My faith in humanity is now completely gone – and I shall never forget that barn with the darkness, overcrowded, boys crawling out to the lavatory, snarls and curses from men trodden on in the process – shouts about potatoes, groans and cries of the sick, my God! It was hell![17]

In some cases the sick were lucky enough to be allowed extra rations by their guards and they soon found themselves given plenty of attention by men who would previously have allowed them to drop dead in the snow.

Even those who had contrived to stick together through thick and thin, and whose relationships were not broken by arguments often found themselves separated. Gordon Barber, had already lost one 'mucker' to sickness:

> In the end you couldn't help it – you just lost blokes. I don't know what happened to Frank, we lost him one day. The guards would stay 'Stop', you'd stop, you were in one batch your mates were in the other. Then they say 'Go' and that was the end. I never knew what happened to Frank or Stevie, but Lofty was with me all the time – he was tall I could always spot him in a crowd.[18]

With the columns being split almost at random it was inevitable that some prisoners were lost in the chaos. Some wandered off to look for food and never found their mates again, others fell out of the columns to rest and were simply ignored by both their fellow prisoners and their guards. The more adventurous among them simply headed out into the unknown on their own, uncertain of what their fate might be but certain they had no desire to keep marching. Ken Wilats soon found himself separated from the main body of prisoners. Having lost his mates when he was taken sick, Wilats found himself at a camp where prisoners were still employed in a timber yard. Here he remained until he had regained his strength and was sent from the working party in an attempt to rejoin his column. He headed to the local station in hope of catching a train westwards:

> The place was a maelstrom. There were evacuees coming out and troops heading for the Russian front, it was a complete mêlée. We waited all day on the station, but nothing came. So we were told to march 15 kilometres to reach them. So we set off up the road – with no guards or anything. The bloke I was with said 'C'mon lets go into the woods and see if we can find a farm and we'll wait for the Russians'. So we got off the road and found this little settlement.

Here they were taken in by a Polish farmer who allowed them to rest in the hayloft by day and come into his home for a meal at night. They soon realised it might not be too healthy a place to remain:

> One day a German officer came looking for fodder for the horses. Another night as we were eating we heard the Germans coming on a horsedrawn sleigh, we could hear the bells. The farmer said 'Quick, quick!' and opened a trapdoor to his cellar and we hid down there. We could hear the German walking about above our heads. But we thought it pretty unfair to take advantage of the farmer because if he'd been caught harbouring us he'd have been shot. So we went on our way. We got back onto the main road and there were crowds of German soldiers all walking towards the Russian front. There were guns and tanks. No one challenged us at all. They were going one way we were going the other. Eventually we joined up with a column of prisoners and stayed with them until we were liberated near Winkelsdorf near Hanover. We were on the road for three months. We were pretty ragged.[19]

Amidst the chaos of the continuing exodus the spectre of theft among the prisoners also raised its ugly head. Men awoke to find their boots had been stolen by others desperate for protection for their feet. Those caught stealing food faced little mercy from former friends and comrades. The guards ignored the prisoners as they attacked the culprits, making them run the gauntlet of kicks and punches from men who could just summon up enough energy to ensure a suitable punishment. When the Germans caught men on one column stealing from the guards' rations they issued threats that the food should be returned. If the food were not returned immediately all the prisoners would miss the next issue of rations. Where once the POWs had stood firm against such threats, now they changed their minds and pointed out the culprits. This was no longer a game, food meant life and the possible punishment of a few men meant nothing compared to filling their own bellies.

The spectre of disease also hung over them. Within days of beginning the march the POWs, few of whom had ever been able to keep really clean within the camps, found themselves filthy. There was little opportunity to wash and few dared remove any clothing for fear of frostbite. They became encrusted with grime and thick with lice. Few had the energy to shave, preserving their strength for the mile upon mile of tortuous marching and the scratching of their bodies whenever the columns halted. One column bedded down for the night in pea straw, little did they know what they were sleeping in, since pea straw turns black when laid in barns. When they awoke they found their faces and clothing stained black, yet continued with the march unconcerned by the colour of their skin.

It was not their outward appearance that bothered the prisoners. They may have been unwashed, with their feet blistered and their crotches rubbed red raw. Their clothes may have been collapsing – indeed one man took his trousers off for the first time in three weeks to find his underpants had disintegrated. But this was not their main worry. What concerned them was what was happening to them on the inside. Soon many were hit by diarrhoea. The poor food, often hastily cooked, assaulted their guts leaving them in agony with 'the shits'. All modesty was a forgotten value as men stopped at the roadsides dropped their trousers and crouched in full view of their comrades, caring only about relieving the pain. They sometimes found themselves the victim of cruel treatment by the guards. On one column those who stopped and dropped their trousers were chased at gunpoint to the front of the column. Almost doubled over in pain, often holding up their trousers, they ran forward, the energy seeping from their body just like the watery faeces seeped down their legs.

As the marches progressed the weather slowly began to turn. First the snows melted. That left the prisoners marching through slush and mud that seeped through their boots, soaking their already wretched feet. Where once they had been able to brush snow from their coats they found themselves soaked by the heavy rains that followed the worst of the winter. But this meant little. The temperatures were slowly rising and the light of spring began to appear. Slowly but surely they began to spot the shoots of flowers appearing on the roadsides as they marched. The avenues of trees were no longer leafless, instead a new life was beginning with buds appearing on the once bare branches. Then, as the weeks turned to months, the sun finally began to show from behind the clouds. With this light came hope. The Red Army had been left far behind and the prisoners were slowly moving towards the Allied lines. Ahead of them no longer lay nothing but a wasteland, instead as they looked towards the horizon they could sense salvation.

Yet for many such hopes would never be fulfilled. Gordon Barber, for example, eventually fell victim to sickness:

> Things started getting a bit dodgy because we all got the shits. That was the worst. By now we'd left the Russians far behind. By this time we were all getting under the weather. We were just walking and hoping we would get home. We looked a sorry state – worrying how long we'd keep walking. The weather was getting nice, it was March or April by then. We tried to stick together but we were getting weaker, and blokes were dying – just falling by the side of the road. You couldn't do nothing for them, you weren't strong enough to carry yourself. The place we got to had just been bombed by the Americans. We knew we were getting near the front. And the Germans were getting a bit easier, they might as well not have been there. Waste of space, they were too old or too ill. You'd look around and think 'where are they?' You could've pissed off but I was in no fit state.[20]

As another marcher later wrote: 'I think if they had shot us and dumped us at this point and in these conditions it would have been a relief.'[21]

It was unsurprising that many of the prisoners started to feel increasingly bitter towards the Germans. Although air raids posed a threat to the safety of the marchers, they did give them an opportunity to vent their anger, as Les Allan remembered: 'When we saw our planes we called out to them "Kill the bastards, kill every man, woman and child". The bombing was our salvation, it certainly lifted our morale. I witnessed the blanket bombing of Hanover, we were marching towards it but we still said "Kill them, bomb them, smash them".'[22]

These air raids may have lifted morale but they also helped to sap the strength of the POWs. Despite their worsening condition the Germans still saw fit to make them work. Hardly able to walk, the forlorn prisoners were herded through towns to play one final part in the desperate attempts by the Germans to keep alive any hope of saving the Reich. To sustain the military in those final weeks of war they needed to keep roads open and the railways running. To this end the columns of prisoners were used to clear up in the aftermath of bombing raids and load and unload trains. Exhausted prisoners – men who had marched hundreds of miles through the winter snows from Stalag XXb – were forced to work 12-hour days at a railway station, surviving on rations of just half a pint of soup and 120 grammes of bread per day. Prisoners found themselves dragging rubble from roads or once more wielding shovels to fill in bomb craters. In the chaotic aftermath of air raids the prisoners were able to search for food, but many took risks that plunged them deeper into despair, as Gordon Barber remembered:

> We were marched through the town down to the station to clear the bomb damage. The worst thing that happened was that we walked in and found a lot of dead animals. There were pigs that had been laying there for two or three days. Some of our blokes cut them up, one of them said 'Let's have this pig. We'll cut the bad bits out and eat the rest.' ' Cause we were bloody hungry. We cooked it up and ate it. Our guts weren't very good before, but when we ate this it was a killer. I can still remember sitting on a plank of wood at the latrine they'd dug. The bloke sitting beside me said 'Ain't it terrible. Do you think we'll make it?' I said 'Yeah'. We sat there watching the American bombing raids, knocking the shit out of this town. All we could see going down into the pit was blood. We had dysentery and malnutrition. I said 'I wish they'd drop a bomb on us'. I don't know how we wiped ourselves, there was no toilet paper. There was water just running out of me. I felt so weak and so horrible, every time I moved I shit myself.[23]

It was little wonder some among them decided to take their chances on their own. Some men had headed off alone through the snow to the farms where their Polish girlfriends awaited their return. Others simply slipped into the woods hoping to team up with gangs of resistance fighters or join up with the Red Army. For many of those who disappeared into the countryside their eventual fate was uncertain, no one knew their names and no one ever recorded what happened to them. Countless men lost their lives in the battles that followed the evacuation and in the ensuing chaos. Those who waited until they reached the relative safety of central Germany had the best hope of survival. 'Bill' Sykes, who had already made two unsuccessful escape attempts from his workplace, was finally able to make his exit whilst marching away from his work camp. Just like his previous 'escapes' there was little attempt at subterfuge. This was less than a 'great escape':

> As the war was coming to a close – on or around March of 1945 – we were marched south with a large contingent of other prisoners. The Russians were approaching the river Elbe from the east, and the Allied forces were approaching the river Mulde from the west, and we were in no-mans-land between the two rivers. After a week or so of marching I was reaching the end of my tether as I was weak from a bad case of dysentery. I decided enough was enough and took it upon myself to make one more 'dedicated' try to escape from captivity. The other ones had just been half hearted one-man protests against the German guards. When I say escape, I use the term loosely, I just walked away. The prisoners – British, American, French, Russian – were incarcerated in a large wooded area surrounded by German guards at 50-metre intervals with orders to shoot anyone approaching the perimeter. I, having reached a point of no return, approached one of the guards who asked me where I thought I was going, I answered that I was going back to England and nothing but nobody was going to stop me.
>
> As at that time I was down to a frail 100 pounds in body weight and had a severe case of dysentery. He appeared to find some humour in this statement, or perhaps it was just my poor German interpretation of my intentions, so to my amazement he turned his back and allowed me to pass through the cordon. He probably thought that I wouldn't get very far and that the next German soldier I met would shoot me anyway. This lead to a chain of events of many days of pure misery, constantly soaked to the skin by cold torrential rain, no food, a bad case of dysentery. What a miserable specimen of the human race I must have appeared. But salvation was at hand, a German family took me under their roof for a few days and gave me a share of the little food that they had and so I survived. I will be forever grateful.[24]

For men such as Sykes the marching was over, they were free, if not yet safe. For thousands of others the marching continued. For some, the columns continued westwards until they met with the advancing Allies. For others their destination would simply breed more uncertainty. They might have been able to see the flashes of Allied artillery in the distance and some among their guards had got rid of their rifles but their war was not yet over and there was a final shock in store for them. Just as they were expecting to be free they were once more marched behind the wire of the Stalags.

NINE

The End

Being liberated was one of life's greatest experiences. However I was still suffering from malnutrition and dysentery and was hospitalised after being flown home. I really don't remember much of VE Day except I was in some pain.[1]

Whilst some individuals slipped away and the rest kept walking through the countryside until liberated, others were marched into the overcrowded Stalags of central Germany. Reaching their supposed safety the prisoners were in for a surprise. Though most had experienced overcrowding in the eastern camps few were prepared for what awaited them. As many of those who had marched for months through the snow and ice of the Polish winter were shepherded into Stalags they were joined by recently captured Allied troops from the western front. As early as the summer of 1944 some camps had reached bursting point as new arrivals entered them from camps in Italy following the surrender in 1943. One NCO, arriving from Italy, found it took him three weeks before being issued with a palliase, and took another three weeks before he was allocated a bunk to put the straw-filled mattress on. Such were the shortages of coal that each stove was given only twelve pieces of coal per day, just enough to keep the stove alight for an hour and a half.

As the British and Americans had steadily advanced eastwards the Germans had relocated camps from their western regions. At Stalag XIIIc in Hammelburg a group of over 200 Indians and South Africans had arrived from France in the autumn of 1944. They arrived in a state of confusion, with most having lost all their identification papers. As the camps bulged at the seams they sank into chaos. Tents were put up as emergency accommodation, which were soon filled by the incomers. The camps soon took on the appearance of shanty towns as spare bunk boards and Red Cross packing cases were hastily nailed together to provide makeshift shelters.

In Stalag Xb, at Sandbostel, which housed POWs alongside thousands of slave labourers, fresh arrivals found little space and even less comfort. Newly captured men from the west were even segregated from the long-term prisoners, being forced to occupy a separate compound between which no contact could be made. When one group of 700 new arrivals were found to be without boots, to alleviate their discomfort the Germans simply issued them with straw slippers. By March 1945 the Red Cross found that all the inmates were sleeping on bare boards, with even the patients of the camp hospital forced to sleep on the wooden floorboards of their huts. Less than a third of the POWs had palliases, and these were filled with heather they had collected on the local heaths rather than the more usual straw. Only 50 per cent of them had been issued blankets by the Germans and the washhouse was without water. Such were the shortages that prisoners were marched 10 kilometres just to collect firewood.

It was little surprise that rats began to thrive amidst such chaos. The only thing that controlled their numbers was that little food was ever thrown away. At Lamsdorf the latrines began to fill with excrement since the Germans no longer had the will to arrange for them to be emptied. As the piles of shit grew so did the horror for the men using the latrines. The piles were so high than rats ran across them, stopping only to bite the exposed backsides of men using the latrines. The terror of these unwanted attentions during what should have been their most private moments meant prisoners perched above the latrines ensuring the rats could not reach their bare flesh.

Such squalor became evident throughout the system of camps. Teeming with weakened men, any attempts to keep the barrack huts clean and tidy were pointless. The floors soon became thick with grease and grime, just like the bodies of the prisoners. What little food they received was cooked in unsanitary conditions, often being prepared in deep urns that were seldom washed out, and then transported from the kitchens in buckets used day after day without washing. The prisoners could not help but compare it to the pig swill it tasted like. At Stalag XIa in Altengrabow, during April 1945 the camp was provided with electricity for just half an hour per day and the British and American prisoners were no longer receiving Red Cross parcels. Coal had not been seen in the camp since February and over 600 prisoners were sleeping on blankets on the bare earth inside hastily erected tents. Half of the 600 men had just one blanket and thus had nothing to cover their bodies as they slept at night. At this late stage in the war there were no delousing facilities and the inmates of the camp had no way of keeping clean. Even worse the latrines could no longer be emptied – the only solution to the problem being to dig a series of overflow pits to prevent the sewage from spreading throughout the camp. It was little wonder that Red Cross inspectors reported the camp as: 'nothing but one big complaint'.[2]

The columns of prisoners fleeing from Stalags in the east were bound for two main destinations – Stalag XIb at Fallingbostel and Stalag VIIa at Moosburg. For the men already in these camps, the new arrivals meant a further deterioration of living conditions that would push them one step nearer to the abyss. Fallingbostel had never been designed to hold vast numbers of men. Its purpose was merely as a transit camp for men heading for working parties. In April 1944 nearly 70,000 prisoners, 2,000 of them from Britain or the Commonwealth, were working Arbeitskommandos supplied by the camp. Positioned in northern Germany, its numbers had been swelled by 4,000 men captured during Operation Market Garden. Though many of the veterans of Arnhem had arrived in the camp with an air of defiance – marching through the gates in step, proudly wearing their red berets, and were led by their soon to be legendary RSM J.C. Lord – they were thrown into life in a camp where they would struggle to maintain that morale.

Their arrival made the accommodation situation within the camp critical. With the coming of winter the whole camp and all the roads and paths within it became a sea of mud. As they trudged around inside their enclosure, trying to fill the long hours of boredom until the next meal, the mud sucked at their boots as if telling them there could be no escape from their misery.

Crammed into vast huts that had never been intended as permanent homes for prisoners, the new arrivals experienced an existence far from the mythological image of the POW camp. Day by day conditions deteriorated. 'Famished, wounded and the majority clad in rags'[3] incoming men, some described as having legs as thin as ten-year-olds, became a burden on the camp authorities. Most were in need of replacement clothing, in place of uniforms damaged in battle, and soon the stockpiles of uniforms were exhausted. As a result long-established prisoners handed out their spare clothing to the new arrivals. George Marsden, captured in Holland, was among those in need of new clothing: 'I still had my cellular pants on, stiff with dried blood, my trousers fastened down the front with safety pins. I'd ripped them diving over wire before being captured, plus my left sleeve was missing from my jacket.'[4] He would receive no new clothing until after liberation.

Clothing was not the only thing in short supply. As each new batch of men arrived they made their homes in whatever space was available. The old dining halls and recreation rooms soon became barrack rooms as new inmates, usually with just one blanket each, dossed down on the floor. As the cold of winter began to bite those lucky enough to have bunks began to burn them, plank by plank, to heat their huts. Many cupboards, once used to store personal possessions, also made their way into the fires. Then, in the final months, the Germans inflicted further hardship on the prisoners by confiscating palliases, tables and stools. Leaking roofs added to the misery, meaning some huts were abandoned as the men searched for a space they could call their own. Soon even those with bunks found they had to share them. This situation was mirrored across the Reich. Men on work details had no fuel except what they could steal and slept beneath blankets that had been unwashed for years. Almost threadbare and thick with grease the thin woollen blankets offered little protection against the winter cold. It was a winter that would live on in the memories of all those who were unfortunate enough to experience it.

At Fallingbostel there were few hygiene facilities and fuel shortages meant the inmates were allowed just one shower per month. In lieu of regular showers the prisoners washed as best they could with whatever was available, as George Marsden remembered: 'there was just a cold water tap at the back of the hut somewhere, no towel so no wash. It was a good job that I was brought up in the recession when people struggled daily to feed their large families.'[5] He soon became aware too of how the latrines were also overused: 'Disgusting, there was one toilet in a concrete building, a hole in the ground which had running water under it, until someone must have been upset because the water was cut off. This was for the use of hundreds of men, most having dysentery, imagine when the stone building was filled and the trail of excrement ran across, sometimes into the hut.'[6]

The fuel shortages that denied them hot water also meant little opportunity to cook the contents of Red Cross parcels. The increasingly hungry, dirty and exhausted inmates seemed to have so much time on their hands but ever less to occupy their minds. The huts were so dark and crowded even those with enough energy to rise from their bunks found the light insufficient to read by. Starved of intellectual stimulation their active minds wandered and they could think of nothing but the very real starvation of their empty stomachs.

With little or no hot water the prisoners were seldom able to wash their few remaining clothes. Even if they could wash clothes there was little space to dry them since the huts were so crowded wet clothes would surely have dripped on a man huddled asleep on the floor. The lack of fuel became an increasing psychological burden for prisoners throughout the Reich. By early 1945 rations were growing ever more basic. As food shortages began to bite the prisoners were forced to take desperate measures. One prisoner at Stalag XIa ate a handful of beans he had been able to scrounge but it was soon discovered they had been chemically treated and the starving soldier died soon after consuming them. With food consumption plummeting the Red Cross couldn't fail to notice the changes in the prisoners between their visits. During one inspection it was noted that in just five weeks the prisoners had gone from appearing healthy to looking like skeletons: 'the food issue by the German authorities is no longer enough to prevent the prisoners from weakening rapidly'.[7] Some Red Cross inspectors went even further. At Sandbostel, where the POWs survived on three potatoes, 200 grams of bread, 30 grams of sausage and 21 grams of margarine per day, they noted there had been several deaths of prisoners weakened by hunger, and decribed what they found within the camp: 'emaciation general .... Low blood pressure ... dizziness .... Signs of famine ... life of prisoners is in jeopardy.'[8]

As the prisoners evacuated from the east crowded into Fallingbostel the men already there did what they could to help them. As the scrawny scarecrow figures shuffled through gates into the main compound efforts were made to ensure they were looked after. They were put into tents erected for them by the guards. Then British doctors checked the condition of each man. Les Allan, who had marched the 600 miles in clogs whilst nursing a fractured ankle, made the mistake of doing his utmost to appear healthy. Maybe it was the sight of the airborne RSM John Lord who had greeted them at the gates in his perfectly creased battledress, or simply that it was so incredible they had survived that nothing would ever seem a strain again, but, when his turn came to see the doctor, Allan stood up and was thus denied one of the bunks allocated for the most sickly of the marchers. The bunks came courtesy of the paratroopers who had been captured at Arnhem. Under the command of Lord, and being among the most recent and thus fittest of the POWs, they volunteered to a man to give up their bunks. It was a show of comradeship and generosity that ensured their survival and was a gesture the men would never forget.

Prisoners held at Stalag VIIa at Moosburg suffered in much the same way as those at Fallingbostel or Sandbostel. Designed to hold just 14,000 men, by early 1945 the population had grown to over 100,000. Swelled initially by Americans captured during the Battle of the Bulge, and then by those arriving from work camps and Stalags in the east, conditions in Moosburg rapidly deteriorated. When one group of emaciated prisoners arrived at the camp they were thought to be unusually pale skinned. They turned out to be labourers from salt mines whose skin had seldom seen the sun. The irony was that whilst they had been digging in the mines salt had become a forgotten commodity for the prisoners at Moosburg. As in the other camps tents filled the gaps between huts, and men slept in whatever space was available as the mud reached their ankles. Recently arrived from hospital, Bryan Willoughby remembered the scenes within the compound:

> It was pretty ghastly – overcrowded. The bunks were in a structure with twelve all together. Bed boards were very scarce, you were lucky to get enough to be reasonably comfortable. People pinched them, there were so many POWs in there. The main thing was lice. I'd take off my shirt and in my armpit it was like greenfly on the back of a leaf. I'd take my shirt off and put it in cold water then put it back on again. As time went on the overcrowding became worse. Towards the very end the floor was absolutely full of sleeping men. You didn't dare go out for a pee in the night 'cause you'd never get to the end of the room without treading on a Russian or maybe a Pole. Everyone was there. I never thought about the smell or washing because you were lucky to get near a tap, they were right at the end of the camp. You'd have to choose your time – late at night or in the middle of the day. If you were dying for a crap you'd find about ten Russians queuing up to occupy one space. Some of them had religious rituals for their washing and it all took time. But I think it was not such a great problem because you got so little to eat, so you didn't go very often. If you eat next to nothing you have nothing to get rid of. I expect we had rats in the camp but I didn't notice them. It wouldn't have worried us, they'd have probably gone into the pot.[9]

With increased overcrowding the segregation of prisoners began to break down and the Germans no longer insisted on compounds being divided up between nationalities. Instead all were thrown in together with a resulting breakdown in discipline. Prisoners within Stalag XVIIc – none of whom had received any new issues of clothing since June the previous year, nor received any *lagergeld* since October – found the camp had become cosmopolitan in character. With 13,000 men crammed into a space designed for just 4,000 it was little wonder the NCOs were unable to keep control. As the German rule collapsed the prisoners became free agents, something that would impact on the countryside around the camp.

With so many prisoners of all nationalities crammed within the camps many prisoners soon noticed the differences between them:

> The Ruskies were very varied, they'd gob on the floor, it was natural to them – you couldn't do anything about it – but some were very civilised. The French were always arguing among themselves, they'd come to blows. The Yanks weren't anywhere near as good as the Brits, they went to pieces quicker. Some would just sit around all day long. If anyone got into that state of mind you would notice it.[10]

In these desperate conditions within the camp some among the prisoners tried to exploit the chaos by attempting to ease their own situation by preying on their fellow 'kriegies'. Bryan Willoughby watched the activities of the bullies in the final days before liberation:

> There were these two Yanks. One a great big John Wayne chap, and his sidekick a George Raft type – a tough guy. They came round and said 'Give us your English cigarettes'. They demanded we hand them over. You couldn't do much about it. They said to this little Yorkshire chap 'C'mon you Limey cocksucker!' He stood up and said 'I ain't a Limey cocksucker'. Looking at him – he was only a little fellow – but I could tell 'George Raft' and his sidekick were going to 'go for a burton'. They would of done. They just slunk off. He was a very tough fellow.[11]

Another Arnhem veteran, Jim Sims, recalled these divisions:

> There was a great deal of bad feeling between the various inmates of Stalag XIb. The Americans shared our Lager but would have nothing to do with us ..... The French disliked everyone, especially the British who had run away at Dunkirk and betrayed the gallant French ... The poor old Russians were treated abominably. The atmosphere in the POW camp was dog eat dog and one soon adapted.[12]

Even in the camp hospitals rations of potatoes and sugar were cut by 50 per cent. By March 1945 the camp hospital at Stalag Xb found itself able to serve just 1,300 calories worth of food to patients each day, and whilst German soldiers in the hospital were served with a variety of vegetables the POWs received swedes at every meal. Only 20 tons of coal were available each week, down from 100 tons a week earlier in the war, and the temperature on the wards never climbed above 13°C. Patients were refused hot showers unless they were suffering from TB. The conditions only helped to slow down the healing process. Some prisoners were even given bread containing sand that had been put into the dough to add bulk. Conditions in one camp infirmary became so bad that sick prisoners refused to remain, fearing the bed bugs were a greater danger to their health than the treatment was of benefit.

With the falling rations what sustenance could be found in Red Cross parcels was once again vital to help protect the prisoners from starvation. Even without fuel for cooking the calories found in cheese, butter and tinned meats could help keep hunger at bay. But for many prisoners the supply of parcels they had grown to rely on had become irregular. By February 1945 one camp hospital reported just 15 parcels left in stock, whereas the previous year there had enough to ensure every patient got a parcel each week. At the camp hospital of Stalag Xb they issued just one parcel per man per month. Despite the shortages, when parcels finally arrived they gave a new lease of life to the dejected prisoners: 'There were long delays before the parcels came around. You got to the stage where you didn't have the energy to do anything. You didn't even have the energy to talk. We were getting to the stage where you could drift off into despair. But when the parcels came there was a sense of relief. Blokes would be up all night gambling with cigarettes or whatever. It was amazing!'[13]

The prisoners at Stalag XIId, including over 400 Indian soldiers mainly employed in German vineyards, found their supplies of Red Cross parcels dried up in early 1945. During the evacuation of the camp from Trier all stores of parcels had been lost and the men were forced to survive on what little food the Germans provided them, or whatever they could pinch. The little food provided by their employers had to be transported from the main Stalag to the work detachments, in one case it was found the 30 kilometre journey took as long as 48 hours. As a result one work detachment complained they received no food for several days and another group survived on less than 100 grams of bread per man per day for two weeks. It was a far cry from the days of the previous autumn when their canteen was still selling razor blades and pale ale.

With food shortages biting, some prisoners were forced to dangerous acts to ward off starvation. Alec Reynolds, working at a copper mine, was one of those who risked all to ensure he was fed:

> Outside there was a great big horse trough and it was filled with our soup – one day it would be spinach, the next carrots. It was the same trough we washed our one set of clothes in. That was all. Red Cross parcels? We hardly ever got them. I used to go out and hide in the toilets after roll call. When the air raids were on I could go over the top of the fence. I'd go to a farm and get spuds. Then I'd go back and hide until the shifts changed. When they went to get their coffee I'd go back to the hut to bed.[14]

For Reynolds the real dangers arose when another man asked to join his nightly foraging expeditions:

> He was a Scottish commando. I said he could come but he had to follow my instructions. Then later a young paratrooper asked to join us. I said no, 'cause the longer it went on, the more chance there was of getting caught. So we went out that night, I saw a light and said 'get down'. I lay on my back so I could see. I noticed we were being followed. We lay still and it was the paratrooper. We had just reached the clamp and I showed them how to take the potatoes. I'd just got my hand in when a torch shone in my face. It was a guard. He said 'Halt or I shoot', I shouted 'Run!' We ran off and the young lad stayed behind. When we got back to the camp we saw the guard marching him down the road. We got back in and they had a roll call. They marched this young lad up the road and shot him. They shot him in the back of the head, the bullet came out of the front but he was alright. They kept him in the camp, in the end he could talk but not very well. They just let him wander about the camp.[15]

All knew the chaos was leading up to one event – liberation. They couldn't be sure when that moment would come, nor how they would react, but they knew it was coming ever closer. In those final days the prisoners readied themselves for that moment. Some began to organise their possessions, others spent long hours straining their ears to hear the sounds of the ever encroaching front lines. Others crouched around hidden radios, listening to broadcasts revealing how close their liberators were, whilst a handful organised themselves into groups, ready to seize control from the Nazis if any attempt was made to liquidate the camps. For all their activity few would have any real control over the events that followed.

When the moment of liberation finally arrived each person had a different experience. Some awoke to find their guards had fled and they were able simply to walk out of their camps. At Stalag XVIIIc many among the 13,000 inmates simply left the camp once they realised their guards had departed. Red Cross inspectors found over 300 men at the railway station fighting for space on a train, desperate to be onboard if it began the journey westwards. Despite efforts to shepherd the men back to the camp the NCOs were unable to control the men who were responsible for what the Red Cross described as 'scenes of considerable disorder and pillage'.[16]

Others watched battles raging around the Stalags as the enemy attempted to defy the Allied onslaught. At Fallingbostel the prisoners watched British tanks blowing up the German barrack huts, it was the first time in years that guns had been pointed away from prisoners rather than towards them. In some places the POWs confronted their guards and took possession of the camps, forcing the guards to flee. By late April Ken Wilats found himself outside Hanover, having marched from East Prussia. With the end rapidly approaching he once again headed off from the column:

> The column had split and was quite small. We had a German officer in charge of us, he was an awfully decent bloke. He called us together and said that the Americans were not far away and they would soon liberate us. He asked us to explain to them that he had been a reasonable guard and had treated us with respect. We agreed. Then a despatch rider came up and the officer told us he was going to have to take it back since the Germans were going to make a stand in the area and so we had to move on. By this time I was mucking in with an American we'd picked up – Freddy Gelfo, a butcher from New York. He said he wouldn't move on so we stayed at the back of the column and decided to hide. We were in the column with two German guards behind us. They were Frenchmen, from Alsace, who'd been forced into the German army. As we were going along after a couple of hours we spotted a barn and ran off across the road. Immediately the two Germans followed us. We thought 'This is it!' But they came into the barn and they took off their German uniforms and had complete French uniforms on underneath! We all headed

back into town and no one was about. There was an avenue of trees that stretched as far as the eye could see. In the distance we spotted a speck of dust that was heading towards us quite quickly. So we hid behind a tree. This tank came up and swung its gun towards us. Freddy called up to them 'Say, are you guys American?' They replied 'Yeah, buddy. Jump aboard.' And so we were free.[17]

American troops were also approaching Stalag VIIa at Moosburg outside Munich. Some of the prisoners had been marched out of the main camp to a place nearby where they awaited the arrival of the Americans. Bryan Willoughby was among them:

We were in a sort of gravel pit, in marquees, and we could hear the sound of tank guns being fired. And we waited, it went on and on for an hour or two. It got stronger and stronger and we knew they were very near. Some of the Yanks couldn't wait and one chap ran up to welcome them and got shot immediately. That wasn't funny. He wasn't killed, fortunately. But he wasn't happy about it. I stayed down. By this time I was beginning to learn a bit of sense, I kept my head down. We knew the war wasn't going to last forever, but there was always a fear that when the end came the Germans could just mow us down with machine guns.[18]

Fortunately their fears were not realised and apart from those men caught in the crossfire of battle most remained safe. Yet such incidents were not uncommon in those final confusing days. When one group of men decided to celebrate their freedom by cooking the last of their food they made the mistake of lighting a fire. A US artillery spotter plane noted their location and ordered a barrage of fire to hit what it thought was an enemy encampment. Two dozen released prisoners were killed.

Not all of those who were killed in the final days were the victims of accidents. Alec Reynolds, whose paratrooper colleague had already been shot by a guard after a failed foraging expedition, remembered the violence: 'When the Americans were close the Germans said they were going to take this paratrooper away to hospital, but they didn't. They took him off and executed him.'[19]

Fortunately such malicious acts were few and for many liberation was a time of unsurpassed emotion. Men dropped to the ground and wept whilst others cheered and danced around the vehicles of the liberating troops. At some Stalags and work camps joyous crowds swarmed around their liberators, collecting food and cigarettes handed out by

the troops. They watched as tanks crashed through gates and brought
down the fences. In the days that followed some among the liberated
men walked in and out through broken fences in a symbolic celebration of their new-found freedom. The emotional impact was such that
some simply didn't know what to do: 'We were free at last, and so overjoyed that we couldn't speak.'[20] But some failed to register any particular emotion: 'I don't remember any emotions at the time of liberation.
We knew it was coming, so it wasn't a shock.'[21] Alec Reynolds described
how uneventful liberation seemed to be: 'There was firing going on so
we knew they were coming. Then up came the Yankees, they had tanks
and everything. They were giving us fags and asking what had happened
to us. Then they said they were off and they left us behind. We just took
it in our stride. No elation at all. You were free and it was up to you to
do what you want to do.'[22] The sickly Les Allan was unable to join in
any celebrations, like so many of the men who had experienced the winter marches his pitiful physical condition controlled his emotions. As he
watched the liberating troops moving on to continue the battle he was
approached by RSM Lord who asked how long he'd been a prisoner.
Hearing the answer 'Five years', Lord sent the emaciated Allan to sit on
a tea chest. Minutes later medics arrived, deloused him with a machine
with tubes that were stuffed up his sleeves and trouser legs, then put
him on a truck taking prisoners straight to an airfield. There was no
time for celebrations. This failure to show any emotion was an indication of how much they had endured and how all that now counted was
to be alive. This stoical attitude would follow many throughout their
post-war lives.

Those arriving among the prisoners were often shocked by what they
saw. The liberating troops, often young men barely out of their teens,
looked at the thin, drawn faces of the prisoners and thought they looked
like old men. From Fallingbostel the War Office representative reported:
'appalling cases of undernourishment'.[23] This was typical British under-
statement. Many were not simply undernourished, they were starving.
Too weak to move from their beds, many simply stayed in their huts
when their liberators arrived. They could not celebrate – their war was
not over, nor would it be over until they had regained their strength and
were returned to a state of physical well-being. For many it would be a
long struggle, for some the full recovery would never come.

Although most troops simply felt immense relief at finally being liberated for some there were other, darker thoughts at play. Many scores
would be settled – sometimes by former prisoners, sometimes by liberat-

ing troops and sometimes by unseen hands. At one mine the British prisoners failed to take action against their guards but watched as liberated Russians caught a cruel overseer and threw him down the mineshaft. In some cases the former POWs pointed out guards who had mistreated them or their mates who were then taken away and executed by the liberating troops. One group of SS men were spotted being led into the woods by a Scottish sergeant armed with a liberated Luger, their fate unseen but their survival unlikely. When one released POW discovered his former guards hanging from the trees of a nearby forest he was uncertain as to whether they had fallen victims to Russian POWs or his own comrades. James Sims watched his fellow prisoners take revenge: 'One really cruel guard was discovered hiding in the next village. He was dragged back to face a kangeroo court and sentenced to be hung. He was hoisted aloft and this didn't bother us one bit.'[24] For some their vengeance was to humiliate rather than to attack. One released sailor, housed by the Americans in a former SS barracks, decided to humiliate the SS man detailed to clean the barracks. Defecating on the floor, he insisted the SS man clean it up with his hands. When he refused a guard was called and the German was forced to carry out the task at gunpoint.

Yet, after all they had suffered, surprisingly few prisoners were bent on revenge. It was not that they did not necessarily feel a great hatred for those who had treated them harshly, but simply that most of those responsible for the abuse of prisoners had disappeared. Knowing the fury that might await them they simply slipped out of uniform and disappeared into the countryside. Others who sought vengeance found themselves too weak to hunt down their oppressors. Alec Reynolds noticed how most of his guards had vanished:

> We were left on our own, then the Americans came. We told them about the young paratrooper who'd been shot and killed. They asked us which guard it was. They gave us a revolver and they said 'You point him out, we'll bring him out and you can shoot him'. But nobody did it. I could have understood it if we had shot him. I don't know why we didn't. Some people can do that sort of thing, I couldn't. I had no hatred for them.[25]

Les Allan, who had suffered much in his time as a prisoner – forced to work in industry despite being a stretcher-bearer, having his jaw broken by a guard, marched 600 miles with a fractured ankle – was convinced it was merely circumstances that prevented the released prisoners from taking revenge after they had been liberated:

> The guards must have been aware of how we felt because the first thing they did was surrender to our troops – not to us. The fighting troops were still governed by the Geneva Convention and the rules of war. But we'd been treated so badly that the Geneva Convention meant nothing to us. There were certain guards we all would like to have got our hands on. Yes, we would have got revenge – if we could have got to them. It must have been on the mind of the British government for months afterwards. When the time came for me to be discharged, when I was on the truck to leave, an officer asked me 'Would you like to stay on in the army?' – it was the first time I'd laughed for years. I said to him 'I wouldn't mind being in the army of occupation in Germany'. He told me he had strict orders that no former POWs were to be allowed to go back to Germany. So I said 'Goodbye'.[26]

For the weak and incapable retribution was provided by the liberating forces. Those able to muster up the strength to throw stones or beat German prisoners with sticks, did so but others were spotted sitting by roadsides asking the advancing troops to open fire on columns of enemy troops marching into captivity. At one camp where 13 German guards were found hiding among POWs dressed in British uniforms, they were handed over to the Russians who executed them.

In the chaos many of those with sufficient energy soon began forays into the German countryside to see what was on offer. Food and drink were high on their shopping lists, as were weapons to deter argumentative civilians. Once fed and watered they found new clothing to replace their ragged uniforms. They entered homes and demanded bath water be heated for them before luxuriating in the water and washing away the accumulated dirt of years of captivity. The baths were more than just a way of getting clean, they were a symbol of freedom, a sign that no one would ever again decide where and when they should be allowed to wash.

With both their guards and their liberators gone Alec Reynolds and his mates went to investigate the local town:

> There was this distillery where they made schnapps. So we went in and found these bottles. I looked at them and said 'That's not schnapps'. Someone else said 'Try it'. So we opened the bottle and just touched the

top of the bottle. It burned my lips. This other bloke swigged a whole lot down. I think it was neat alcohol. He just passed out. We just took him into this house and asked the people to look after him.[27]

Released from captivity Bryan Willoughby was among a mixed group of prisoners who were also left to their own devices:

Up to the liberation the Germans fed us – in inverted commas. But after liberation we just looked after ourselves. We went into a factory to look for food, then around the villages and town trying to find food, but it was very difficult. We eventually found odd bits, eggs and what have you. But we were under no one's authority for two weeks. So we just looked after ourselves. We just hung around.[28]

For some, freedom did not involve the spectacle of liberation by the advancing armies, rather they just wandered off alone. Emerging into the chaos of a collapsing nation many found it an ideal opportunity to enjoy the mayhem, yet for others it was a time of danger and uncertainty. In Austria one group of prisoners took shelter in a barn after the flour mill where they worked was evacuated. Hiding up by day, they spent the nights scavenging for food. Australian prisoner, Alexander Mansfield took his turn to feed his mates but was shot and killed by a civilian. After waiting so long for freedom it was a tragic end to the war. Not all were so unfortunate, such as Robert Hallam and his group of mates who left the column they were marching in and headed towards the front line hoping to link up with the Russians. Stopped by German troops they were made to work for three days. Escaping for a second time they decided to head towards the advancing American army. Once more they were recaptured, this time being returned to the column they had originally escaped from. Upon their return their guards explained that they had not been reported as missing since the guards were afraid of punishment.

D-Day veteran 'Bill' Sykes was among those who found themselves alone. Having simply ignored his guards and walked away from captivity the 18-year-old Sykes wandered alone through the German countryside for five days. Ravaged by dysentery and facing bitterly cold rainstorms the youngster was in a desperate situation. Salvation came from an unlikely source:

I was picked up by a German patrol and questioned as to my intentions.

The major in charge placed me under the guard of an older Sergeant – who had been a prisoner of war in England during WW1 who spoke a fair amount of north-country English – with instructions to take me down to the local jail. Sergeant Paul Tauber was a man full of surprises – first he took me to the local beer tavern where they fed us with whatever small portions of food were available. We drank dark beer with a chaser, which in my state of health was pretty lethal and it didn't take much to get us both totally inebriated. I was very grateful for this magnificent old soldier's hospitality. That was the first of Paul's surprises – next, he excused himself and came back dressed in civilian clothes and said in a broad north-country accent, 'I don't know where you're going son, but I'm going to make my way back home'. We parted company with many handshakes and Paul went on his way into the evening darkness with the rolling gate of a sailor who had drunk too many rums. I never saw my saviour and new friend ever again. I do hope he made it home safely. As for me, I was in no state to travel and have no idea where I slept that night but in my sublime state of inebriation I slept the sleep of the righteous. Next morning, I awoke with a terrible hangover, which took days to disperse, and I staggered onto what appeared to be the village green and sat under a tree where I succumbed to the after effects of the drinks we had consumed and sank into blissful oblivion. Later I found that I was in the small village of Wermsdorf, and much to my relief a German family apparently saw my plight and provided me with shelter for several nights in a hay loft above their garage and gave me whatever food that they could spare. I am ever grateful to them for their kindness. The moral of these two stories is that not all Germans are bad. To close out the particular hectic few weeks in the life of an ex-prisoner, I ought to mention that one evening I met up with a contingent of Russian soldiers on the village green who were celebrating crossing the river Elbe by drinking bottles of vodka. They insisted that I join them in their celebration and of course it was an invitation that I could not refuse, as I did not want to be exiled to Siberia. After the Russian soldiers went on their merry way I made one of my better decisions and decided that the time had come to surrender myself to the American Armed Forces. I later found myself in a hospital in Nuremberg and a week or so later was homebound to a hospital in Nottingham.[29]

Not all were so sick they had to rely upon the hospitality of German civilians. Instead many of the ex-POWs decided the time had come to take whatever they needed or wanted. Now free, they began to scour the countryside for souvenirs. Many had already clothed themselves in bits and pieces of German uniforms since these were usually the only clothes they could find that weren't falling to pieces. Now many began to collect German equipment. They hunted for Nazi daggers, ornamental swords and weapons of all descriptions, in particular the legendary Luger pistols. Musical instruments, ornaments, impressive German beer steins, candlesticks, cameras, watches, fountain pens, razors – anything that was portable was stuffed in haversacks ready to take home.

Some among them filled their packs and pockets with jewellery that they stole from local houses. Corporal David Robb of the Argyll and Sutherland Highlanders was among them. Released from a work camp he went looting with some Russians. His haul included a gold cigarette case, diamond brooches, gold earrings set with rubies, bracelets, platinum brooches, amethyst cuff links and a gold compact. When he returned home he attempted to sell his loot and the jeweller estimated the total value of the goods at £1,020 – a small fortune in 1945. The problem was that the jeweller believed them to be stolen and reported him to the police. Although following an investigation the police accepted no crime had been committed and let the matter drop, local Customs Officers were less understanding. They decided that since import duty had not been paid the goods should be confiscated until the corporal was able to pay. With Robb in hospital recovering from TB there was no way he could raise sufficient money and his loot was lost forever.

Bryan Willoughby also went hunting for 'souvenirs' that would never reach home:

> I kept an eye out for stuff worth looting. I filled two kit bags of things I thought I could sell. Lugers had a price of £10 a time. So I had Lugers and knives. That was the feeling at the time, you didn't keep things as souvenirs you kept them to make a bit of money. Unfortunately when the RAF came to pick us up they weren't as easygoing as the Yanks. They said 'You can't have that or that, only the bare essentials' so I lost all my loot. Every bit of it. I should have sold it first but I didn't have the market.[30]

Once free, many had one other thing on their mind – women. In the words of one prisoner they spent their new found freedom: 'scooping up any stray crumpet'.[31] James Witte was among them. Having had a sexual relationship with a Belgian woman whilst employed in a German factory, Witte was eager to continue his physical life. He soon befriended a German war widow who initially rebuffed his amorous advances. Eventually she responded:

> This time she allowed me to play with her breasts. Greatly heartened by this, and somewhat hardened, I put my hand up her skirt and let it stray to the flesh above her stocking top, but when I slid my eager fingers up her suspenders and towards her knickers she stopped me. By this time I had a great erection which she couldn't fail to notice. I mentioned this to her, whereupon she undid my trousers taking my penis out. I ejaculated right away much to her amusement.[32]

Whilst the men who had reached the safety of central Germany were already beginning to rebuild their lives, others were not so fortunate. For those who had not been evacuated westwards, or had chosen to remain behind to await the arrival of the Red Army, a very different fate awaited them. As the camps were evacuated many of the inmates of camp hospitals were raised from their beds to begin the march westwards. The bedridden were often left behind, as were enclosures full of Russian prisoners. At Stalag XXa the bed-bound prisoners and medical staff found the hospitals besieged by Russian POWs who attacked the cookhouse and stole food. The starving Russians were growing increasingly desperate and with no guards left to control them they were free to raid the hospital and surrounding villages.

Another group of 50 British prisoners were left behind in a Russian camp. Too sick to be moved the men – many with pneumonia, diphtheria or frost bite – were simply left on a straw-covered floor with no one to tend to them. At Stalag XXb a group of POWs were forced to remain behind to bake bread for the German army. They worked on even whilst Russian shells were whistling over the camp or exploding around them. All across Poland and Czechoslovakia hundreds of POWs of all nationalities disappeared into the countryside. Their intentions were many and varied. Some could not face the prospect of marching for weeks across the frozen countryside and simply went into hiding. Their knowledge of the local surroundings gained during the years of working in the countryside proved invaluable – many found hiding places on the farms where they had once laboured for the enemy. With the German population fleeing the Red Army the local farmers were free to take over their lands. Many prisoners joined them, settling down in the farmhouses. As late as September 1945 British officials were still finding pockets of prisoners living in villages across eastern Europe, with many making brides of the local girls who had long been their lovers. One of those who stayed behind was Corporal Albert Heafield of the Gordon Highlanders. Captured in 1940 he had worked on a farm at Katzke near Danzig from August 1941 until February 1945. At the farm he had started a relationship with a woman, Eva Schulz, whose husband had been killed in action in 1941. The following year she gave birth to Heafield's child. On 3 February he left the westward bound column and returned to Frau Schulz and their child, remaining there until the Red Army reached the area. He eventually returned home and began the process of applying for permission for his family to be allowed to join him in England.

In Czechoslovakia many of the remaining prisoners gravitated towards Prague where the Foreign Office reported 'considerable numbers' of them living in civilian homes with no immediate intention of moving out. In the words of the diplomats they had 'gone native'.[33] They chose to avoid the official reception centres since they distrusted the Russians and whenever they heard of trains heading westwards they converged on railway stations, jumping on board in the hope of reaching the Allied lines. Most were unlucky, instead of passing into freedom the Soviets refused them passage through the front lines and they were forced to make their way back to Prague. By the end of September 1945 6,000 British former prisoners of war had passed through the Czech capital.

Some had more martial intentions. Rather than going into hiding they joined up with bands of partisans, helping to clear up pockets of German troops. When a group of former POWs were found by a team of British agents sent into Austria to find prisoners, they didn't await transport home. Instead they asked for weapons and civilian clothes and headed south to team up with Tito's partisans. In Poland and Czechoslovakia the local fighters also found recruits from among former prisoners. Some among the POWs who had originally been held in camps in Italy already had links with partisan groups, having joined up with them following the surrender of Italy in 1943. Now released from camps in Austria and Germany, a few headed south to rejoin the fight or merely to thank the Italian civilians whose generosity had sustained them in their struggle to evade the Germans. One South African had a particularly good reason to head back to Italy. When he had been recaptured he had left his brother still fighting with the partisans. Now free he headed south in an attempt to make contact.

This free-spirited sense of adventure – hardly surprising in men who had been imprisoned for so long – was a dangerous game, especially with the Red Army controlling eastern Europe and parts of Austria and Germany. Amidst the anarchy of spring 1945 the former prisoners had every reason to be suspicious of the Red Army. Most prisoners had seen the behaviour of the Russians in the Stalags and knew how ruthless they could be. They also knew how much the Poles they had worked alongside feared the Russians and had heard German reports of the brutal treatment meted out by the advancing army. As early as April 1945 the Foreign Office had reported they feared the Russians would not release the prisoners westwards, rather they would hold them in eastern Europe and send them home via the Black Sea. But before such evacuations could take place the prisoners had to survive the arrival of the Red Army. Countless POWs may have lost their lives in the battles that raged across eastern Europe in early 1945. No one was on hand to count the dead or mark their graves. Marching prisoners were targeted in mistake for German columns and lone men were simply shot down by Russians uncertain as to their identity. Even as late as summer 1945 those former prisoners still at large faced immense danger. One of them, Gunner Pritchard, was shot and killed by the Russians in August 1945, a full three months after hostilities had ceased. More fortunate was Royal Engineer Alan Edwards, who also came into conflict with his erstwhile allies. Captured in 1940 Edwards had served five terms of imprisonment for refusing to work. In early 1945 he was one of the thousands marching westwards through the Polish winter. Whilst on the march he escaped and went into hiding. When the Russians arrived he was put into a camp alongside other refugees, including freed slave labourers of all nationalities and other wandering ex-POWs. Escaping from the camp, he was first robbed of all his documents and possessions by Red Army soldiers and was then put into a 'concentration camp' since he was unable to prove his identity. After two weeks of trying to convince the guards as to his identity, he was finally released. Heading home by bicycle he once more came into conflict with the occupation forces when two Russian MPs tried to steal his transport. Edwards argued with them and received a bullet in his leg for his trouble. Now in desperate straits – wounded, alone in a war ravaged country and without any identification – he was saved by the intervention of a local woman. Wanda Skryzpkowska took him in and dressed his wounds, nursing him back to health. Whilst still in hiding they married and eventually in November 1944 Edwards received permission to return to England with his new bride.

Such hostility from the Russians were not isolated cases. When the Red Army liberated entire camps of POWs they often kept them behind the wire, not allowing them access to the longed for freedom. It was not just their freedom that was curtailed. At Stalag IVc the incoming Russians immediately emptied the remaining parcels from the Red Cross stores, leaving the prisoners to fend for themselves. Some camps were visited by Red Army officers who requested the prisoners volunteer to join them. Some took up the offer, accepting weapons from their liberators and continuing the war they had long thought had passed them by. Fearful of Russian intentions the War Office took action and sent men on secret missions to facilitate the rescue of prisoners. In March a team recruited from among Austrian POWs in Britain were parachuted into their home country to locate former prisoners on the run in the region. However the agents were soon found by the Russians who, though accepting their story, decreed that since they were dressed in civilian clothing they should be shot as spies. They were saved by the sergeant detailed to carry out the execution. After stealing their watches he let them escape, allowing them to go back into hiding in the local villages. In the same region there were further reports of Russian hostility to escaped British prisoners. One group who had teamed up with the Red Army to round up German troops were executed once their work was finished.

Those more fortunate men who had been liberated in the west soon began the journey home. Some followed the 'stay put' orders received from London and the instructions of the liberating troops, and awaited the liaison officers who would process them and organise transport home. Yet large numbers of men at work camps had simply never received any orders and so made off into the unknown. All across the Reich liberated POWs began to search for transport home. Many simply stole whatever transport was available and headed in the direction of Brussels. Prisoners working at a quarry in Austria borrowed a car from a local man and ferried the entire contingent of POWs between the camp and the British lines in northern Italy. When their last journey was complete they returned the car to its owner. Whilst many prisoners were being counted by staff sent to process them others simply headed for the channel ports and cadged lifts on ships heading back to 'Blighty'. Then they thumbed lifts straight home, never bothering to be officially demobbed from the army.

All across Germany civilian cars, motorcycles and delivery trucks helped to move men homewards. Often drunk, either on beer or emotion, they waved at the Allied troops still advancing into the heart of Germany. Some 'liberated' bicycles and mustered up all their reserves of energy to pedal westwards. Others chose tractors or even fire engines to make the journey. Alec Reynolds found a most unusual form of transport, one which would take him right across Germany:

> Everybody else stayed at the camp but we went into town. By this time
> I had a little Beretta pistol and a Luger. I'd got conjunctivitis, so I had
> a patch over one eye and these pistols – I looked like a pirate. Myself,
> the Scottish commando and another chap went into town and went into
> this big house. The French people who worked there fed us. One said to
> us 'I've got to get wood.' I asked him what he needed wood for. He said
> 'For the truck'. He had a wood burning truck. So we got some wood and
> we just headed off towards home. All my kit was left behind. I wasn't
> bothered. We had no idea where we were going or how far it was.[34]

With his POW colleagues, two Frenchmen and a French girl dressed in military uniform, Reynolds headed west. Travelling by day, staying in farms at night, and eating whatever they could beg, borrow or steal, they eventually crossed the entire country before being put into trucks travelling to Liège. Given an American uniform he was then put straight on a flight back to Great Missenden. From the airfield he made his way straight to his sister's home in Watford.

Liberated by the Americans, Ken Wilats was told to go to the parade ground of a barracks in a nearby town that had recently been captured:

> The place was swarming with released prisoners of war. So Freddy and I
> thought we wouldn't go in, instead we thought we'd have a look around.
> The place was in a state of flux so we thought we'd have a bit of an
> adventure. Then they said there would be an important announcement
> made on the parade ground. We dawdled around and eventually stood
> at the back of about a thousand men, all facing this general. He got
> onto the platform and gave us all the usual spiel about being liberated
> by the American army. We noticed soldiers behind us erecting these bar-
> riers right behind us. Then the general said 'Gentlemen, I'd like you to
> know we are going to get you home as quickly as possible, and we are
> starting right now. About turn!' So we were at the front of the queue, we
> went through the barrier went straight to a plane and were home that
> evening![35]

Few were able to get home quite so swiftly. Converging on towns and cities in Belgium the prisoners began the final leg of their journey home.

Bryan Willoughby found himself in Liège where as fortune would have it he was wearing an American uniform given to him by his liberators: 'I found myself among a group that was 90 per cent Yanks. And the Yanks were paying out! Everyone was getting a big handful of money. So we queued up. While I was in the queue this lad tells me to say I was such and such a number and belonged to the North Carolina Regiment. So when I got to the table I gave them my name and supposed regiment and got the money!'[36] The uniform that had helped them to fill their pockets in Liège would have a less impressive impact when he and his British comrades reached Brussels:

> We were put in a hotel. Every man had a bed! – 'Look, Sheets!' So one or two of the lads said 'Let's go for a quick drink'. So we went across the road into the first café we saw. We were sitting there drinking and the first thing that happened was that we were set on by Canadians – they thought we were Yanks! One of the lads I was with had a peg leg and he unscrewed it and put it on the bar. The Canadians were horrified, so that put a stop to that.[37]

Most ex-prisoners enjoyed their stay in Brussels, making up for lost time in the restaurants, bars and brothels that had become such a feature of the Belgian capital's nightlife. Recognising them as POWs the MPs ignored the drunken men and merely escorted them back to hotels rather than arresting them for breaking the curfew or being drunk and disorderly. Once their brief stay in the city was complete each group of men were driven out to an airfield to begin the journey home. Bryan Willoughby only just made it back in time to meet the transit:

> It was too early to go back to the hotel so we went from café to café. Then we picked up this woman and her daughter and they insisted on coming along with us. So we went into more cafes and did a bit of dancing, then had some more booze – I spent all the money the Yanks had given me. I didn't get back to the hotel until six o'clock in the flaming morning. When I got there they were marching out of the gate! So I just fell in with them. I was not anywhere near sober. Then we flew back.[38]

As they left the barracks some were struck by the significance of the moment – their war was finally over. One of them, Ken Clarke, captured during the retreat to Dunkirk, later wrote of his emotions: 'Bewilderment, I think, is the best way to describe my feelings, at being free to walk about without a gun hovering behind me, not having to wonder when the next meal would come and not needing to collect butt ends from cigarettes so that I could re-roll them for a few puffs later.' He also explained why he walked out to the plane with just the clothes he stood up in, leaving behind his treasured clarinet which had brought him so much comfort during the long years of captivity: 'I suppose that with the excitement of the war being over, the years of sweated labour and imprisonment ended, the long dreadful march finished, thoughts of being back in England now took over. Nothing else really mattered at that moment.'[39]

Liberated by the Americans, Gordon Barber was put into an ambulance to take him to an airfield ready for the return journey to England. Despite medical treatment he remained weak from the exertions of the long march:

> They thought I had something wrong with me, 'cause I was still making such a mess. They kept me in hospital for a couple of days then they took me by ambulance. It was a rough ride, I was still shitting myself all the time. I asked the driver for toilet roll but he didn't have any. I still remember what I used to clean myself up – I used my *lagergeld*, the old camp money. It was worthless. Then they loaded me on a Dakota full of wounded men, to go home.[40]

As they lined up on the runways of airfields, the released prisoners were counted and recounted – just like in the old days of the seemingly ceaseless *Appels* – then were given numbers and told to await their homeward-bound flight. As they waited they were informed that much of their luggage would have to be left behind, since space restrictions would allow for no more than 30 kilos per man. Anxious not to leave behind much of the loot they had acquired since liberation they began sorting out what they really needed to take home with them. Lightweight items like Nazi memorabilia – hats, helmets, swords, medals, badges – were kept, whilst heavier goods often including items of furniture made by some of them whilst in captivity, were abandoned.

It was not the separation from such possessions that had an emotional impact on the returning men. What concerned many was that they were separated from their friends at the last moment. After years of 'mucking in' together, and sharing the privations of the long march, men were split up as they were counted off into the waiting aircraft. Those men who lost their mates at the last minute were sent into a whirl of conflicting emotions, excitement that they were finally going home and deflation that they were without their companions. It was simply a matter of space, when the correct number of men were aboard, the plane would take off. Speed and efficiency were the order of the day, worrying about the separation of friends was an irrelevance.

For many the flight home was their first time in an aeroplane. Others looked back on their previous flights, such as the ill-fated trip to Arnhem. Yet few were frightened by the experience, they were simply overjoyed to be going home. Some perched in the bomb bays or fuselages of bombers more used to destruction than salvation. Others sat inside transport aircraft or occupied the seats most commonly used for paratroopers. As they approached the coast of England pilots called men forward in turn to get their first glimpse of the land they had spent years dreaming of, and which some had once given up hope of ever seeing again. As the pilots finally announced they were once more flying above English soil the ex-POWs were hit by a wave of emotion. Some cheered whilst others sat deep in thought. Some clapped, sang or hugged the men beside them whilst others sat in tears, their thoughts on all those who would never be returning home. It was a time of rejoicing and remembering, for both celebration and contemplation.

Then finally the wheels touched down, they were safe and free. Yet there were still a few more formalities to go through. Most were deloused, some had all their body hair shaved off and were scrubbed down with lotions and potions to kill the vermin. Others were simply dusted with powder and declared safe. Many of their uniforms were gathered together and incinerated, although some men desperately attempted to save their kit from the flames. It would provide a permanent reminder of their condition in those final weeks and months of war.

Baths, showers, shaves and haircuts were the order of the day, with men who had worn shoulder length hair once more appearing as soldiers. They collected brand new uniforms, with unit badges, stripes and medal ribbons sewn on by the Women's Institute, then collected leave passes, travel warrants and pay. Then they were free to go.

Clad in their new uniforms, shod in polished boots that had replaced their clogs, the former prisoners began their journeys home. Some sent telegrams or made telephone calls to alert their anxious families. Others simply set off in the direction of home wanting to save the hallowed meeting until they were once more face to face with their families. Ken Wilats was among those who chose not to send word of his arrival:

I thought I'd surprise them. I got the train to London, then got on the train to Balham at platform 9 of Victoria Station. I walked from the station to my home and my parents were out at the pub. My brother was at home. He had only been a young lad when I left to go to war – so he didn't really recognise me. I said 'I'm Ken' and he couldn't believe it. Then my parents came back and they were very tearful – emotional and delighted. That was the end of the story.[41]

However, not all were able to head home quite so quickly. The lean months of winter had left many too sick to face the trials of reintegrating into society. Their weakened bodies fell victim to all manner of sickness and disease. Many were admitted to military hospitals and treatment prevented rapid reunion with their families. When families did visit many walked through the wards unable to find their husbands or sons. They simply failed to recognise them. They had gone off to war in the prime of their lives, as strong, fit young soldiers but had returned as shadows of their former selves. The poor diet had weakened their teeth, left their skin drawn tight over fleshless skulls, and given them stoops. Likewise, their hair had lost its lustre, fallen out or turned grey. These were young men inhabiting the bodies of the middle-aged. In this condition some implored their families not to visit them, preferring to save their reunions for the day they could walk confidently into the family home.

Whether the journey home was immediate or after hospital treatment all among the ex-prisoners experienced feelings of trepidation. As they sat down in trains or buses they were alone for what seemed the first time in their lives. Stripped from the close confines of the Stalags and work camps, they were finally free to take in all they had experienced in the years that had passed between capture and liberation. No longer with their mates at their shoulder laughing and joking, their minds began to wander back to the good times they had shared and the horrors they had experienced.

Some 'palled up' with other former prisoners or men heading back on leave, others made the journey in silence, their minds racing with thoughts of what lay ahead of them. Maurice Newey, released after years in camps in Italy and Germany, later wrote of arrival at his family home in York. Having walked through the still city night he finally greeted his parents then made his way to bed. All across Britain in the May of 1945 there were thousands of men sharing this moment, as they returned to the peace of home after years of the pain and hardship of forced labouring for the Germans. Newey might have spoken for them all: 'I stretched out in the comfortable bed relishing the feeling of the sheets. An overwhelming desire to cry came over me and tears rushed to my eyes, I shut them tight but one tear managed to escape and tickled my cheek as it ran down. After a while I became calmer and felt unutterably weary. I let myself relax and I drifted into a dreamless sleep. I was home, in my own bed.'[42]

TEN

Every Day a Bonus

No more lining up for parcels
Same old pushing shoving throng
Same old laughter, same old faces
Same old voice 'It won't be long!'
No more standing late on rollcalls
Cross the surging restless foam
We'll be overjoyed, elated
This is England! This is home![1]

'Life in a POW camp, as I experienced it, was not the cops and robbers theatrics as portrayed in "Hogan's Heroes", it was a constant battle to survive.'[2]

And so they came home – men who had changed, returning to a land that had changed. They had spent years musing on what they might do once their shackles were cast aside and they were free once more to rebuild their lives away from the deprivation and disease of the Stalags. Hours of discussion had passed with men planning the meals they would eat, the women they would chase, what work they wanted to do. In short, how they would maximise the freedom that had been won for them by the supreme efforts of the liberating armies – efforts that they would never forget and always be thankful for.

Yet many returned home with a shadow over their lives that would take years to erase. George Marsden was among them. His experience of arriving home was perhaps symbolic of the uncertain future faced by many of the returning prisoners, as he later wrote of his typically subdued homecoming: 'made my way home on the train alone, caught a bus to Sheffield, and sat on the doorstep waiting for my mum to get back from shopping. So that was that, no flag waving, no fuss, the end of an exciting time of my life, some happy, some not very good at all.'[3]

The first days of freedom back home were a chance to see whether they could realise these wartime musings. The men who had written poems – rather eulogies – to the prospect of liberation, with titles such as 'The Jubilation of a Repatriated Prisoner' or 'It's All A Day Nearer' would soon find out if their dreams would be fulfilled. Back in the spring of 1944, when liberation seemed so far away, one POW had written his thoughts of the future:

> I think that the ordinary things of life which we hardly noticed will in future mean more to us. Such commonplace things as an armchair and a coal fire, or a real bed complete with smooth, white sheets and without bugs. These, I maintain, will forever give us an extra, subtle satisfaction, even though we may not be fully conscious of it. ... I don't think little setbacks and annoyances will ever affect us again as they once did. .... You can't stop either the clock or the calendar and before long we'll be looking back thinking of this as a period of cold storage, but finding life so much more grander than it was by sheer contrast.[4]

As the returning prisoners arrived back in the UK they were soon packed off to their homes, they were not eligible for foreign service for at least six months and started life back home with a period of six weeks leave, being given double rations for the first 28 days. They were then called to a medical board to see if they were still fit for military service. Those deemed unfit were then given an additional eight weeks 'terminal leave' before being discharged from the army. The conditions were not the same for all since some still had plenty of time before they would be returning to their families. The Commonwealth and Dominion troops were all far from home and would have to await the long journey across the oceans before they would see their loved ones again. Unlike prisoners released in the Mediterranean who shipped directly home the Australians and New Zealanders who arrived back in Britain were given 28 days leave before they would be expected to return home. The Canadians were given just 14 days leave before returning to service. More generously the Indians were allowed a period of three months leave and the South Africans were warned they were likely to remain in the mother country for 'some months'.

Once they had crossed the threshold of their homes it was time to start rebuilding their lives. However nothing was that simple. In the time they'd been away much had altered. Women throughout the land were occupying many of the jobs previously held by men. Young children had grown up with little real memory of their fathers and older children had left home and moved on. Parents and grandparents had died and wives and girlfriends had moved on – sometimes emotionally and sometimes physically. Even the look of people had changed. The prisoners were shocked to see how much make-up was worn by British women. They were used to the clear faces of central European women and they felt the women at home were wearing masks. Furthermore, the physical landscape of the world they returned to had suffered – prisoners came home to find whole areas flattened by enemy bombing, some returning to 'homes' they had never seen before. Nor did they return to a land of plenty – a land where they would be able to sate their cravings for food and leisure. They came home to a bleak Britain, still gripped by rationing, a country exhausted by six years of war.

For most the shocks began even before they reached home. As they sat clutching their kitbags on trains and buses they listened to the conversations around them. They attempted to pay bus fares only to find drivers and conductors laughing at them because the prices they expected to pay had risen so much in the passing years. Small talk about events and people they had no knowledge of were confusing. Discussions about the constraints of rationing meant little to men who just weeks before had fought over bread crusts or potato peelings. Some found themselves craving a bar of chocolate only to find the vending machines of railway stations empty, their contents having succumbed to the rigours of rationing many years before. Men attempted to enjoy their freedom by walking into shops and spending their money, a privilege denied them for so long. Yet, when one ex-prisoner returned to shop where he had always previously bought his cigarettes he was informed they were reserved for regular customers only.

Such irritations were the least of their worries, what was of greatest concern was the mental and emotional burden they had carried home from the Stalags. The experience of imprisonment meant that the return home for married men was not always marked by a great outpouring of emotion. They had dreamt of the day they would walk through the front door of their home and whisk their wife upstairs to bed for the long awaited reunion. Like everything else about their return home, such grand intentions were often undermined by the reality of the situation. Many felt uncomfortable with their wives, the lack of contact over so many months and years left a gap that could not immediately be bridged. Furthermore some lacked the physical strength to make love and wished to do little more than rest. W.G. Harvey, who had ironically helped build POW camps in France in 1940 for the expected influx of German POWs only to be later captured himself, recalled his return to his wife: 'I remember kissing Edith but after that time apart we both felt rather strange with each other and I suppose in my rundown condition I would seem aloof and miserable. It was at least a fortnight before we could come together in the normal relationship of husband and wife, due entirely to my physical condition.'[5] In a bizarre contrast to this, some prisoners found that peppering their food acted as a strong aphrodisiac. After having been denied pepper for so long they found it stimulated those parts of their body that had long lain idle.

Harvey was not alone. Plenty of ex-prisoners were self-conscious about their appearance. The ravages of the final months of war had stripped the flesh from their bones, leaving them emaciated, with eyes and cheeks sunk hollow into their skulls. Hair had lost its shine, gone grey or fallen out. Gums had receded, indeed many among them had lost their teeth. Their skin was grey and lined and many admitted feeling they had grown old during their time as 'guests of the Third Reich'. Not only that but some had all their body hair shaved off during the delousing programme. They felt self-conscious about the appearance of their bony, hairless bodies, not wanting to be seen naked by anyone.

There was genuine concern that many of the long-term POWs would need psychiatric help. In late 1944 the War Office had compiled figures showing how much help would be needed. With around 100,000 British soldiers held in Germany, of whom 58,000 had been in captivity for over three years, it was expected that around 71,000 of them would be in need of 'mental' help. In reality few would ever receive any serious counselling. In an effort to help the returning prisoners rebuild their lives plans had been drawn up by the War Office to help families understand the men who returned. Written by POWs who had been in captivity earlier in the war, the documents helped illuminate the mental state of the liberated men. A list of points was to have acted as a guide for families yet was never issued. Instead the ex-POWs were left to make the best of the situation upon their return, often being faced by families with an unrealistic notion of how they should behave. This was a pity since the proposed leaflet had offered much useful advice about how to best aid rehabilitation. Families were urged to be good listeners but not to pressure the men to talk if they didn't want to. They should also answer any questions carefully to help the returning man understand how society had changed during his missing years. Business or personal matters should be ignored until the man was ready to put his mind to such matters. Families were told to expect men to be moody: 'He will very likely be very cheerful and talkative at times and then very quiet and depressed for a spell. He may get upset rather quickly too. That's all natural and will pass in time if you don't worry him about it. Show him that you sympathise with him when he needs it but don't let him think you are pitying him.'[6]

It was also recognised that POWs should be allowed to do whatever they liked at first, urging families to let a man stay in alone if he wanted to whilst agreeing to let him go out all the time if he so desired. Wives were also given pointers as to how they might expect their husbands to be with them: 'He may be rather shy of showing affection at first. He has been starved of it for a long time. Give him a chance to realise he is at home with those who love him.'[7] Other tips included not overfeeding ex-prisoners and not allowing them too much strong alcohol since their weakened bodies would not be able to cope with it. Finally they were offered one important piece of advice: 'Remember a prisoner of war is not a sick man unless the doctor has said he is one.'[8]

The British government approached the whole issue of the returning POWs with trepidation. There had already been psychiatric evaluations made of POWs who had returned home in January 1945. Of the 31 men all but two were medically downgraded on the advice of army psychiatrists – and the other two had been admitted to a psychiatric hospital. There were others aware of how the returning men would need careful handling. As early as December 1944 the BBC had proposed broadcasting a talk by a Colonel Chapel, himself an ex-POW who had been repatriated earlier in the war. Chapel's talk was an honest assessment of the mental state of POWs:

> But do you understand quite clearly just how he feels when he realises that all the places and faces that he has dreamt about and thought of so often in captivity are not quite as familiar as he had thought and hoped they would be? People and places too – thanks to Hitler and his bombs – change quite a lot, you know, in four or five years ... After all, we are more or less 'Rip Van Winkles' coming back to life again after a long period of isolation from the world we knew ... Please don't laugh at us if we ask a question which seems foolish and out of date ... We are all a bit touchy. The kind of question I mean is 'What are points?' 'Why can't I buy sardines without points?'[9]

Such questions about the complexities of the rationing system and how prisoners and their families needed to be prepared were simple common sense. However the War Office decided against allowing the broadcast, preferring instead to present a much more formal talk by a General Adams which was devoid of the emotional aspects of Chapel's planned speech. As a result of the 'stiff upper lip' approach of the War Office both families and prisoners entered this new period of their lives with little preparation.

Whilst they rebuilt their relationships with their families the ex-POWs had to realise there was much about life to which they needed to adapt. Long forgotten details of home life seemed unreal – the soothing ticking of clocks, tables laid for meals with tablecloths and cutlery, open fires rather than the stoves of central Europe, the taste of common British vegetables rather than the pickled cabbage and boiled turnips they had grown so familiar with. Where there had once been no choice now they had choice – whether to stay in or go out, what to eat, which radio station to listen to. They overheard conversations on subjects they knew nothing of. Accepted details of everyday life such as the Mulberry Harbours were a complete mystery to them. All were small, seemingly insignificant details of normal life, but were complicated dilemmas to men who had endured captivity.

These problems were no less trying for single men, since at least the married men had someone to return to. Many came home to their bedrooms in the family home they had left years before. They looked back at their previous lives and realised how much they had changed. The passing years had seen them outgrow their childhood homes. The 18- and 19-year-old boys who had gone to war six years before had returned as men – men whose experience of the horrors of war had matured them beyond belief. Yet despite their new found maturity and the desperate yearning for female company some men found they could no longer approach women. Years of captivity had eroded their confidence and they felt uncomfortable in mixed company. Some attended dances but were unable to ask women to take the floor. It would take time for them to learn to live fully, and soon many families realised the brave face shown in the letters from the POW camps had been little more than a mask concealing a reality few outsiders could have imagined.

The attention given to the return of the prisoners caused discomfort for some among them. No one could begrudge families wanting to visit them, nor blame them for wanting to hear tales of war. However, many among the prisoners simply wanted to be left alone. After so long in enforced captivity, crammed into huts alongside other men, they yearned

group photo showing Gordon Barber (back row, second from right) and 'Lofty' Griggs (back row, third from right); Frank Turton (middle row, first on left) and Ken Wilats (bottom row, first on right), next to him is Phipps who had a nervous breakdown (see p.195)Barber, Turton and Griggs saved Wilats's life when he fell sick during the long march westwards.

Gordon Barber today in his eighties

The kitchen in the Stalag hospital where Bryan Willoughby was treated (National Archive)

Above: Bryan Willoughby in 1940

Right: Bryan Willoughby in 2004 at Arnhem

The house in Wermsdorf in which Sykes, suffering from dysentery and malnutrition took shelter after escaping from a POW column in Spring 1945.

Left Above: Sykes' POW ID tag from Stalag XIIA

Left Below: Eighteen year old Eric 'Bill' Sykes with the
7th Battalion, Parachute Regiment in 1944

Right: Sykes in 1994 after parachuting into Normandy on the
50th anniversary of D-Day

Originally captioned 'A Hero Comes Home to Devon' the cheery atmosphere belied the reality of the homecoming for many ex-prisoners. Few among them considered themselves heroes and many struggled for years to cope with their wartime memories. (Imperial War Museum CP12833F)

for solitude. Instead many became curiosities, constantly receiving visitors who wished to view them. Few wanted the attention, preferring to rebuild their lives quietly without the constant questioning of well-intentioned friends and relatives. Above all they wanted to fit back into society with as little fuss as possible.

Feeling they had wasted so much of their lives in Stalags and work camps the ex-prisoners realised they needed to change and put behind them the memories of what had gone before. They couldn't continue with the lives they had known. Everything needed to be moderated. Table manners needed to be learnt all over again. They had to remember to use cutlery rather than their fingers and not to lick plates clean in desperation. They also needed to remember that few among the civilian population expected to hear every sentence punctuated by swearing. Some had even attended lectures to prepare them for civilian life, however the advice sometimes left a lot to be desired. At one lecture former POWs were advised to modify their table manners, being told: 'When you go home, don't say pass the fucking butter! Say pass the fucking butter – please!'[10]

Though such comments may have provoked laughter, there was a serious side to the experience of returning home from war. Although all of society was attempting to readapt to peacetime conditions the ex-prisoners perhaps had it harder than most. All the demobbed soldiers needed to reconstruct and restart their lives but for the prisoners the circumstances seemed more extreme. The curtailment of their freedom had stripped away many of the certainties of life and replaced them with doubt. Freed from Stalag VIIa at Moosburg, ex-paratrooper Bryan Willoughby came back ready to rebuild his life:

> I wasn't ashamed of having been a POW. I was 25 when the war ended. I'd got no job. I didn't know anything. As ignorant as a pig, I was. I got a job in insurance through the recommendation of a friend. There was no time to dwell on my experiences. Other things were more important, like scratching a living. I had time to make up. I don't think it's generally realised just how little we knew of life, when we came out of the army. The ordinary things of life people would be expected to know we didn't. All that had to be learnt. Like the business of trying to buy a house – what to do, what not to do. We'd spent our youth thinking of something else – trying to stay alive.[11]

As the POWs struggled to adapt to fit into the civilian world, much of the burden was carried by those family members closest to them. Some of the unconscious behaviour of former POWs went unexplained, they made decisions that confused their wives and children but which, with the passing of time, became clear. Some children of former POWs were denied normal childhood treats by their fathers. Ex-POWs didn't want to visit zoos and see animals held in small cages, nor allow caged pets to be kept in their homes. Upon arrival home one former POW immediately opened a birdcage and allowed its inhabitant to fly away. The very thought of any living thing being confined in so small a space brought back intense memories of their own incarceration. At mealtimes they could not tolerate seeing food being left on plates, or rejected by ungrateful children. To men who knew such scraps could mean the difference between life and death such behaviour was unacceptable. One former POW disrupted a civic event in Swansea when the pensioners for whom the event was organised were refused food until the local dignitaries arrived, in his fury he upended one of the tables, which in turn collapsed the rest of the tables in the hall. Whilst most people attending the event were furious other former POWs stood by him and offered support, fully understanding his emotions at seeing people being forced to wait to eat.

In light of such tensions it was to the credit of most families that they allowed their husbands or sons to adapt to civilian life in their own time. George Marsden was one of those who endured a lifelong struggle with his memories of the degrading squalor in which he was held at Fallingbostel. With the support of his wife he was able to attempt to rebuild his life: 'My life was affected, in that I became subdued. I think every night about certain things and have been unable to go away on holidays or be away from home. I have been back to Normandy, but was agitating to return home again, we have never been abroad on holiday, but I have a good wife who has looked after me.'[12]

The men who had received years of support from their wives whilst they were POWs became conscious of the mental anguish their wives had suffered – not knowing how long his captivity might last, nor if they would ever meet again – and were concerned at how it had affected their relationships. One later wrote: 'My biggest regret was not that it marred my life, but also caused hardship and trouble to my wife and children. Much to her credit she never reproached me for it. Looking back I wonder if it was worth it or just an unmitigated folly.'[13]

These men were not alone in suffering. Though most hid their feelings, few could not help but feel they had contributed little to the eventual victory and owed much to others. Many among them remained reluctant to talk of their experiences and despite all they suffered they considered themselves fortunate compared to so many. They saw the conditions of labour endured by prisoners in the Far East and blessed their good fortune to have been captured in Europe or North Africa. They could also remember the appalling deprivations forced upon Russian POWs and the brutality shown towards the forced labourers from concentration camps. Some among them had witnessed at first hand the ultimate horror of the Nazi regime, something which helped put their own sufferings into context. 'Bill' Sykes was among them:

> Eventually after many days and nights of aimless wandering, I was picked up by forward echelon troops of the American forces and dispatched to a hospital near Nuremburg, suffering from a bad case of dysentery and malnutrition. During my time at this location I met an American Army Sergeant who indicated that he had a Jeep and was going to travel to a concentration camp at Buchenwald, and seeing no one else had volunteered to travel with him, would I be interested. I said certainly, why not. I had travelled this far and survived, so why shouldn't I see for myself the crimes of man's inhumanity to man. Anyway, I figured that in my current physical condition I would be right at home amongst the skin and bone fraternity. Once again how wrong could I be. The scene that I witnessed was one of infinite horror where piles of dead bodies, in various stages of decomposition, were scattered about the camp. The living could not be distinguished from the dead. A place of horror, disbelief and anger against the perpetrators. To those unbelievers out there, I can attest to the fact that Hitler's 'Final solution' the 'Holocaust', or whatever one wishes to call the terrible acts of inhumanity, did occur and was as violent and horrific as portrayed in later documents.[16]

Looking back, men like Sykes realised their own suffering seemed minimal – indeed they had been fortunate to survive when so many had perished. Instead of wallowing in self-pity, they held their heads up high and continued with life.

Whilst the plight of the Far East prisoners has been highlighted over the years, the realities of imprisonment by the Germans has received scant public attention. Former POWs were unaware of how little the people of Britain knew of their sufferings, nor would they learn of them for many years to come. Although they did not face the same levels of brutality and systematic cruelty that others endured at the hands of their Japanese captors, they suffered enough to ensure their lives were changed forever. Yet somehow much of what they experienced was forgotten or simply never made public. For every man whose memoirs of suffering were published it seemed a hundred others told their stories of escape and evasion. And the public wanted heroes not victims. Those who spent long hours tunnelling to freedom seemed to embody the defiant spirit of the wartime years, not the men who spent five years slaving for the common enemy. These ex-POWs had suffered more than many others – most had endured defeat in battle, faced the humiliation of captivity and been powerless to prevent the enemy from enlisting them to work on the farms or in the factories of the Reich.

Maybe some felt ashamed of having worked for the enemy, maybe they were frustrated that so many years had been wasted in the mind numbing drudgery of slave labour. Maybe they were just too exhausted to tell their story. Some quite simply thought that no one would ever believe their tales of the disease and deprivation endured in the Stalags and work camps. Ex-POW copper miner Alec Reynolds explained why he seldom talked of his experiences as a POW:

> It's rarely that I ever talk about it. I never thought I'd suffered. My boys never knew where I'd been or what I'd done. For years no one could get anything out of me, but I talk about it more now. Being a POW was just part of life. The real shocks were when you first went away into the army. You had no idea what was going to happen to you. Then when you first go into battle, it was just confusion. Anyway, the 1930s had been grim so the POW camp wasn't too much of a shock. At home as a kid there were ten children in a two bedroom house. There wasn't much food, you just ate what you could find. The ones who worked always ate first. We had soup nearly every day. It was a big pot with everything in it. You'd put water in each day and heat it up. The thing is, it wasn't that different when I was a prisoner, so it was no shock. I'd been brought up with that sort of life.[17]

Arnhem veteran Bryan Willoughby also had a quite simple explanation for why he spoke so little of his experiences in the post-war years: 'For 15 or 20 years after the war you didn't tell your stories. The quickest way to clear a room was for somebody to tell their war experiences. People were fed up with it – they'd had their fill of war.'[18] Others realised they would have to put the whole thing behind them if they wished to progress in the new post-war world. Ken Wilats, who had barely survived the first day's march from Stalag XXb, recalled his life after liberation:

> I didn't throw myself into life upon my return. Things in Britain at that
> time were very bad. You came home, you met a woman, you fell in love.
> You needed to look round for a job and somewhere to live. You had an-
> other goal to achieve in life. You were coming back to a country that had
> been devastated, there were no houses, rationing was still in place. If you
> were going to get married you had to look at the moment and carve out
> a new life for yourself. We settled down into a routine that would have
> been impossible before the war. We were trying to make our way in the
> world after a five year break – as were many other people. We felt we had
> lost a few years of life – five years is a big slice of your life – but so had a
> lot of others. But it was the same for a whole generation.[19]

In common with many ex-POWs, Wilats recognised that in a lot of ways
their war years had actually been spent in greater safety than many others. Despite the deprivation and disease, the monotony and the mental
torment, life could have been a whole lot worse:

> The fighting troops must have suffered tremendously. Without being too
> smug – having done what one could, which wasn't a lot quite frankly,
> and then having been taken prisoner – providing you kept your head
> down, lived a quiet life and weren't too antagonistic towards the Ger-
> mans, you didn't have too much to worry about. It was boring and one
> was on tenterhooks about the future but by going out to work you set-
> tled into a daily routine. So it was a boring but strange existence.[20]

Even to this day many among the prisoners look at the 'youngsters' who
fought the battles that led to their liberation and hold them in great es-
teem. Having lost in battle they cannot help but admire those who per-
severed to bring the victory. Maybe hiding beneath this admiration and
respect were the seeds of the reasoning behind why so little of the POW
story has ever become fully known to the general public. Although few
among the men who suffered defeat would ever admit to any feelings
that they themselves had personally failed, maybe there was a nagging
doubt in their minds that the public would never accept the fact they
had never tried to escape nor been part of the 'goon baiting' cliques of
the Oflags and Stalag Lufts.

Some of the POWs attempted to reveal the truth of what they had experienced but found no one really wanted to hear their version of events.

When Arthur Dodds, who had been imprisoned at work camps within the Auschwitz concentration camp, appeared at a talk organised by his local council he found the audience was not interested in his tales of horror. They responded with cheers and applause to the tales told by a veteran of the battles around Arnhem but sat in silence as Dodds spoke. At the end of the meeting the audience crowded around the paratrooper but ignored the POW. It would be many years before he would speak of his horrific experiences again.

Such experiences led some ex-POWs to carry a grudge against the people who imprisoned them. As one man captured in Greece later wrote of his observations of the treatment of the Germans following the collapse of the Reich: 'The enemy is being treated too good.'[21] Lance Bombardier Norman Osborne, a commercial artist from Brighton, put it somewhat bluntly when answering a post-war military intelligence questionnaire: 'All Germans should be killed.'[22] Even 60 years later some are unable to forgive the Germans for the misery they endured and the sufferings they knew whilst working as slaves for the Third Reich. One former POW explained how he feels:

> If I meet a young German it is fine. I admire them. But if I meet a German of my generation I don't want to know. A mate of mine used to run a pub. One of his customers was a young German dentist working in England, they became quite friendly. One day he brought his family, including his parents, in for a meal. He was talking to the dentist and asked if his father had been in the war. He said 'Yes, he was an SS officer.' According to his wife my mate jumped over the bar and ran towards them with his fists flailing, he was knocking chairs over. He lifted the table out from under them and threw it over. They left in such a panic that they jumped in the car and immediately crashed into a wall. Some things are difficult to get rid of. They well up inside you. I have no time for my generation of Germans. Even now they are trying desperately hard to make excuses, but there is no excuse for what they did. They say 'We never knew about the concentration camps!' But if us POWs knew about the camps the German people must have. Human flesh doesn't smell like roast beef. The smell of burning flesh covered miles and miles of countryside. They must have known. As far as I'm concerned they should put a big monument up to Bomber Harris in Whitehall. They say we should apologise for Dresden, that we shouldn't have done it because the war was almost over. It wasn't almost over for me. My only regret was that they didn't do more Dresdens. Bomber Harris was great as far

as I'm concerned. The only apology should be by them for starting on us.[23]

The Germans were not alone in continuing to be blamed for the suffering of POWs. The Italians were also guilty of many breaches of the Geneva Convention, with many of those captured in North Africa having reported they were almost dead from starvation within a month of reaching the Italian mainland. As one former prisoner described it, they received: 'criminally unsanitary and inhumane treatment'.[24] In the words of another returning prisoner: 'They treated us a darned sight worse then the Huns, and that's saying something!'[25]

Yet although many ex-prisoners continued to bear a grudge against those who had imprisoned them, others bear their wartime enemies no ill will. Not all of the working prisoners experienced brutality. Many among them suffered from disease and malnutrition yet remained convinced their own guards had played no role in any ill treatment. Quite simply, it was war itself that caused their suffering rather than any Germans they could personally blame. D-Day veteran 'Bill' Sykes was one of those who had no animosity towards his captors:

> Having never been subjected to any acts of physical violence against my person whilst incarcerated in two Stalag prisoner of war camps, and two work camps, I can say that I never personally witnessed any acts of brutality by the German guards against any prisoners that I was in contact with and can also say that I never felt any malice towards them. I can only attest to the fact that the German guards that I came into contact with acted strictly according to the Geneva Convention. One must remember that these guards were members of the Wehrmacht, and not stormtroopers of the Waffen SS or other brutal organizations.[26]

There was also the issue of those fellow prisoners who had collaborated with the enemy. The War Office issued questionnaires to returning British and Commonwealth troops to find out about any treachery that had taken place within the Stalags and work camps. Many of the returning POWs include names and details of the offenders and their actions. Their crimes were many and varied: Sergeant Hales at Arbeitskommando E251, who betrayed two men planning to escape. South African Corporal Cloate who disappeared from the Stalags after agreeing to broadcast for the Germans. From Moosberg two other South Africans, Laue and Lochenberg, were also named as was an Australian, Boyse. From Stalag IIIa at Luckenwalde came the revelation that six British and Commonwealth prisoners – including a Canadian named Rose – had been involved in a ruse where they entered the cells of the newly captured. Once there the lights would be turned out and the Germans would enter and pretend to beat him up. This fake beating allowed the collaborators to gain the trust of the new prisoners in the hope of then being able to extract information from them. There were plenty more offenders named, such as Canadian Jim Nicholls who reported the illicit radio at Arbeitskommando E351, or Liverpudlian Private Edmeeds, Corporals Perry, Street and Quickenden, Gunner Brandt, Private Ormond, BSM Harris and Sergeant Major Homer at Thorn. A Private Chappell of Stalag XXId was reported for having been considered over familiar with the Germans whilst in the Stalag. The fears of his fellow prisoners were confirmed when he was spotted in Berlin wearing civilian clothes. Not all the revelations gave specific details, indeed some among the returning POWs chose to classify any NCOs who had imposed discipline within the Stalags as having been collaborators, such as CSM Bruce at Stalag XXIa whose supposed offence was reporting disturbances to the Germans, or RSM Parslow of the Royal Artillery who was the 'Man of Confidence' at Stalag IVd. Parslow was reported for failing to help the men under him and for believing they should not hinder the Germans whilst they were working. There were also officers reported such as a major named Bolton, who was reported as having: 'no time for POWs' since they were a "cause of bother"[27] to him.

Some of those reported to Military Intelligence had played a more active role in supporting the Nazis than those who had merely used their position to help themselves. Small numbers of British prisoners had joined another Nazi organisation, the British Free Corps. Their representatives, often British soldiers of German extraction or former members of the British Union of Fascists, toured the Stalags eager to find volunteers for their cause. To their disappointment they received short shrift from the vast majority of POWs who preferred captivity to treachery. Some of those who volunteered were destined to become infamous for their propaganda efforts. Others were adventurers or men who simply took the opportunity to find a way out of the boredom of work camps and Stalags. In 1945 two traitors, John Kenneth Pritchard and Private C. MacDonald were spotted in Estonian SS uniforms heading towards the front. Pritchard was not seen again until he reappeared in the UK alongside returning prisoners, concealing all indications that he had volunteered for the enemy. His efforts were wasted since there were enough men who had witnessed his treachery and passed on his name to Military Intelligence. They were able to pin down Pritchard since he had filled in a questionnaire issued to all returning POWs. Though he made no mention of his activities he gave the name of MacDonald as one of his associates. It was a clear sign to the investigators that they had found their man.

For some the questionnaires were used to record a positive side to the experience of being a prisoner. More POW's than used the forms to reveal collaborators utilised them to record their thanks to NCOs whose devotion to duty had helped them through the darkest days of captivity. They offered praise and thanks to those who had struggled to keep them fed and who had helped organise their lives in face of great hostility from their guards and work camp bosses. Many also chose to note their thanks to the civilians who helped them whilst in captivity. In particular they gave thanks to those – especially the Czechs – who had taken great risks to feed them during the long march westwards.

Whatever the reasons, the experiences of the POW labourers soon disappeared from the mainstream history of the war in Europe. Even the military report into POW conditions sat in the archives for many years, gathering dust and unavailable for public scrutiny. The SHAEF report into the abuse of POWs highlighted their plight, yet remained unseen by the British public. It concluded their treatment had 'at all times failed to comply with the requirements in that regard of the Geneva Convention'. And that 'the degree of such failure has increased in every respect with the progress of the war. ... at no time and in no place ... have the requirements of the convention been fully or adequately observed'.[28] The report made clear that most prisoners lived in cramped conditions that were under-ventilated, often not weather proof, with crowded beds, thin blankets, bug ridden straw mattresses, and that they were kept alive only by Red Cross parcels. The report made clear their labour was: 'calculated, directly or indirectly, to contribute to the German war effort,' with 'excessively long hours' in 'dangerous and unhealthy conditions'. Furthermore the report admitted the prisoners had been: 'compelled to work in localities subjected to Allied air attacks with resulting casualties' and had been 'frequently compelled to work when sick, or suffering from injury, in spite of protests by their own medical officers'.[29] Furthermore it was admitted there had been little protection for many POWs who were faced by hostile civilian foremen, many of whom carried weapons in defiance of the Geneva Convention.

Yet despite such post-war recognition of the mistreatment of prisoners there were plenty in the War Office whose view of the men forced to work in Germany seemed outdated. Maybe they had retained their faith in a gentlemanly approach to war, believing German honour would ensure fair treatment for the men behind the wire. Even those men awaiting repatriation had not received full sympathy in London. In September 1941 the Army Council wrote that although the men were 'compelled to perform this work against their will' they were of the opinion that: 'provided the work which prisoners of war passed for repatriation are required to do is of a light nature and care is taken to ensure there is no possibility of injury to their health, such work will tend to benefit the prisoners who might otherwise suffer from the boredom resulting from inactivity'.[30] Then in 1942 staff in London expressed regret that prisoners had downed tools whilst working on a project to build a causeway they believed would improve access to a naval base: 'It is therefore considered particularly unfortunate that the prisoners of war should have sought to impose their view on the camp authorities by unjustifiably refusing to continue work instead of relying upon the action of the protecting power on the receipt of their written protest.'[31]

This lack of understanding of what labouring in German industry entailed was perhaps understandable in the early war years. For all the doubts about the Nazi regime few could have believed the horrors that would eventually be revealed. No one had expected POWs to be starving to death or collapsing from disease. Yet when it happened how did they excuse failing to compensate the individuals concerned? Many of the firms for whom the POWs slaved would later become household names. The German industrial giant Siemens was a major employer, even detailing prisoners to work in munitions factories and having the POWs living in conditions described as 'unsatisfactory' by Red Cross inspectors.[32]

For those men who slaved for the enemy there was no solace found in public recognition of their sufferings. A mythical image of POW camps became engrained in the public consciousness via a stream of war movies and books whose camps were far removed from the everyday experiences of a majority of prisoners. They simply created a world unknown to those who had toiled in the hellish depths of Silesian mines or spent their war years confined to the agricultural villages of East Prussia. As one explained:

I have seen a lot of films depicting Stalag life. The camps look like holiday camps and every inmate looks well fed and drinks beer from 'shops'.

They are always well turned out and the Germans are always portrayed
as stupid. One of the worst things was the smell from bodies and open
wounds – this is never referred to in films'.[33]

It was not the fault of the writers that the public perception of prisoners
of war grew into something so far removed from the actual truth. Most
of those who wrote down their experiences had honestly attempted to
represent their life behind the wire. To some degree all had included the
boredom of life as a POW, but they had submerged the misery beneath
the more interesting and exciting aspects of Stalag life. A further factor
was that most of the stories published in the immediate post-war years
were written by officers whose experiences were far removed from those
ranks forced to labour for the Nazis. This was not a conspiracy to hide
the truth about Stalag life, it was simply that few among the stories revealing the drudgery of POW life had any appeal for the reading public
or cinema audiences. As one POW later admitted: 'Who's going to sit
through an hour and a half film about somebody at a working party?'[34]

With the passing of the years it seemed to the vast mass of former
POWs that their stories would never be told. A number of writers published stories that exposed the realities of life in work camps but they
failed to capture the imagination of the reading public or to make a dent
in the ever growing mythology of POW life. Adrian Vincent's *The Long
Road Home* was one of the most notable exceptions. Vincent's story, described by one reviewer as being 'The most honest prisoner-of-war story
I have read in the last ten years', told of a world without heroes where
men simply made the best of their lives in the hope that they might one
day be free.

With the passing of time more writers attempted to redress the balance. When Elvet Williams told his story of captivity in alpine work
camps he entitled it simply *Arbeitskommando*. Williams, who in the
company of a mixed group of Britons and Australians was able to escape via Yugoslavia, summed up the difference between officer escapees
and other ranks when he wrote: 'Escape from such a life meant release
from bondage rather than captivity.'[35] Unlike many previous writers he
was firm in his assessment of his employment by the enemy. He and his
fellow prisoners had been: 'slave labourers hired out to civilian contractors'.[36]

In the late 1980s serial escaper John Elwyn also told his story of life
in the Stalags and on working parties. He didn't shy away from revealing the violence he had witnessed between prisoners at Lamsdorf, nor

the degradation suffered by the men who marched from France following the defeat of the BEF. He brutally expressed the condition he and
his fellow prisoners were reduced to: 'The evolutionary clock had been
put back to the era of survival of the fittest. Man's primal instincts had
taken over. How thin is the veneer of civilization!'[37] His words served to
reveal a world known to few whose knowledge of POW camps had been
based around *The Colditz Story* or *The Great Escape*.

It would take another 15 years before historians finally fully and very
successfully confronted the reality of the last desperate months of captivity as endured by thousands of the prisoners. The publication of John
Nichol and Tony Rennell's *The Last Escape* in 2002 was the first time
the story of the long marches westwards was fully told. For the prisoners who thought their plight had been consigned to the rubbish bin of
history this book was a revelation. After suppressing the memories of
their ordeal for so long few former POWs who read it were unaffected
by the experience. Among them was Gordon Barber, who after five years
of captivity had weighed just over 8 stones when he was liberated, who
had considered himself a 'survivor' in the harsh world of the Stalags and
work camps, and who had never given up hope of surviving his ordeal.
His wife watched as the book brought back painful memories of deprivation, disease and death: 'He cried his eyes out when he read it.'[38]

Yet if the rigours of those final months were at long last being pub-
licised the sufferings of those prisoners employed as slave labourers for
the Third Reich were still all but forgotten. Few but the members of
ex-prisoners' organisations across the Commonwealth remember their
plight. Leslie Allan, the founder and General Secretary of the National Ex-Prisoner of War Association is among them. Even to this day he
campaigns for official recognition of their sufferings. Yet when he has
talked to politicians and Ministry of Defence officials he has constantly
been blocked. On numerous occasions he has been asked why, if conditions were so bad, he and his fellow prisoners didn't write home and
complain: 'Just imagine me telling my mother and sister the real facts in
a letter? We knew they were going through a hell of a time themselves,
so we gave them a light hearted view of life – "Yes, I'm fine, don't worry
about me, I'm having a great time" – so as not to worry them.'[39]

Hoping to raise awareness of how successive British governments
have long ignored the plight of the POWs he wrote:

Germany has put together a financial package to compensate those
who were subjected to slave labour under the Nazi regime. However,

ex-prisoners of war are excluded, with the full approval of the Ministry of Defence. Far East prisoners of war, who were in the hands of the Japanese, have recently been awarded compensation by our government. Sadly, many of our members who were prisoners of the Nazis will not be receiving such compensation because the government considers that their treatment was not bad enough ... These were the men who fought the rearguard so that the evacuation of Dunkirk could take place, the men who took on Rommel's Afrika Korps in the Western Desert, or who parachuted into Arnhem or fought their way ashore at Normandy. Crimes against prisoners of war held in Germany were endless, but for political expediency a conspiracy of silence has been the policy of the UK. To date not one UK POW held by the Nazis has been compensated. Not one![40]

For Les Allan, who has worked tirelessly for justice for the POW slave labourers employed by the Nazis, the failure to recognise their sufferings has remained a bone of contention ever since their return from war. To him, it is clear they were not prisoners but slaves, since they were not treated according to the Geneva Convention: 'People think you have to have a man standing over you with a whip to be a slave. Our guards didn't have whips but they did have very efficient guns. Even if you had every comfort in the world and all the food you could want, how would you like to work for five years at the wrong end of a gun?'[41]

Whilst the official Allied Supreme Headquarters report damned the Germans for their mistreatment of POWs, politicians seemed to offer a different view. The military report considered the Germans were at fault for failing to abide by the Geneva Convention, yet the governments placed the blame squarely on the shoulders of individual guards. Thus there could be no claim for compensation since the German regime had not been responsible for the crimes against POWs. To men such as Allan this is a ridiculous notion – why were the Nazi leaders considered responsible for the actions of their troops against civilians yet not for the treatment they inflicted on the POWs? It was the German government who failed to recognise his status as 'protected personnel' and therefore the German government who was responsible for the breaking of his jaw with a rifle butt whilst at work.

In the minds of so many ex-prisoners how could the German government not have been responsible for their sufferings? The failure to provide food to prisoners on forced marches was a breach of the Geneva Convention. The differences between rations given to German soldiers in hospital and Allied POWs in the beds alongside them was also a breach of the Convention. Wages that were never paid, arbitrary punishments of prisoners without the due process of law, the use of POWs in armaments factories, the guarding of prisoners by armed civilians, the forced employment of NCOs and medical personnel, the murder of escaping POWs by their guards – all were illegal and all were widespread. These were recognised by both the Red Cross and the official SHAEF report on the treatment of POWs, yet British governments have continuously failed to show any interest in their cause.

The failure to recognise the sufferings of the prisoners has long appeared to be a conspiracy:

On my Army Book it says I was granted the 1939-43 Star. Later Churchill made a statement saying the giving of medals and ribbons is to give pride and pleasure to those worthy of wearing them. Then he devalued our medal from the 1939-43 Star to the 1939-45 Star. We wouldn't have objected but it was his wording about not being worthy. We were treated like pariahs. We've never had any official recognition. The Yanks eventually gave their prisoners all a medal. I can always spot an ex-POW, he is the one at the parades with the fewest medals. Members of Parliament have been an absolute disgrace. Some, before they became ministers, they promised us justice. But when they got into government – nothing. We blame it on the political stance of the post-war days, the Allies were desperate to befriend the Germans. So they whitewashed everything that happened to us in Germany. Even now we just can't seem to break into the MPs. We couldn't get lottery grants, even though they were giving grants to ludicrous things. We just wanted some money to help produce the newsletter. We applied for a grant, after it was refused three times we didn't ask again. We are still proud men. Now it would be begging, that's something I'm not prepared to do. It's not for us to crawl to them.[42]

Chief among the complaints from ex-POWs is that they seldom received the wages they were supposed to be paid. One man, supposedly receiving 70 pfennings a day, found he received a total of just 15 reichsmarks for nine months work. As he later commented: 'we received the money just when they felt like paying you'.[43] Many of the returning prisoners also found that non-existent payments had been deducted from their credits when they returned home. Their credits – the wages accrued whilst in captivity, to which was added a bonus for their period of service – were something all the prisoners had looked forward to. Yet they were losing out from these real wages for money they had either never received, or which had been all but useless to them. A stretcher bearer taken prisoner whilst part of the rearguard protecting the retreat to Dunkirk, Les Allan was one of the 'protected personnel' forced to work by the Germans. He worked on farms and in factories for four years before he was finally recognised as a 'protected person' and exempt from work. His wartime treatment by the Germans and his post-war treatment by the British government caused him much concern. All the time he was slaving for the enemy deductions were being made from his pay. This was supposedly then paid to the German government to make up for the wages they paid him. This was a marvellous concept except for one small hitch – he never received any wages from the Germans. Yet when he returned home from captivity his wartime credits showed the deductions made for the unpaid wages. Sixty years on he has still never been compensated for his loss and when talking to politicians he always resorts to sarcasm and tells them: 'We paid for our holiday'.[44] Adding insult to injury, Allan also discovered that prisoners of the Japanese returned home to receive their full wartime credits since the Japanese had not paid them. This iniquity between how the two sets of prisoners – Far East and European – are treated by the British government continues to annoy Allan:

> The governments say 'But the Far East prisoners had a hell of a time'. Yes, they did. But that doesn't mean the rest of us were in holiday camps. We didn't have as hard a time as most of them, of course we are all glad we were prisoners of the Germans rather than the Japanese, but surely we are entitled to our credits? But the British government took our money away.[45]

Ken Wilats, one of those working prisoners who has never received any payment for his forced labour in the farms and quarries of the Third Reich, still finds the echoes of those experiences resound through his mind as vividly as they did sixty years ago:

> At the age of 21, five years is a big slice of your life. As you grow older your thoughts don't gravitate to the future, they go much more easily to the past. Old men tend to reminisce and World War Two is probably the biggest event in most of our lives. I must have gone over it in my mind ten thousand times – especially if I can't sleep at night. I can trace the war from 21 January 1940, when I was called up, right through to 20 May 1945, when I came home, in absolute detail. I can remember every-

thing precisely and I can pinpoint anything. I suppose it's a comfort to remember. I regret the waste of time but it could have been a lot worse. I know I wasn't a very brave soldier but I hadn't been trained to be a brave soldier. I didn't go to war to kill Germans but to stop them killing me.[46]

Perhaps it is fitting to conclude with the words of Les Allan, who has devoted years of work to the cause of the men who endured so much at the hands of the enemy and who has struggled long and hard to get official recognition. Like so many of his fellow prisoners he kept quiet about his experiences for many years, even failing to tell his wife the truth of how he had spent the war years. He quite simply never thought anyone would believe him. Once he had finally faced up to the truth and admitted to his family what had really happened he decided it was time to rebuild and gain something positive from what had been such a negative experience:

All ex-prisoners of war are on the same level. Even today, if I was talking to a serving officer I would call him 'Sir'. But if I was talking to Earl Haig, who was in Colditz, I'd just say 'hello' – you wouldn't say 'Sir' – because he'd be on my level. All ex-prisoners immediately talk to each other no matter what their status in life is. It's a common bond, it's real and nationality is irrelevant. It's a great thing to have, it gave me friends for life. Hopefully it made me a better man. A prisoner of war has known every human emotion except the final one – death. He has known fear, happiness, misery, hardship – everything, and in extremes. In all honesty, I wouldn't have missed it for the world, but if I had to go through it again I'd shoot myself.[47]

Notes

PREFACE

1   *Arbeitskommando* – Elvet Williams (Victor Gollanz - London 1975)

CHAPTER 1, Into the Bag

1.   Public Record Office – FO916/14
2.   Ken Wilats – Interview with author.
3.   Gordon Barber – Interview with author.
4.   Ken Wilats – Interview with author.
5.   Gordon Barber – Interview with author.
6.   Ken Wilats – Interview with author.
7.   Gordon Barber – Interview with author.
8.   Public Record Office – WO32/184189
9.   Ken Wilats – Interview with author.
10.   Gordon Barber – Interview with author.
11.   Ken Wilats – Interview with author.
12.   Gordon Barber – Interview with author.
13.   *At the Fifth Attempt* – John Elwyn (Leo Cooper – London 1987)
14.   Gordon Barber – Interview with author.
15.   Public Record Office WO32/18489
16.   Gordon Barber – Interview with author.
17.   Gordon Barber – Interview with author.
18.   Imperial War Museum – E.G. Laker 85/18/1
19.   Imperial War Museum – James H. Witte 87/12/1
20.   Public Record Office – WO32/15543

21.   Eric 'Bill' Sykes – Letter to author.
22.   Eric 'Bill' Sykes – Letter to author.
23.   Eric 'Bill' Sykes – Letter to author.
24.   Eric 'Bill' Sykes – Letter to author.
25.   Bryan Willoughby – Interview with author.
26.   Bryan Willoughby – Interview with author.
27.   John Mercer – Interview with author.
28.   Jim Sims – Letter to author.
29.   George Marsden – Letter to author.

CHAPTER 2, Abandon Hope All Ye Who Enter Here

1.   Jim Sims – Letter to author.
2.   Ken Wilats – Interview with author.
3.   Eric 'Bill' Sykes – Letter to author.
4.   Eric 'Bill' Sykes – Letter to author.
5.   *At the Fifth Attempt* – John Elwyn (Leo Cooper – London 1987)
6.   Ken Wilats – Interview with author.
7.   Gordon Barber – Interview with author.
8.   Public Record Office FO916/241
9.   Bryan Willoughby – Interview with author.
10.   Bryan Willoughby – Interview with author.
11.   Bryan Willoughby – Interview with author.
12.   Public Record Office FO916/252
13.   Eric 'Bill' Sykes – Letter to author.
14.   Imperial War Museum – Maurice Newey 90/4/1
15.   Bryan Willoughby – Interview with author.
16.   Public Record Office FO916/520
17.   Gordon Barber – Interview with author.
18.   Imperial War Museum – Thomas Crawcour 99/36/1
19.   Eric 'Bill' Sykes – Letter to author.
20.   Gordon Barber – Interview with author.
21.   Gordon Barber – Interview with author.
22.   Imperial War Museum – James Witte 87/12/1
23.   Gordon Barber – Interview with author.
24.   Imperial War Museum – F.W. Daniels p357
25.   Leslie Allan – Interview with author.
26.   Leslie Allan – Interview with author.
27.   Leslie Allan – Interview with author.
28.   Ken Wilats – Interview with author.
29.   Public Record Office WO344/140/1
30.   Gordon Barber – Interview with author.
31.   Imperial War Museum – Gilbert Lawrence 02/25/

CHAPTER 3, Industry

1. Public Record Office FO916/252
2. Public Record Office WO344/287/1
3. Public Record Office WO224/27
4. Alec Reynolds – Interview with author.
5. Alec Reynolds – Interview with author.
6. Imperial War Museum – L.F. Barter pp/mcr/159
7. Public Record Office FO916/519
8. Alec Reynolds – Interview with author.
9. Alec Reynolds – Interview with author.
10. Imperial War Museum – L.F. Barter pp/mcr/159
11. *The Long Road Home* – Adrian Vincent (Allen & Unwin – London 1956)
12. Public Record Office FO916/520
13. Public Record Office WO224/11
14. Public Record Office WO224/11
15. Imperial War Museum – M. Newey 90/4/1
16. Ken Wilats – Interview with author.
17. Les Allan – Interview with author.
18. Imperial War Museum – M. Newey 90/4/1
19. Public Record Office FO916/252
20. Public Record Office FO916/871
21. Public Record Office FO916/34
22. Public Record Office FO916/844
23. Imperial War Museum – F.W. Daniels p357
24. Public Record Office WO344/16/1
25. Public Record Office WO224/13
26. Les Allan – Interview with author.
27. Public Record Office – Red Cross reports on Stalag XIIIc.

CHAPTER 4, The Land Army

1. Gordon Barber – Interview with author.
2. Gordon Barber – Interview with author.
3. Ken Wilats – Interview with author.
4. Gordon Barber – Interview with author.
5. Gordon Barber – Interview with author.
6. Gordon Barber – Interview with author.
7. Imperial War Museum – William Hymers 88/58/1
8. Les Allan – Interview with author.
9. Gordon Barber – Interview with author.
10. Gordon Barber – Interview with author.

11. Ken Wilats – Interview with author.
12. Gordon Barber – Interview with author.
13. Les Allan – Interview with author.
14. Gordon Barber – Interview with author.
15. Gordon Barber – Interview with author.
16. Gordon Barber – Interview with author.
17. Ken Wilats – Interview with author.
18. Ken Wilats – Interview with author.
19. Ken Wilats – Interview with author.

CHAPTER 5, A Place Not Called Home

1. Public Record Office FO916/34
2. Public Record Office WO224/34
3. Public Record Office FO916/241
4. Public Record Office WO224/27
5. Ken Wilats – Interview with author.
6. Imperial War Museum – Howard Bates 03/57/1
7. Ken Wilats – Interview with author.
8. Eric 'Bill' Sykes – Letter to author.
9. Alec Reynolds – Interview with author.
10. Public Record Office WO224/13
11. Ken Wilats – Interview with author.
12. Gordon Barber – Interview with author.
13. Public Record Office WO224/13
14. Gordon Barber – Interview with author.
15. Ken Wilats – Interview with author.
16. Gordon Barber – Interview with author.
17. Les Allan – Interview with author.
18. Ken Wilats – Interview with author.
19. Bryan Willoughby – Interview with author.
20. Eric 'Bill' Sykes – Letter to author.
21. *At the Fifth Attempt* – John Elwyn (Leo Cooper – London 1987)
22. Gordon Barber – Interview with author.
23. Ken Wilats – Interview with author.
24. Imperial War Museum – J.H. Witte 87/12/1
25. Eric 'Bill' Sykes – Letter to author.
26. Eric 'Bill' Sykes – Letter to author.
27. Gordon Barber – Interview with author.
28. Imperial War Museum – W.G. Harvey
29. Imperial War Museum – M. Newey 90/4/1
30. Imperial War Museum – M. Newey 90/4/1
31. Les Allan – Interview with author.

32. Imperial War Museum – F.W. Daniels p357

CHAPTER 6, Friends, Enemies and Lovers

1. Public Record Office FO916/520
2. Imperial War Museum – J.H. Witte 87/12/1
3. Ken Wilats – Interview with author.
4. Gordon Barber – Interview with author.
5. Gordon Barber – Interview with author.
6. Public Record Office WO224/9
7. Gordon Barber – Interview with author.
8. Gordon Barber – Interview with author.
9. Public Record Office WO344/287/1
10. Public Record Office WO344/160/1
11. *The Long Road Home* – Adrian Vincent (Allen & Unwin – London 1956)
12. Ken Wilats – Interview with author.
13. Gordon Barber – Interview with author.
14. Ken Wilats – Interview with author.
15. Imperial War Museum – M. Newey 90/40/1
16. Imperial War Museum – F.W. Daniels p357
17. Gordon Barber – Interview with author.
18. Imperial War Museum – F.W. Daniels p357
19. Imperial War Museum – J.H. Witte 87/12/1
20. Imperial War Museum – J.H. Witte 87/12/1
21. Imperial War Museum – J.H. Witte 87/12/1
22. Imperial War Museum – J.H. Witte 87/12/1
23. Public Record Office WO224/35
24. Gordon Barber – Interview with author.
25. Ken Wilats – Interview with author.
26. Gordon Barber – Interview with author.
27. Ken Wilats – Interview with author.
28. Imperial War Museum – J.H. Witte 87/12/1
29. Imperial War Museum – M. Newey 90/40/1
30. Bryan Willoughby – Interview with author.
31. Bryan Willoughby – Interview with author.
32. Bryan Willoughby – Interview with author.
33. Imperial War Museum – F.W. Daniels p357

CHAPTER 7, Danger, Disease, Decay and Death

1. Public Record Office WO344/16/1
2. Public Record Office WO224/11

3.   Jim Sims – Letter to author.
4.   Public Record Office FO916/250
5.   Public Record Office FO916/544
6.   Les Allan – Interview with author.
7.   Public Record Office WO32/15543
8.   Public Record Office WO32/15543
9.   Alec Reynolds – Interview with author.
10. Imperial War Museum – J.H. Witte 87/12/1
11. Jim Sims – Letter to author.
12. Imperial War Museum – D.W. Luckett 90/4/1
13. Public Record Office FO916/844
14. Bryan Willoughby – Interview with author.
15. Imperial War Museum – F.W. Daniels p357
16. Public Record Office FO916/844
17. Public Record Office WO224/11
18. Gordon Barber – Interview with author.
19. Public Record Office WO224/48
20. Public Record Office FO916/844
21. Ken Wilats – Interview with author.
22. Public Record Office WO32/11125
23. Alec Reynolds – Interview with author.
24. Alec Reynolds – Interview with author.
25. Gordon Barber – Interview with author.
26. Public Record Office WO32/11125
27. Public Record Office WO32/11125
28. Public Record Office WO32/11125
29. Les Allan – Interview with author.
30. Public Record Office WO224/16
31. Imperial War Museum – F.W. Daniels p357
32. Imperial War Museum – F.W. Daniels p357
33. Public Record Office WO224/9
34. Imperial War Museum – A.J. Richardson 92/10/1
35. Public Record Office WO224/9
36. Ken Wilats – Interview with author.
37. *Spectator in Hell* – Colin Rushton (Pharaoh Press – 1998)

CHAPTER 8, The Column of the Damned

1.   Gordon Barber – Interview with author.
2.   Les Allan – Interview with author.

3. Gordon Barber – Interview with author.
4. Gordon Barber – Interview with author.
5. Ken Wilats – Interview with author.
6. Gordon Barber – Interview with author.
7. Gordon Barber – Interview with author.
8. Imperial War Museum – W. Bampton 94/49/1
9. Gordon Barber – Interview with author.
10. Gordon Barber – Interview with author.
11. Ken Wilats – Interview with author.
12. Gordon Barber – Interview with author.
13. Public Record Office WO344/80/2
14. Imperial War Museum – M. Newey 90/4/1
15. Gordon Barber – Interview with author.
16. Les Allan – Interview with author.
17. Imperial War Museum – W. Bampton 94/49/1
18. Gordon Barber – Interview with author.
19. Ken Wilats – Interview with author.
20. Gordon Barber – Interview with author.
21. Imperial War Museum – W.G. Harvey
22. Les Allan – Interview with author.
23. Gordon Barber – Interview with author.
24. Eric 'Bill' Sykes – Letter to author.

CHAPTER 9, The End

1. Jim Sims – Letter to author.
2. Public Record Office WO224/34
3. Public Record Office WO224/35
4. George Marsden – Letter to author.
5. George Marsden – Letter to author.
6. George Marsden – Letter to author.
7. Public Record Office WO224/11
8. Public Record Office WO224/33
9. Bryan Willoughby – Interview with author.
10. Bryan Willoughby – Interview with author.
11. Bryan Willoughby – Interview with author.
12. Jim Sims – Letter to author.
13. Bryan Willoughby – Interview with author.
14. Alec Reynolds – Interview with author.
15. Alec Reynolds – Interview with author.

16.   Public Record Office WO224/47
17.   Ken Wilats – Interview with author.
18.   Bryan Willoughby – Interview with author.
19.   Alex Reynolds – Interview with author.
20.   Imperial War Museum – J.H. Witte 87/12/1
21.   Bryan Willoughby – Interview with author.
22.   Alex Reynolds – Interview with author.
23.   Public Record Office WO224/35
24.   Jim Sims – Letter to author.
25.   Alex Reynolds – Interview with author.
26.   Les Allan – Interview with author.
27.   Alec Reynolds – Interview with author.
28.   Bryan Willoughby – Interview with author.
29.   Eric 'Bill' Sykes – Letter to author.
30.   Bryan Willoughby – Interview with author.
31.   Imperial War Museum – J.H. Witte 87/12/1
32.   Imperial War Museum – J.H. Witte 87/12/1
33.   Public Record Office FO916/1202
34.   Alex Reynolds – Interview with author.
35.   Ken Wilats – Interview with author.
36.   Bryan Willoughby – Interview with author.
37.   Bryan Willoughby – Interview with author.
38.   Bryan Willoughby – Interview with author.
39.   Imperial War Museum – K. Clarke 01/25/1
40.   Gordon Barber – Interview with author.
41.   Ken Wilats – Interview with author.
42.   Imperial War Museum – M. Newey 90/4/1

CHAPTER 10, Every Day a Bonus

1.   Imperial War Museum – F.W. Daniels p357
2.   Eric 'Bill' Sykes – Letter to author.
3.   George Marsden – Letter to author.
4.   Imperial War Museum – F.W. Daniels p357
5.   Imperial War Museum – W.G. Harvey
6.   Public Record Office WO32/11125
7.   Public Record Office WO32/11125
8.   Public Record Office WO32/11125
9.   Public Record Office WO32/11125
10.   *Travels with a Leros Veteran* – Pauline Bevan (PB Books – 2000)

11. Bryan Willoughby – Interview with author.
12. George Marsden – Letter to author.
13. Imperial War Museum – W.G. Harvey
14. Veronica Taylor – Letter to author.
15. Veronica Taylor – Letter to author.
16. Eric 'Bill' Sykes – Letter to author.
17. Alec Reynolds – Interview with author.
18. Bryan Willoughby – Interview with author.
19. Ken Wilats – Interview with author.
20. Ken Wilats – Interview with author.
21. Public Record Office WO344/140/1
22. Public Record Office WO344/240/1
23. Public Record Office WO344/270/1
24. Public Record Office WO344/270/2
25. Les Allan – Interview with author.
26. Eric 'Bill' Sykes – Letter to author.
27. Public Record Office WO344/290/2
28. Public Record Office WO219/5044
29. Public Record Office WO219/5044
30. Public Record Office FO916/34
31. Public Record Office FO916/252
32. Public Record Office FO916/519
33. Jim Sims – Letter to author.
34. Ken Wilats – Interview with author.
35. *Arbeitskommando* – Elvet Williams (Victor Gollancz – London 1975)
36. *Arbeitskommando* – Elvet Williams (Victor Gollancz – London 1975)
37. *At the Fifth Attempt* – John Elwyn (Leo Cooper – London 1987)
38. Gordon Barber – Interview with author.
39. Les Allan – Interview with author.
40. Les Allan – Interview with author.
41. Les Allan – Interview with author.
42. Les Allan – Interview with author.
43. Public Record Office WO32/15543
44. Les Allan – Interview with author.
45. Les Allan – Interview with author.
46. Ken Wilats – Interview with author.
47. Les Allan – Interview with author.

Sources

UNPUBLISHED SOURCES

Gordon Barber – Royal Horse Artillery. Interview
George Marsden – Duke of Wellington's Regiment. Letter to author.
Alex Reynolds – Royal Artillery. Interview
Jim Sims – Parachute Regiment. Letter to author
Eric 'Bill' Sykes – Parachute Regiment. Letter to author
Ken Wilats – 2/5th Queens Regiment. Interview
Bryan Willoughby – Parachute Regiment. Interview

Public Record Office

WO219/5044 SHAEF Court of Enquiry on treatment of American and
           British Prisoners of War
WO32/11125 Rehabilitation of Returned POWs
WO32/11129 Rehabilitation of Ex Prisoners of War Returning to Civil
           Life
WO32/15543 SHAEF Board of Enquiry on the Treatment of American
           and British P.O.Ws
WO32/18489 Reports on treatment of POWs
FO916/14   Welfare of POWs in Germany 1941
FO916/15   Welfare of POWs in Germany 1941
FO916/15   Welfare of POWs in Germany 1941
FO916/16   Welfare of POWs in Germany 1941
FO916/34   Conditions of Labour in POW camps 1941

FO916/57   Ill treatment of POWs in Germany 1941
FO916/241   Red Cross reports on Stalag XXB 1942
FO916/250   Letters from International Red Cross Committee enclosing camp reports.
FO916/252   Conditions of Labour in POW camps 1942
FO916/266   Ill treatment of prisoners of war in Germany 1942
FO916/167   Welfare of RAMC prisoners of war in Germany 1942
FO916/519   Conditions of Labour in POW camps 1943
FO916/520   Conditions of Labour in POW camps 1943
FO916/544   Ill treatment of POWs in Germany 1943
FO916/613   Activities of IRCC 1943
FO916/844   Conditions of Labour in POW camps 1944
FO916/871   Ill treatment of prisoners of war in Germany 1944
FO916/889   Bombing of POW camps in Germany 1944
FO916/898   Treatment Of 1st Airborne Division taken POW at Arnhem
FO916/950   Welfare of Indian Prisoners of War in France 1944
FO916/1166 Ill treatment of prisoners in German hands 1945
FO916/1184 Bombing of Prisoner of War camps 1945
FO916/1202 Treatment of British Prisoners of War and Internees by the Russians in Austria and Czechoslovakia 1945
WO224/9   Red Cross reports on Stalag IIID Sept 1941 to Dec 1944
WO224/11   Red Cross reports on Stalag IVa April 1941 to Feb 1945
WO224/13   Red Cross reports on Stalag IVC May 1941 to March 1945
WO224/16   Red Cross reports on Stalag IVG Jan 1944 to April 1945
WO224/26   Red Cross reports on Stalag VIIIA Oct 1943 to Nov 1944
WO224/27   Red Cross reports on Stalag VIIIB
WO224/31   Red Cross reports on Stalag IXC April 1941 to April 1942
WO224/33   Red Cross reports on Stalag XB August 1942 to May 1945
WO224/34   Red Cross reports on Stalag Xia Jan 1944 to April 1945
WO224/35   Red Cross reports on Stalag XIb Jan 1944 to Feb 1945
WO224/37   Red Cross reports on Stalag XIId July 1944 to Feb 1945
WO224/47   Red Cross reports on Stalag XVIIIC November 1943 to Feb 1945
WO224/48   Red Cross reports on Stalag XXA 1941 to 1945
WO224/51   Red Cross reports on Stalag XXID 1941 to 1944
WO224/102   Red Cross report on Bau und Arbeitsbattallion No 20 Dec 1941 to Sept 44
WO224/103   Red Cross report on Bau und Arbeitsbattallion No 21 Oct 1941 to Sept 44
WO224/104   Red Cross report on Bau und Arbeitsbattallion No 21 Sept 1941 to Feb 43
WO224/105   Red Cross report on Bau und Arbeitsbattallion No 48 Feb 42 to Feb 43

WO224/244   Red Cross reports on Stalag VIIIb 1942
WO344   Directorate of Military Intelligence – Liberated Prisoner of
                War Interrogation Questionnaires

Imperial War Museum

James H. Witte (87/12/1)   E.G. Laker (85/18/1)
Jim Sims (83/52/1)   William Hymers (88/58/1)
Dr H.C.M. Jarvis (89/16/2)   Thomas Crawcour (99/36/1)
Maurice Newey (90/4/1)   Howard Bates (03/57/1)
D.W. Luckett (90/4/1)   John Tonkin (p461)
F.W. Daniels (p357)   A.J. Richardson (92/10/1)
W.G. Harvey (no number)   Gilbert Lawrence (02/55/1)
L.F. Barter (pp/mcr/426)   Ken Clarke (01/25/1)

PUBLISHED SOURCES

A Crowd is Not Company, Robert Kee (Eyre And Spottiswoode, London
     1947)
Arbeitskommando, Elvet Williams (Victor Gollancz, London 1975)
At the Fifth Attempt, John Elwyn (Leo Cooper , London 1987)
The Bolo Boys, Mac MacIntosh (Victoria Press, Maidstone 1989)
The Conquest of The Reich, Robin Neillands (Weidenfeld & Nicolson,
     London 1995)
Five Days in Hell, Jack Smyth (William Kimber, London 1956)
The Guarded Years, Douglas Baber (William Heinemann, London 1955)
The Iron Cage, Nigel Cawthorne (Fourth Estate, London 1983)
Last days of The Reich, James Lucas (Arms & Armour Press, London
     1986)
The Long Road Home, Adrian Vincent (Allen & Unwin, London 1956)
My Life, Bert Hardy (Gordon Fraser, London 1985)
The Password is Courage, John Castle (Souvenir Press, London 1954)
Prisoners of the Reich, David Rolf (Leo Cooper, London 1988)
Report from Germany, Leonard O. Mosley (Victor Gollancz, London
     1945)
Silent Invader, Alexander Morrison (Airlife, London 1999)
Spectator in Hell, Colin Rushton (Pharaoh Press, London 1998)
Travels with a Leros Veteran, Pauline Bevan (PB Books 2000)
Years Not Wasted 1940-1945, Keith Panter Brick (The Book Guild 1999)

Index